MW01107145

The Fundamentals of Global Governance

The Fundamentals of Global Governance

Jim Whitman

First published 2009 by
PALGRAVE MACMILLAN

Palgrave Macmillan in the UK is an imprint of Macmillan Publishers Limited, registered in England, company number 785998, of Houndmills, Basingstoke, Hampshire RG21 6XS.

Palgrave Macmillan in the US is a division of St Martin's Press LLC, 175 Fifth Avenue, New York, NY 10010.

Palgrave Macmillan is the global academic imprint of the above companies and has companies and representatives throughout the world.

Palgrave® and Macmillan® are registered trademarks in the United States, the United Kingdom, Europe and other countries

ISBN-13: 978–0–230–57253–9   hardback
ISBN-10: 0–230–57253–7   hardback

This book is printed on paper suitable for recycling and made from fully managed and sustained forest sources. Logging, pulping and manufacturing processes are expected to conform to the environmental regulations of the country of origin.

A catalogue record for this book is available from the British Library.

A catalogue record for this book is available from the Library of Congress.

10 9 8 7 6 5 4 3 2 1
18 17 16 15 14 13 12 11 10 09

Printed and bound in Great Britain by
CPI Antony Rowe, Chippenham and Eastbourne

For Maureen Loveland

Contents

Preface

In the course of teaching over several years, I noted that many students find the concept of global governance difficult to approach, since a good deal of the literature is either conducted on the basis of already highly elaborated positions, or because it is dedicated to specialist areas with which they are not closely familiar. A large part of this difficulty is in the nature of the scholarly enterprise, since any general definition of global governance immediately invites questions as to its meanings, purposes, mechanisms, beneficiaries, legitimacy and accountability; who or what can count as an actor; what differentiates global as opposed to international governance; and how 'global governance' relates to established concepts in several fields. That said, there are a number of fine works that are both scholarly and accessible, notably the published output of James Rosenau over many years, and numerous edited works cited at various points in this volume. But although there is now a considerable body of literature on global governance and the term circulates very freely, it remains difficult to specify with clarity – and without inviting contention of quite fundamental sorts – what characterises global governance as an activity. That is the purpose of this book.

The eight 'fundamentals' discussed in Chapters 2 through 9 are founded on the simple and essentially un-contentious definition quoted in Chapter 1: 'Efforts to bring more orderly and reliable responses to social and political issues that go beyond the capacities of states to address individually.' This description accommodates the principal themes that have developed in the literature over many years, without necessitating an argumentative focus on a single aspect or perspective. For the purpose of clarity, two contrasting uses of the term 'global governance' are distinguished. The first, here termed 'summative', regards global governance as the overall order of the world – the sum of all governances, high and low; formal and informal, with all their inconsistencies and inadequacies. The second is 'sectoral' – that is, efforts dedicated to ordering a specific area of human endeavour or addressing a serious issue. Under globalised conditions, these are necessary abstractions rather than fixed categories.

The propositions that stand as the theme for each of the central chapters describe fundamentals of global governance as a form of activity, broadly applicable to any particular instance, explicit purpose or arena of operation. The elaboration of the propositions draws on the established literature but it is also an attempt to convey the kinds and degrees of difficulty involved in our attempts to comprehend the world we have made for ourselves, to conceive and agree consensus about ends and means, and to act comprehensively and consistently. Chapter 10, 'the human rights regime as global governance', grew from an awareness that it is easier to pose than to answer the question, 'What would an adequate global governance be the governance *of?*' While I do not believe that a definitive answer to this is possible, I submit human rights for definitive inclusion.

It would be difficult to discuss the fundamentals of global governance from almost any perspective without encountering limits of various kinds, not only political and practical, but also limits to our capacity to comprehend the possibilities latent in the complexity and speed of our human systems. At the time of writing (October 2008), we appear to have averted a meltdown of global finance. One might regard this as evidence of the effectiveness of national, international and private actors acting in a concerted and timely manner on what few would dispute is a truly global scale. But even as we wait to see whether the crisis has run its course and to see what aftershocks might ensue, we could usefully reflect on the summative and sectoral forms of global governance we had in place in the years preceding the crisis and ponder whether global finance was unique, and whether in their current state our systems of governance and global governance are proof against making an ungovernable world.

Acknowledgements

It is a great pleasure to express my thanks in writing for the honour of being the first Visiting Fellow in Peace Studies at the University of Calgary in the Spring of 2007, where much of the research for this book was conducted. The Fellowship was a rich and fulfilling period and I greatly appreciate the splendid conditions and the very considerable freedom that came with it. Everywhere I went in the University of Calgary, I encountered open doors and a positive ethos. I had many stimulating and worthwhile meetings with colleagues in Law, Education, Psychology, Strategic Studies and Social Work; and the staff at the University Library and the Law Library were untiring in their eagerness to help me with every request, no matter how obscure.

Professor George Melnyk, acting on behalf of the Consortium of Peace Studies, initiated the invitation and guided me at every turn. His honesty, forthrightness and utter reliability made everything easy. What mattered a great deal more to me than his brisk efficiency was his thoughtfulness, warmth and concern for my well-being, in matters both large and small.

During my time at the University, I was accommodated by the Calgary Institute for the Humanities under the directorship of Professor Wayne McCready, with whom I enjoyed a relaxed and intellectually stimulating relationship. The Institute provided for my every need and the Institute administrator, Denise Hemel, could not have been more helpful. I was made to feel very much a part of the Institute from the day I first walked in. The Education Faculty also supported my Fellowship and I would like to express my thanks to Professor Tim Goddard for his good offices and for his interest in the work of the Consortium of Peace Studies as well as his attention to securing the conditions of my stay. Dr. Yvonne Hébert facilitated my Internationalisation Grant from the Faculty of Education. I also appreciated the warm personal support and intellectual engagement of Professor Hank Stam of the Department of Psychology.

The Department of Peace Studies at the University of Bradford remains a special place and I am sensitive to the privilege of working with fine colleagues. I am particularly grateful to Malcolm Dando, Paul Rogers, Shaun Gregory, Nana Poku, Tom Woodhouse and Nick Lewer. We also have more than our share of inspired and inspiring students. One could not ask for a more stimulating environment than to be in the company of people from around the world whose common trait is an unembarrassed and often steely determination to make the world a little better.

The cover image was produced by Bob Colameco, whose teaching career extends back at least as far as the year he befriended me. And the zen of spot welding was the least of it.

This book is dedicated to my partner, Maureen Loveland, with a smiling, tender awareness that these years together have been too good not to be true.

Glossary

AIDS	Acquired Immunodeficiency Syndrome
CFC	Chlorofluorocarbon
CT	Convergence of Technologies
EST	Expressed-Sequence Tags
EU	European Union
FAO	Food and Agriculture Organisation
GDP	Gross Domestic Product
GOARN	Global Outbreak and Alert Response Network
HIV	Human Immunodeficiency Virus
IFI	International financial institution
IGO	Intergovernmental Organisation
IMF	International Monetary Fund
IPCC	Intergovernmental Panel on Climate Change
IO	International Organisation
INGO	International Non-Governmental Organisation
IR	International Relations
LTCM	Long-term Capital Management
MP	Member of Parliament
NATO	North Atlantic Treaty Organisation
NBIC	Nanotechnology, Biotechnology, Information Technology and Cognitive Science
NGO	Non-Governmental organisation
OECD	Organisation for Economic Cooperation and Development
OTA	Office of Technology Assessment
PCB	Polychlorinated Biphenyls
SARS	Severe Acute Respiratory Syndrome
SOA	Sphere of Authority
TB	Tuberculosis
TRIPS	Trade-Related Aspects of Intellectual Property Rights
UDHR	Universal Declaration of Human Rights
UK	United Kingdom
UN	United Nations
UNDP	United Nations Development Program
UNICEF	United Nations Children's Fund
US	United States

USPTO	United States Patent and Trademark Office
WFP	World Food Program
WHO	World health Organisation
WTO	World Trade Organisation

1
Global governance: of, by and for whom?

Is it truly the case, as we are sometimes told, that 'global issues require global solutions'?[1] What would acting in this way entail, and do we currently have the means to do so? What would be required of the familiar structures, actors and processes of politics? Are these fixtures either necessary or sufficient? Would something new need to be created, or could we engineer 'global solutions' by making running adjustments to our already existing organisations of political community? Are global issues now properly the work of international organisations, or should we think instead of supranational ones, or possibly configurations of state and non-state actors? How would the agents of 'global solutions' secure and maintain all of the important mainstays of democratic politics: legitimacy, authority, accountability, inclusiveness, and representation? On what basis would 'solutions' be enacted – and if necessary, enforced?

Such questions are not entirely abstract. They arise quite directly from the challenges posed by concrete matters that most people would regard as global, at least in some respects: the HIV/AIDS pandemic; climate change; criminal and terrorist networks and the kinds of social, financial and electronic networks that facilitate and finance them; and the proliferation of weapons of mass destruction and the capacity to acquire or manufacture them.

However, it is not difficult to assign the qualifier 'global' to any matter that is of considerable human consequence and which cannot be contained within geographical or political boundaries – qualities which certainly pertain to the examples immediately above and many more besides. So it might reasonably be asked whether such qualities necessarily mean that we now have 'global issues' that are in some ways significantly different from, or even a step change beyond the stuff of national and international politics. Are not nations and the

1

international system already fully engaged with these issues (albeit with all of the contention and competition that routinely attends them)? Besides, not all conditions or relations with global qualities are issues, or a least issues in ways that are open to solutions. For example, global trade is regulated by means of national laws and international regulations and agreements, most notably the World Trade Organisation (WTO). These regulations are problematic in practical ways and are certainly highly contentious in political terms, but trade is a dynamic feature of our ways of life, not a problem that can be solved. In addition, the assertion that global solutions are required for global issues can be a useful rhetorical device for national political purposes, such as distributing responsibility for the creation and/or worsening of a situation and for its rectification. As early as 2001, when President Bush asserted that 'the solution [for climate change] ought to be global', what he had in mind was the involvement of developing countries in shouldering the costs and burdens.[2]

All International Relations (IR) theorists appreciate that the international arena itself has at least one encompassing context – the planetary environment. It is clear that the global physical arena of animate and inanimate processes is subject to a considerable number of anthropogenic impacts, hence crises such as biodiversity loss and climate change. But the activities that create these effects can at least in principle be forbidden, restricted, controlled or regulated in line with our understandings of security and sustainability. Was the Montreal Protocol (which provided for the phasing out of ozone-damaging chlorofluorocarbons (CFCs)) a 'global solution to a global issue'? If so, why should we now speak of 'global solutions' – and indeed, global governance – when international politics should be sufficient, at least in principle?

But while scepticism about superficially attractive phrases such as 'global solutions for global issues' is appropriate, it is difficult to sustain the position that the international system is wholly or largely adequate for the regulatory burdens being generated by globalising processes. Note how in the following, a robust defence of the centrality and integrity of states and international system facing a variety of globalising forces, the emphasis is given to authority rather than ability; to states and the international system more as institutions than as actors; and with no mention of the vastly expanded regulatory burdens that come with globalisation – and especially environmental ones:

> Transnational activities are a striking feature of our era which signal some of the ways and directions in which human relations on the

planet are changing at the present time. These changes are important. They are technological, economic or social circumstances that statespeople must deal with. They may adversely affect state institutions and may even undermine them or weaken them in certain ways. But they do not constitute or involve moral or legal claims that challenge the authority of state sovereignty. They do not constitute a global political institution that is a rival or alternative to the society of states. At the present time, there is no rival or alternative to the society of states for organising and conducting political life on a global scale.[3]

It is certainly useful to be able to think of human activity and organisation in terms of arenas (physical, economic, political, military) and levels (global, international, national, local). However, the international system is a necessary abstraction, not a free-standing entity either above or outside of the planetary environment or the societies and peoples that comprise it; nor is it impermeable to the effects of their myriad dynamics. Acknowledging this in outline terms is much more straightforward than getting to grips with its implications. So however considerable the standing of states and the international system relative to other actors, it does not necessarily follow that states in any variety of configurations will be sufficient, on their own, for regulating matters that can reasonably be described as global – and there is abundant evidence to suggest that for many purposes they are not.[4] To argue such is not to argue for 'rival or alternative' structures, but to suggest that we need to think less categorically about human social order and the organisation of political community, with a view to dealing effectively with the expanding and perplexing range of regulatory challenges now facing us. And as part of the still incomplete progress from Cold War mind sets, we need to bear in mind that states must deal not only with other actors (and other, powerful states especially), but also with complex dynamics – some of them unwilled, often unanticipated – which vex both human systems and natural systems.[5]

Turning our attention from structures to activities, a related difficulty is that what counts as a significant actor at the international and global levels has not remained fixed. Hierarchies of power now have more analytical purchase in specific contexts rather than in absolute terms. States still matter, but so too do a range of non-state actors – and they matter *to* states: to the compass of their effective power; to their perceived legitimacy; and to their relationships with each other. Although these points have been a commonplace in the globalisation literature for some time, the state remains a central focus of thinking about world order, partly because of the persistence of Realism in International Relations theorising; partly because globalising forces are so pervasive and unsettling, for states themselves and for their citizens.[6] A world which depends on states and the international system for a great deal of its systemic stability is at the same time globalised and still globalising. This is why changes in the viability, relative standing and deployable power of states are one of the most important measures we have of tracking the trajectories of globalisation and of assessing its many meanings. The conceptual challenges presented by this are as considerable as the practical ones. It has made theorists of all of us.

But in international politics, theory and practice arise together; they are necessarily complementary because all actors, including states and the international organisations they create, must act with imperfect knowledge; with an understanding of causal relations that is incomplete at best; and with consequences that are not entirely predictable. So for example, the application of international sanctions is based on a theory developed at the end of World War I;[7] and more recent is the notion that democracies do not go to war with another – former US President Clinton and George W. Bush's assertion that this is the case[8] is a hotly contested matter in the theoretical literature.[9] Politics is not only the art of the possible: it is also the uncertainty and risk of the possible. And clearly, the uncertainties and the risks are increasing.

Of course, the discipline of IR has a theoretical base and depth that extends beyond the bounds of pressing matters of public policy and inter-state relations; and other related disciplines – International Political Economy, Political Sociology, Strategic Studies – inform it and shape its agendas. But so too do current events: terrorism most recently, but also global environmental crises; infectious diseases; trade disputes; widespread financial turmoil. Sometimes, deliberation is conditioned by urgency, while at other times, change is more incremental, with the drama of change visible only at the 'tipping point' – an observation often made by those advocating immediate and concerted action to forestall the catastrophic and irreversible effects of climate change.

One of the fascinations of the global governance literature is that its compass can be dealt with in terms of the range of significant actors, or in terms of relations or situations that require considerable and frequently novel forms of steering, organisation or control. In practice, one can scarcely write meaningfully about global governance without considering both together, so particular studies tend to emphasise one aspect over the other, while recognising that they are mutually constitutive. Although much the same could be said about the study of IR, global governance offers considerable challenges to the study of IR, especially with respect to significant actors, with states normally occupying a realm that is elevated if not exclusive (a theme dealt with in Chapter 5). Even as the developing literature on global governance implicitly poses the question, 'What would an adequate theory of global governance be a theory *of*?, it is becoming increasingly difficult for IR theorists of any disposition to avoid revisiting the basics: 'What would an adequate theory of International Relations be a theory *of*?' A response to either informs the other.

Global governance *of*: the compass of global governance

In the absence of supranational organisations, and despite the frequency with which the term 'global institutions' has begun to appear, any particular form of global governance might well be considerable, but no one holds the view that we can have global governance of the globe – that is, of human social life in its entirety. The global governance literature is not a search for the political equivalent of a unified field theory in physics. Rather, it is an attempt to describe sets of relations which appear to have outrun our theoretical embrace. These include a dizzying variety of forms of human relatedness – within and between nations, peoples and communities, often remote from one another; and between the full span of human systems (political, industrial, economic) and natural systems.

Before dealing with the subjects of global governance, it is important to note that the term 'global governance' is also used in a summative, descriptive sense – to convey the sum total of all the world's many orders. 'Global' in this sense denotes inclusiveness rather than coherence and comprehensiveness, even for any particular issue area. As expressed by James Rosenau: '...global order is conceived...to be a single set of arrangements even though these are not causally linked into a single coherent array of patterns. The organic whole that comprises the present or future global order is organic only in the sense that its diverse actors are all claimants upon the same earthbound resources and all of them must cope with the same environmental conditions, noxious and polluted as these might be.'[10]

It is the character of our large-scale crises as much as the fact of them which has brought the global governance concept to such prominence. For all of the considerable differences between them, the HIV/AIDS pandemic, climate change, biodiversity loss and global financial turmoil have a number of features in common: they are rooted in individual behaviours; they are largely unrestricted by borders and boundaries; they span a number of diverse realms (for example, rainforest ecology and international trade in the case of biodiversity loss); and they cannot be contained or addressed by nations acting on their own. Globalisation has not by any means overwhelmed states and the international system, but it has certainly expanded, or perhaps 'deepened' the arena in which they must act. National and international governance issues remain, but even they are now frequently conditioned by global issues – the multiple impacts of HIV/AIDS being a case in point.[11]

It is not difficult to appreciate why so much of the global governance literature is devoted to sector-specific concerns: once a number of human and/or natural dynamics manifest themselves as a crisis in the international system or as an issue which is pervasive, serious and challenging if not unprecedented for one or more states it quickly comes to be regarded as a global issue. Yet few global issues will be open to 'global solutions'. This is because whatever might count as a global governance actor and whatever might count as the activity of global governance, the largest part of managing any human situation (including crises) entails managing relations. This is not to discount or dismiss the importance of scientific investigation, quantitative measures and technical expertise, but '...to challenge our ideas of "relations" as flimsy nets external to the elements which they relate and leaving those elements unaffected, most of all where those elements are human minds. We are not separable from the multitude of relations which we sustain. Like our societies, we *are* systems of relationship.'[12] Seen in this light, environmental issues – even those on the largest scale – are fundamentally relational problems: strongly contested and/or unsustainable practices within and between human and natural systems. The same applies for any other issue over which we exercise governance – and the relational quality of these efforts is evinced most clearly in the work of states to secure themselves in their environment – an important element of which is maintaining the order and stability *of* their wider environment: international *relations*.

Although we can speak of international relations in general terms (as the sum of all inter-state relations), there is no generic form of activity that goes under that term: instead, 'international relations' is the quality of certain forms of state-directed activity. Similarly, we can speak meaningfully of global governance both as a condition and as a form of activity, but there is no generic global governance. Whether we can limit global governance as an activity to certain issue areas, or to particular actors or configurations of actors are important considerations for global governance theorising, together with what might comprise the 'global' quality of such governance. But as set out at the start of this chapter, there are some conditions (or issues) which have an indisputably global character, however much states and the international system are implicated as the responsible causative or rectificatory agents. How states (and very often) a panoply of non-state agents combine to address such matters is now centre stage in the literature that is concerned with global governance as an activity.[13] Scepticism about global governance from a theoretical perspective notwithstanding,[14] it is difficult to imagine that states and the international system, applying the familiar mechanisms of politics and diplomacy, will be sufficient on their own to address matters as pervasive and embedded as HIV/AIDS, or to ensure a change in the habits of millions and sometimes billions of individuals (discussed further in Chapter 2).

Depictions of sector-specific global governance are frequently top-down in character, but they are (at least implicitly) not exclusive – after all, no one pretends that the climate change regime exhausts whatever might be included in 'global environmental governance'. On any sober assessment of the challenges involved, it will clearly entail the governance of many physical environments that together comprise our world – in addition to the global governance of various sectoral activities (energy generation; commercial fishing; the airline industry) that can have a deleterious effect on the planetary ecosphere. And at a still lower level are relevant individual behaviours, most notably patterns of consumption and travel (further discussed in Chapter 2). We can see in this how in depicting global issues (and the possibility of 'global solutions'), the matter(s) to be governed and the actors involved either actively or passively arise together. In the following, Sir John Houghton, former co-chairman of Scientific Assessment for the International Panel on Climate Change, outlines the task of addressing global warming in a form that is essentially a call to global governance:

> Global pollution demands global solutions. To arrive at global solutions it is necessary to address human attitudes very broadly, for instance those concerned with resource use, lifestyle, wealth and poverty. They must also involve human society at all levels of aggregation – international organisations, nations with their national and local governments, large and small industry and businesses, non-governmental organisations (e.g. churches) and individuals.[15]

We need not speculate about the limits of global governance as an activity below an admittedly difficult to determine 'global' threshold since in any event, widening and intensifying global dynamics are likely to ensure that the number and range of issues that easily come within the compass of global governance are likely to increase. Certainly there is no current shortage:[16] the planetary environment (really a theme, which itself carries a plethora of terribly difficult, interlinked issues); health; finance; and possibly matters such as terrorism and human rights (the subject of Chapter 10).

It is worth bearing in mind that what constitutes initiatives that amount to global governance is only partly a matter of the qualities of the subject addressed. In the absence of any kind of authority to mandate a global governance initiative, what we are witnessing is the evolution of responses by sometimes novel combinations of established and aspiring actors to events and situations which matter greatly to them, or to those they represent. As the Commission on Global Governance expressed it, global governance '…is a broad, dynamic, complex process of interactive decision-making that is constantly evolving and responding to changing circumstances'.[17]

So global governance as it is now widely understood has been less an invention than a development, much as we have come to use the term 'globalisation'. And if globalisation facilitates, amplifies or accelerates the emergence of global threats, it also performs something similar in terms of the responsiveness of affected parties.

In many respects, then, a simple definition of global governance suffices to outline the scope of global governance as an activity: 'Efforts to bring more orderly and reliable responses to social and political issues that go beyond the capacities of states to address individually.'[18] This general characterisation is a helpful one, but still leaves open the question of what kind of order – and in whose interests.

Global governance *by*: global governance actors

If what were once commonly regarded as national and sub-national actors can no longer be confined to clearly bounded arenas (something implicit in the term, 'transnational corporation'), this is in part because the arenas and levels of human activity have become so porous, so easily traversed. Comprehending this world in the making is becoming ever more difficult as the span of actors and issues increase in number, and as movement and developments between them become more dynamic – and in some cases, less predictable. Indeed, characterising a situation as a global issue (whether or not it can also be deemed a crisis) signals that it is not merely a relatively novel agenda item in international politics, even if the most obvious and immediate response takes the form of cooperative endeavour on the part of our largest organisations of political community, especially international organisations.

Given the attention that is usually focused on the performance of international organisations as mainstays of global governance,[19] it is easy to overlook how important they are in enabling states to acknowledge a large-scale matter as a *political* one. What makes some developments and some situations political is that they affect the organisation and maintenance of communities in key areas to a degree which necessitates action (or at the very least, contention about action), at the community level. So, for example, if pollution can be externalised – say, dumped in a river and washed out of sight, out of mind, there are no immediate political consequences. If, however, the community's fish supply is thereby depleted, or a community downriver finds its way of life endangered, the actions are invested with considerable political meaning. In an era of global environmental issues, the same principle applies, but in vastly more complex ways, not only for communities, but also in respect of planetary-level physical processes as well. The political meaning of environmental problems is not fixed, or something that can be measured scientifically. Determining political meaning – and from there, political responsibilities – is often a large part of the substance of environmental negotiations. The well-established structures and mechanisms of international organisations are central for this purpose as well as for the more procedural aspects of framing detailed agreements and monitoring compliance to them.

There can be little doubt that states and the international organisations they have created will remain crucial to most forms of global governance, including unexpected crises such as the outbreak of Severe Acute Respiratory Syndrome (SARS), as well as longer-running and/or more routine governance matters – in this case, the global governance of health. As in other areas of human security, globalising dynamics can worsen existing conditions, such as rapidly facilitating the spread of SARS. But globalising dynamics can also improve the prospects for effective governance – and, staying with our example, global health is no exception.[20] In matters of worldwide connectedness or inclusiveness, it is now becoming common for large, dedicated national and international organisations to serve as much as the centres of extensive networks as significant, solitary actors:

As a form of sectoral global governance, the control of epidemics poses some particularly difficult challenges. To begin with, the international system and the global physical environment – the realm of viruses and bacteria – are incommensurable. We have limited knowledge of the full extent of the microbial world; pathogens are capable of rapid, adaptive mutation; and our preventive governance measures, however extensive and effective, cannot eliminate the fact of human vulnerability to disease. Yet preventive measures, even non-specific safeguards, are an important bulwark against disease outbreaks becoming epidemics, and epidemics pandemics. The inevitable need not be catastrophic. Ensuring this is the business of a considerable range of actors – states most prominently; international law and organisations; regional organisations; the scientific and medical communities; and non-governmental and commercial organisations of many kinds. Ensuring timely cooperation between all of them, against the pull of powerful interests and potentially considerable costs – all sometimes in an atmosphere of fear and suspicion – is the daunting task neatly gathered under the term, 'global governance of epidemics'.[21]

Of all the world's international organisations, it is the United Nations, its programmes, funds and agencies that feature most prominently in accounts of global governance by – and on some accounts, *as* – international organisation.[22] Most notably, the UN's subsidiary bodies perform both normative and functional roles, instigating and organising a wide variety of global governance activities, including aspects of development, environmental protection, food provision and intellectual property, to list but a few. Because of its standing and universal membership, the UN can initiate global conferences on even quite divisive normative subjects (the human rights of women, and of children, for example) and also undertake active, practical roles itself, as we see in the work of WFP, UNICEF and UNDP – often in partnership with non-UN actors, many of them local. Of course, all such UN-directed activity is subject to the political interests and pressures of its member states, often through funding arrangements which are both directive and restrictive.

A great deal of scholarly attention has been devoted to the 'architecture' of global governance – essentially, high-level international organisations and regimes tasked with creating and maintaining order within and between human systems.[23] In some ways, the architecture metaphor is quite apt: it suggests planning; solidity if not permanence; and an ability to accommodate large affairs, or numerous particulars. On the other hand, it is also oddly static. We surely require structures, but we must also be sensitive to dynamics. The largest and most extensive 'architectures' created at the international and regional levels concern economic and financial management, most prominently the Bretton Woods Institutions. Yet these were created before the capacity of private traders to contract trillions of dollars of exchange electronically – and rapidly; before the emergence of hedge funds and private equity firms as powerful, system-level actors; and before computerised stock market trading – all of which have generated turbulence and even crises in the global financial system.

Does the emergence of new or familiar but greatly empowered actors in global finance challenge the global governance of this arena, or could we say that to the extent that they shape and direct it (not necessarily for the good of all, or for stability and predictability), that they too are agents of global governance? If the 'global governance by' question in any particular field identifies many actors, from a variety of levels of human organisation, then global governance need not be confined to multilateral forums. What follows from this is that considerable interest in the global governance literature includes not only how well our larger, established governance actors have coped in a world of changing dynamics, but also to what extent non-state and private actors now share the stage with them – and with what implications. Forms of global governance activity arising from the expansion of the global governance actor arena have been described as 'governance without government':

...[S]ystems of rule can be maintained and their controls successfully and consistently exerted even in the absence of established legal or political authority. The evolution of intersubjective consensuses based on shared fates and common histories, the possession of information and knowledge, the pressure of active or mobilizeable publics, and/or the use of careful planning, good timing, clever manipulation and hard bargaining can – either separately or in combination – foster control mechanisms that sustain governance without government.[24]

The conditions brought about by the collapse or critical debilitation of a state's central authority can assume a modicum of stability and order, one form of 'governance without government', albeit with power-based relations likely to be ascendant over structured forms of accountability.[25] However, what is more notable is the number and variety of governance activities now taking place 'below' or outside the direct purview of states and international organisations, a trend that has been underway for many years,[26] but which has greatly expanded in recent years and gained considerable momentum. Forms of advocacy, of norm creation and consolidation, standard-setting, and self-regulation are in themselves nothing new, but the capacity of transglobal networks and coalitions to affect changes at the international level are a significant development, creating a global politics – an arena in which states and the international system contend (and at times cooperate) with a wide range of non-state actors, either singly (as with Amnesty International, or Greenpeace), or in purposeful configurations (the Jubilee Campaign on developing world debt; the campaign to ban land mines). Although it is not difficult to cite examples of 'governance without government' initiatives to improve the plight of the disenfranchised or to diminish violence and destructiveness, the 'for whom and for what purpose?' question still applies. Non-state actors include organisations which are a good deal more self-interested than the frequent references to progressive NGOs might suggest. The interested parties behind the development of the 1994 Agreement on Trade-Related Aspects of Intellectual Property Rights (TRIPS) entailed contention between states, of course, but non-state actors were not a homogeneous group, with private sector activism pulling in several directions. As one analyst expresses the negotiations leading to the TRIPS agreement, 'Structural factors tipped the scale in the direction of privileged agents and their preferred policies, but [...] [t]he global governance of intellectual property is a dynamic process: focusing on the relationships between micro and macro level factors helps to show how agents reproduce and transform the structure through their actions.'[27]

As globalisation continues apace, the reconstitution of innumerable forms of human relatedness is coming to be recognised as one of its more significant outcomes. As a consequence, it is now widely held that greatly enhanced modes of communication, together with a growing awareness of the power of globalising dynamics for various parties and purposes has brought about the emergence of a 'global civil society'. The concept has a long lineage:[28] one can see a line of continuous development of civil society across centuries to our present, globalised condition when viewed '...not as an object but a complex set of relations that emerged historically in compromises made between Western publics and emerging state powers'.[29] In recent years, 'global civil society' has commanded a good deal of analytical notice.[30] Clearly linked as it is with the idea of 'governance without government', it is also notable that the concept carries the hopes of many in the possibilities of a progressive global politics,[31] not only for practical engagement with what we have characterised here as global issues, but also for the advancement of norms. However, global civil society has no distinct membership, shape or continuity; nor does it have agency. We might best regard it as a condition of relatedness which in active modes can turn associational links and enhanced means of interaction between disparate groups to common political purposes. But there is nothing inherent in such a very wide range of peoples and organisations that promises benign purpose or that precludes contention within and between its many possible configurations – something clearly evident if we consider corporations to be as much a part of global civil society as NGOs.[32]

Any organisation or group capable of wielding global governance, or of participating significantly in activity we can so characterise, is exercising power – and with every accrual of power, all of the social provisions against its absolute forms and other abuses come into play: legality, authority, legitimacy, accountability. The difficulty with many of the early characterisations of non-state global governance actors is that the novelty of empowerment was privileged over questions of accountability. The emphasis has shifted as some more worrisome accumulations of power and authority have become more visible, including organised crime syndicates, private military companies, largely unregulated financial operations and terrorist networks. Even so, there remains some faith that the extent of the diffusion of various forms of power 'downward' (from states) and 'outward' to widely diverse actors provides a sufficient safeguard against state-like or state-level abuses of power:

> It has been estimated...that the number of transnational corporations exceed 35,000 and that, in turn, these have over 200,000 subsidiaries. While these figures indicate that sizeable areas of global life rest on a form of governance that lacks democratic accountability, they also suggest that the dispersal of authority in globalized space is now so widespread that severe violations of democratic values cannot readily be concentrated in hegemonic hands.[33]

But scepticism about this position properly begins prior to the 'retreat of the state',[34] not least in respect of economic matters. As Rodney Bruce Hall and Thomas Biersteker point out, 'One salient analytical cut into the emerging issue of private authority in the international political economy is the debate about whether the state is complicit in the transfer of its once sovereign prerogative (such as the setting of exchange rates, the maintenance of a stable currency, or trade management).' They continue:

> In such cases, is the state complicit in the devolution of its authority to private actors? Has the state delegated authority, enabled it, or

simply allowed authority to slip away, and for what purposes? Or is the state merely impotent to do much about this devolution of authority? Has the state no mechanism with which to combat the collusion and coordination of firms with interests in minimizing state authority through the development of 'private regimes'?[35]

It is becoming clear that as the number of significant governance actors increases and as sources and forms of considerable power and authority move 'outward' from states and the international system, the regulatory burden is likely to increase – at the very least in terms of confronting these new sources of power, holding them to account and dealing with the direct and indirect consequences of their activities.

James Rosenau has observed that 'If governance on a global scale involves the norms and practices that constrain and empower social, economic, and political entities engaged in collective behaviour in a globalized space, then all of these agents...need to be sorted out. [...] Obviously, an understanding of governance on a global scale is bound to be hampered until it yields an incisive conception of the agents that sustain it.'[36] But the globalised expansion of the arena of significant action and an increase in the number of actors has not merely enlarged the game: it has transformed it. So perhaps we need to think less in terms of actors in the sense of agents of global governance on one hand and those acted upon on the other – and more in terms of participants in shifting relational patterns of activity which continually shape the kinds and degrees of order and turbulence in our world.

Global governance: for what and for whom?

Issue-based studies of global governance (say, of the global environment, or global health) do not on the whole invite questions of the sort, 'for what purpose?' At a minimum, the definition of global governance quoted above – 'Efforts to bring more orderly and reliable responses to social and political issues' – suffices, at least as far as the immediate, functional fulfilment of basic human needs and planetary stability are concerned. These activities can still be controversial, since they inevitably entail negotiation and bargaining over responsibility and costs. But in conditions where threats of a fundamental kind can quickly globalise, contention is more likely to gather around the particulars of practical engagement than about hidden agendas. However, global governance is not merely an extended form of crisis management; and such global governance as is now extant concerns the distribution of power and the construction and maintenance of orders that plainly advantage certain states, organisations and peoples at the expense of others, or at the cost of irreversible environmental damage. That portion of the global governance literature concerned with fundamentally inclusive and humane global governance[37] has its complement in studies which depict global governance in terms of more self-interested, less beneficent initiatives to shape the contours of our globalising world. One need not regard these as conspiratorial simply because a good portion of them involve a range of non-state actors (criminal organisations notwithstanding). Many involve a degree of state/on-state cooperation – not least the pervasiveness of free market capitalism, the structure of which is founded not only on treaties and international organisations, but also the initiatives of numerous private actors, especially transnational corporations.

Basic and sharply contrasting views on how best to characterise global governance sometimes turn on what is taken to be the more significant arena of action. Those concerned with inequitable social orders, the hope of a global social policy and the more beneficent possibilities of global civil society and networked forms of political action tend to emphasise the aspects of global governance at those social, largely sub-national and transnational levels. Those more concerned with the actors, issues and mechanisms that largely fall within the compass of international relations tend to privilege these matters over related but distinct actors and outcomes. This has led one analyst to suggest that 'Global governance is best described as a muddled blend of *parapolitics* and *metapolitics*, that is, a Janus-faced combination between the continuation of politics within the societal sphere on the one hand, and the assignment of roles to international politics and transnational economics on the other.' The author goes on to argue that 'global governance has a transatlantic organisational bias' and that 'more often than not, ideas about global governance are inherently economistic'.[38]

However, one need not abstract the international realm from lower-level social ones in order to conceive global governance as a pernicious consolidation of the forces of exclusion and domination. Mark Duffield's general depiction of the changing relationship between state and non-state actors is, within the span of the global governance literature, unexceptional: 'While states and governments remain important, and will continue to do so, increasingly they exercise their authority through complex international, national and sub-national governance networks linking state and non-state actors.'[39] But from this observation, he goes on to depict global governance as an emerging strategic complex; not so much a small number of powerful actors pursuing a common goal, but a much larger configuration, the dedicated and co-opted alike, shaping world order:

> [L]iberal peace is embodied in a number of flows and nodes of authority within liberal governance that bring together different *strategic complexes* of state-non-state, military-civilian and public-private actors in pursuit of its aims. Such complexes variously enmesh international NGOs, governments, military establishments, IFIs, private security companies, IGOs, the business sector, and so on. They are strategic in the sense of pursuing a radical agenda of social transformation in the interests of global stability. [...] [T]hey have expanded to constitute a network of strategic governance relations that are increasingly privatised and militarised.[40]

The fundamentals of global governance as an activity

Men and women of widely differing intellectual disposition, political allegiance and practical ambition see in global governance myriad possibilities for good and for ill – and in this regard, the problems of getting to grips with global governance are similar to those that globalisation presents. Indeed, a number of themes are common to both, most visible in polarised positions on matters such as whether globalisation and/or global governance are advancing and consolidating hegemonic domination, while others see in one or both possibilities opening up for the currently disenfranchised, either through the spread of prosperity[41] or through the emergence of global civil society and a range of other relatively novel forms of associational politics. The question of whether in summative terms global governance can be regarded as a political project with a strategic orientation accommodating the interests of an elite returns us to fundamental conceptual questions: the problems of state power in an anarchic world central to nearly all IR theorising;[42] its relationship to globalising processes and whether global governance consolidates them or mediates them;[43] whether we might do best to concentrate on empirical studies, or on political vocabulary;[44] – all the while beset with changes to our social and physical environments we struggle to comprehend for practical, let alone political and intellectual purposes.

The kinds of 'solutions' spoken of as being available for global issues should probably be regarded as shorthand for political endeavour on the largest possible scale: inclusive of actors both high and low; intensely political; daunting in terms of organisation and coordination; and often at odds with the established momentum of organisations and the fixed aspirations of individuals. This is the stuff of global governance as an activity, whatever the likelihood of global 'solutions'. Its characteristics, essentially in the form of the challenges it must face, are the subject of the next eight chapters.

2

Global governance in most senses and in most cases will link the local and the global; and the individual and the national/international realms

The US Congressman Thomas ('Tip') O'Neil once asserted that 'all politics is local'.[1] There is a degree of provocative simplification in this, but also some seasoned political shrewdness. Political engagement or ascent is driven less by any objective measure of the scale or seriousness of an issue than by how much it matters to individuals. This is often felt in terms of immediate, practical concerns such as job security, disposable income and perceptions of hazard. But there is a good deal more than highly localised and self-interested impulses behind the capacity of individuals to accept or assert the need for making any issue a political one requiring a concerted response. Compassion, a sense of justice and concern for the quality of life of future generations also manifest themselves quite routinely in everything from the politics of foreign aid[2] to the 'Make Poverty History' campaign.[3] Politicians are not always able to detect, inspire, lead or channel the felt concerns of their constituents, but they know it is essential to success – and all the more over issues that initially meet with indifference or hostility.

The dynamics between a government and its citizens run in both directions. In the case of law-making, sometimes laws consolidate changed or changing social norms, in effect making law what has already been established as custom. (The gradual codification of the rights of women and the decriminalisation of certain classes of drugs are two examples.) At other times, laws are enacted and enforced in advance of social norms, as was certainly the case with civil rights legislation in the United States of the 1960s.[4] At both national and international levels, what counts as governmental responsibility or democratic responsiveness is a matter of political contestation, both inside and outside of legislative chambers. However, in modern states, most decision-making on important matters is not subjected to direct

18

public deliberation, a condition summed up by the post-electoral phrase 'democratic mandate'. Although in any state that is more than nominally democratic, there is at least some check on the excesses of governments though the routine electoral cycle, a democratic mandate of four years or longer can carry a good deal of legislative freight, not all of it either the substance of an election manifesto or a response to an unexpected development or event. (For this reason, the inadequacies of majority-led 'participatory democracy' have in recent years given rise to a movement toward fuller, more engaged and engaging forms of 'deliberative democracy'.[5])

As the pressures of globalisation encroach with greater frequency and impact on even the most powerful states, some of the decisions and positions adopted by governments can be deeply unpopular, or at least contentious and divisive to significant degrees. Individuals can and do develop sudden and vociferous opposition to globalisation, or aspects of it, when it threatens their personal security, or touches a raw nerve in some other way. And what is true about states' accommodation of the harsh realities of globalisation is no less true of their efforts to frame concomitant global governance arrangements that attempt – (so the political justifications run) – to maximise benefits and minimise costs. Those left out in the cold are understandably unimpressed with the logic of this hybridised form of utilitarianism. For example, consider the following characterisation of the exigencies of global governance:

> Global governance, thus far, is about negotiations among government and corporate representatives charged with the responsibility of defending national and corporate economic interests. Government representatives are chosen for their ability to skilfully trade off weaker domestic interests for the stronger, if necessary. That is the assigned task of those involved in trade negotiations and it is a weighty and complex assignment.[6]

One may read into this that although it may be reasonable to say that all politics are local, some locales are more important than others; and that political priorities close to home can be shaped, driven or determined by dynamics and interests quite remote in origin but powerful in effect. In other words, local politics cannot be insulated from globalising dynamics – economic, social, cultural and environmental as well as political. One hardly need explain to someone whose means of earning a living has been transferred to a low-cost foreign establishment that the local and the global are explicitly linked, or that interests and priorities determined at national and international levels have a direct bearing on individuals. These and similar cases are now commonplace, but the frequency of trade-offs occasioned by globalisation and the impacts these have on millions of individuals mask a deeper and longer development of ways in which the relational qualities of individuals as persons and as actors has been expanding for many decades.

On the matter of the standing of individuals as persons, an important development in international law has been the trend since the end of World War II toward the inclusion of individuals as subjects (rather than 'objects') of international law – that is, individuals acquiring a legal personality, both liable to certain strictures of international law and able to make claims within its compass. This trend had its strongest impetus in the war crimes trials in the 1940s and with the establishment of the United Nations Charter, but has expanded considerably since then, extending to individual liability in other fields.[7] Furthermore, the establishment and development of universal human rights (discussed more fully in Chapter 10) is itself an implicit challenge to the power of sovereign states: relations of absolute power cannot be reconciled to the human rights regime, thus conditioning the relationship of all citizens in every country to their respective states.

The standing of individuals within the national and international realms has its counterpart in the affective power so many of us have accrued. There is now a critical mass of human beings who are sufficiently empowered in various ways such that their mundane and hitherto quite innocent actions make their individual and collective 'carbon footprints' dangerously large. Our consumerist behaviours (frequent international jet travel; food and perishable goods sourced from the four corners of the world; goods and services reliant on non-renewable energy sources) eventually manifest themselves as crises: disappearing fish stocks; water scarcities; climate change; and biodiversity loss through habitat destruction. The parlous state of the global commons is as it is because of the way millions of us live – in a word, unsustainably. The source of the degradation of natural environments (local and regional as well as global) is located not in politicians' 'lack of political will', but in individual choices (and for the desperately poor, in the absence of meaningful choice). In democratic countries, governments more often do the bidding of the majority of citizens than is commonly acknowledged, even when this 'bidding' is by default. (How many of those who profess concern over climate change travel less frequently by car or plane?)

Given our globalised condition, what counts as local has become highly conditioned in almost every important particular; and when we recognise that our individual choices and defaults are linked to outcomes we would never countenance directly, we implicitly distinguish local politics from politically meaningful choices made locally. The relational and environmental linkages between distant locations are becoming more numerous, more intense and more immediate and the injunction to 'think globally, act locally' is a recognition of this. So too is our heightened awareness of the ethical and environmental consequences of even the most banal consumer choices. Of course, it is through various forms of social organisation that individuals are enabled to make such powerful impacts on both human and natural systems. Industrial and commercial enterprises create abundance in the form of goods and services, with a range of consequences often uncosted or even acknowledged (much as pollution carried away downstream or downwind was once a 'disregarded externality'.) At the same time, outside of the largest part of the developed world, poor governance (and struggling forms of governance in poor countries), together with many forms of 'greed and grievance'[8] enable or invite exploitation of natural resources that can be devastating at a local level – and in the longer run, catastrophic at the global level, too. The illegal allocation to the logging industry of 21 million hectares of rainforest in the Democratic Republic of Congo[9] is a case in point: it would destroy the ways of life of the peoples who inhabit this region; and it would be disastrous for biodiversity and planetary ecosystem stability. (The Congo rainforest is the second largest in the world.) The cumulative impacts from similar depredations elsewhere on this scale are likely to be quite dramatic.[10] But there are markets for these timber products; and the markets comprise the consumption patterns of millions of individuals far from the localities where the negative impacts will be felt most sharply and immediately.

The cumulative effects of individual actions extend well beyond the realms of our physical environments. Assisted by computerised information and telecommunications systems of several kinds, the initiatives of currency speculators, computer hackers and terrorists (to list but a few) are capable of producing systemic effects at the highest levels of social and political organisation. The former Chair of the US Federal Reserve Board, Alan Greenspan was given to wonder how the 'irrational exuberance' of share traders can be factored into monetary policy[11] – an implicit recognition that time-limited, individual and small-group behaviours can have extended, large-scale economic effects – in this case, '...escalated asset values, which then become subject to unexpected and prolonged contraction [as was experienced] in Japan over [a]decade'. Likewise, global transport links facilitate considerable movements of people, both legal and illegal. The aggregate statistics on these movements are a poor expression of the willed initiative of many millions of people, be they tourists, economic migrants, the displaced or refugees. Cumulatively, however, the effects can be impressive: emigrants from Latin America sent home £32 billion in remittances in 2006, a sum that exceeded the combined flow of aid and foreign direct investment;[12] and tourism generates 11 per cent of global GDP, with the number of tourists expected to double to 1.6 billion by the year 2020.[13]

One can trace at least in general terms the lines of causation from individuals and their needs and wants – and their considerably amplified means of acquiring them – up to the most serious global issues, including but not confined to global environmental crises. So it is plain that the cumulative effects of innumerable individual choices are creating regulatory burdens of unprecedented size and complexity, matters which at their worst are comprehensively life-threatening. Yet the socio-political and socio-economic conditions that make this possible are not a seething, lawless free-for-all. Governments are not distant bystanders to these developments, however much one might want to argue that globalisation has greatly disempowered states. Industrial and commercial enterprises are licenced, regulated and taxed for national purposes; and a vast panoply of international business regulation[14] exists to maintain standards and coordinate the links that provide the legal and normative infrastructure that makes a good deal of international and global interchange a matter of routine rather than risk. In fact, 'Our international world is the product and preoccupation of an intense and ongoing project of regulation and management.'[15] One need only consider how many national and international regulations, standards, norms and laws need to be in place in order for international airline travel to be possible, let alone safe, reliable and readily available. In addition, a great many non-state actors, from International Non-Governmental Organisations (INGOs) to transnational corporations work to ensure favourable conditions for themselves or for their constituents by creating or strengthening norms, or by contending against them. We can witness this in the struggles over intellectual copyright issues, the conditions of world trade, developing country debt and environmental standards.

These and other forms of organising and regulating international and global exchanges accord with generally accepted understandings of global governance, of which the following is not an exceptional definition: 'The complex of formal and informal institutions, mechanisms, relationships and processes between and among states, markets, citizens and organisations – both intergovernmental and non-governmental – through which collective interests are articulated, rights and obligations established and differences are mediated.'[16] One can see in that definition the socio-political and socio-economic means by which a globalised world has been created and is maintained – to the benefit of some, at least. But that same highly regulated world also includes all of the world's gross inequities, unsustainable practices and impacted crises in which we the prosperous are implicated, sometimes directly but more often than not indirectly. All politics might well be local, but an increasing number of human choices have a political quality, with immediate consequences that are often insubstantial to the point of invisibility, or that accumulate elsewhere, over time, and in places distant from the preoccupations of what are generally thought to comprise local politics.

The large-scale outcomes of our individual and/or local activities (such as national carbon footprints) are mediated – and indeed, made possible – by political, economic and socio-cultural systems, as is the North-South divide in almost every human essential. The extent to which any of us adds to the already considerable stresses in the complex interaction of human and natural systems[17] is not an expression of the human predicament, but of human organisation.

But to discern causal linkages between activities at individual and local levels and their cumulative effects at a global level is only to reveal what is likely to be the highly intractable and intensely political nature of global governance initiatives that attempt to align these realms. To get a sense of this, consider the findings of a 2006 Pew Research Center survey conduced in the United States: 'Despite widespread agreement among survey respondents that there is solid evidence that global warming is happening, and a broad sense that its effects can be mitigated, dealing with global warming remains a relatively low priority for the American public. Asked to rate the importance of various issues, [global warming] is among the lowest of 19 issues tested [...] The only issue rated as less important than global warming is gay marriage.'[18] Within and beyond the United States, the relatively cheap and unrestricted means of travel by car and plane that contribute so much to climate change (in the UK, they account for one-third of carbon emissions[19]) are now deeply embedded in ways of life and in popular expectation. There might well be a majority understanding that we have already reached the high-water mark of cheap and easy human mobility, but that will not necessarily play out in terms of a political willingness to shoulder the burdens and the consequences for making it more restrictive and/or expensive – and politicians broadly reflect this, in ways which certainly appear to validate Tip O'Neil's aphorism. So for example when former UK Prime Minister Tony Blair was questioned by MPs on the subject of climate change and the difference that the imposition of a tax on aviation fuel might make, he asserted, 'I do not think you're going to have any political consensus for saying we're going to slap some huge tax on cheap air travel.'[20]

Clearly, actions that in aggregate terms can have powerful global impacts need not be explicitly political, or purposeful beyond the satisfaction of needs that are immediate and/or local. But the exercise of effective global governance in both preventive and rectificatory modes will be both. If they are going to make any large-scale difference, the initiatives put in place to reverse global warming are going to impact the way we live as individuals. We can see this from either end of the telescope: governments currently contending in international forums that they are not going to subscribe to environmental standards that inhibit economic performance; and injunctions that we should switch to low-energy light bulbs and take public transport to our places of employment. The politics of the environment and the clear necessity to bring local and global into some broadly agreed conformity would appear to validate James Rosenau's assertion that '[d]omestic and foreign affairs have always formed a seamless web....[and that] we can no longer allow the domestic-foreign boundary to confound our understanding of world affairs'.[21] But although our world can fairly be characterised as seamless in terms of causal dynamics, it is hardly smooth in relational terms – that is, the ways in which individual/local activities and their global consequences are seamless are not at all comparable to the ways in which political engagement and initiative within and between levels ranging from local/domestic to international are seamless. Indeed, the more seamless the world becomes, the more difficult it is to frame regulatory agreements that are necessarily inclusive but not an ineffective 'least common denominator' compromise.

Nor is the necessity for global governance arrangements confined to matters arising from the desired ends and willed actions of individuals, or to sites where 'local' is fixed and discrete. Information and communications technologies not only enable individuals in familiar ways: they also combine to form 'systems of systems' – and, although the systems behaviours that result are often unplanned and even unanticipated, these become arenas for a surprising range of dynamics that have important impacts in the 'non-virtual' world. For example:

> The two-day outage of one of the world's largest peer-to-peer (P2P) internet services has raised concerns about the technology's robustness. P2P networks are touted as the future on internet distribution for video and TV, since the high bandwidth that would normally be provided by central servers is instead shared between individual network members, removing the problem of data bottlenecks. But on 16 August [2007], the Skype internet telephony network, which depends on P2P, crashed. Millions of users' computers had rebooted simultaneously during a routine update of Windows software. This reduced the network's resources, and when the multitude of freshly rebooted computers sent their combined log-in requests to Skype, its servers buckled.[22]

The Skype case is of little long-term significance, but it is indicative of the new forms of seamlessness we have created for ourselves: highly complex, tightly coupled and densely interconnected information and communications technologies that can generate governance issues of considerable magnitude, however well governed the local systems that comprise them. This became abundantly clear during the global credit crisis which emerged in August 2007. The root of the crisis was in unwise lending practices (high-risk, or 'sub-prime' mortgages in the United States), together with other forms of 'packaged debt' which were sold on a worldwide basis in order to disperse the risk. But when the US housing market stalled and defaults rocketed, the extent of the debt exposure of some of the world's largest financial institutions began to emerge. Liquidity in the world's financial markets evaporated, requiring considerable injections of cash by reserve banks. (The US Federal Reserve alone pumped US$17 billion of short-term funds into the world's financial system and by the end of the first week of the crisis; central bank interventions around the world totalled US$300 billion; and Goldman Sachs bailed out one of its own hedge funds with US$3 billion, as did Barclay's Capital, to the tune of US$1.6 billion.[23]) Much worse was to follow one year later.

Although the source of the crisis can be traced to the accumulation of ill-considered lending in the US$9 trillion US mortgage market – in origin, a matter at once both individual and local – the most notable feature of the crisis is that there was no global oversight, in the sense that no one had any clear picture even of the sum of the debt involved, let alone which institutions were perilously exposed once liquidity dried up.

The Chairman of the US Federal Reserve could only estimate a figure of between 50 and 100 billion US dollars, shortly afterwards revised upwards to 250 billion dollars.[24] As the crisis intensified and expanded, institutions were reluctant to reveal their degree of exposure, since institutional viability became so immediately sensitive to systemic stability – which made the interest rate and liquidity release judgements by central banks all the more difficult.

So the world's many financial systems – highly interactive, computer-assisted and operating around the clock – are seamless not only for intended, functional purposes: they also facilitate relations of ungrasped and possibly ungraspable complexity and speed. After the fact, it is not difficult to discern how the world financial system came to this pass. As the manager of one large hedge fund described the matter, 'Trillions of loans have been bundled, diced, synthesised, refinanced. Now the music has stopped and they have to be owned and financed properly.'[25]

From the perspective of global governance, the spectacle is quite instructive. After all, many sector-specific studies of global governance are devoted to global finance, often from an international organisation perspective. Certainly in this case, the governance of global finance as the work of international organisations has left us with some serious gaps. And another well-known global governance perspective – global governance as the exercise of control by a combination of state and non-state actors – appears in mirror form: a crisis of global governance arising from the inadequately regulated behaviour of non-state actors (hedge funds; banks; private equity groups), with results that necessitate a multi-billion dollar bail-out of global finance by states.

From any one or even several global governance perspectives, what stands out most starkly is that there were no global governance arrangements in place to prevent this crisis. The global governance exercised after the fact was almost entirely rectificatory – indeed, almost all of the effort expended was toward the urgent need to diminish financial instability and restore confidence, not toward a global governance that might prevent such a thing happening again. A year before the crisis, the chairman of the US Securities and Exchange Commission called for more restrictive controls on the trillion dollar hedge fund industry. But '[his] demands for regulation may face an uphill struggle as [US] Federal Bank chief Ben Bernanke has said he believes free market discipline, rather than constricting rules, are the best way to regulate hedge funds'.[26] That same market discipline necessitated Mr Bernankle's predecessor, Alan Greenspan, to organise a publicly-financed buy-out of the hedge fund Long-Term Capital Management in 1998 after its collapse had threatened comparable turmoil in global finance.[27]

The fallout from this crisis is likely to see the link between the individual/local and the international/global work out in the form of mortgage defaults, foreclosures and falling employment, as financial institutions pass on at least some of their losses to their customers – matters which will in turn reverberate in economies around the world, at local, national and international levels. The pertinent links between individual/local and international/global are certainly numerous and dynamic; and now, if not before, some of the more pernicious and destabilising possibilities are clear. At the same time, it is not difficult to appreciate the kinds of interest-based resistances to the advent of restrictive measures (including forms of global governance) since the less regulated an operating environment, the less costly it is, at least for the most powerful, least directly affected constituencies, whereas restrictive controls are likely to be costly, politically and/or financially. Even as the August 2007 financial crisis was unfolding, political leaders called not for tighter controls or more effective global governance, but for 'greater transparency'.[28] Both the 1998 and 2007/08 interventions to stabilise global finance could be considered instances of global governance, albeit of a fire-fighting sort and certainly not steering, controlling and regulating in the sense of providing for a modicum order, stability and predictability.

And notably, they are directed not toward rectifying the way in which innumerable, small instances of debt can accumulate and disperse without any overarching tabulation (let alone control) only to emerge as a crisis of huge proportions. It is clear that most forms of effective global governance will need to take account of the dynamics that can be generated at quite low levels of human activity. Given the realities of national and international politics, this could hardly entail 'top down' directives, not least because there is no dedicated source of political authority at the global level. But since states can and do act to ensure kinds and degrees of stability at a global level, what is required is perhaps greater *political* seamlessness – connectivity between forms and levels of the organisation of political community.

Connecting local activity, international politics and global governance

Conceiving and enacting systems of global governance is not merely a matter of overcoming political resistance or 'lack of political will' once causal pathways and malign possibilities are made obvious. As we have seen, the individual actions over widely scattered locations can and do accumulate in ways that have impacts – often unforeseen and rarely sought – on multiple and overlapping arenas: on stressed physical environments, on hugely complex and dynamic financial systems and on contending interests played out within political systems. These cannot easily be abstracted one from another, sequenced and prioritised. For example, partly as a consequence of the way that globalising dynamics have greatly diminished the degree of remoteness inherent in our understanding of 'local', political ends and means for matters near and far can and do become tangled. An interview with Tony Blair in 2007 reveals the degree to which local/global and domestic/international considerations are becoming more tensioned, with issue-based political initiatives serving wider, mediating roles between political arenas:

> Perhaps the biggest change in [Tony Blair's] 10 years [as UK Prime Minister] is the way the global has overtaken the local. 'Foreign policy is no longer foreign policy.' Your dilemma as a national leader is that 'your country wants you to be focused on the domestic and yet the truth is the challenges you're facing are often global'. For example, it's important for us to take domestic action on climate change but, in truth, 'the purpose of it is to give yourself traction on international leadership'.[29]

The reverse is also true: governments can and do lever domestic resistance to restrictive legislation by appeals to international obligations – and in at least some environmental matters, to global obligations.

The many practical difficulties entailed in aligning the local and individual with the global *through* the structures and mechanisms of national and international politics becomes clear when we review why the international politics of the environment are so problematic, despite the clarity and implications of a number of global environmental crises. Given any detailed account of the state of the global commons, the trajectories of anthropogenic change and the number and nature of both interested and affected parties, some form of global governance (as defined above) would seem to be indicated – that is, environmental controls that include but extend beyond those already established in the national and international arenas. But the international politics of the environment do not take place in a realm that is removed from the pressures, sensitivities, expectations and fears that comprise local politics, nor from the fixed habits and/or aspirations of millions if not billions of individuals. This brings the individual and the local much nearer to the prospects for, and mechanisms of, global governance than is commonly appreciated in studies of international relations.

Yet bilateral and international contention over environmental matters is difficult enough. The international system is cooperative to some degree – it is, after all, a system – but it comprises competing sovereignties. While these are not always hostile, the frequency with which European politicians talk of 'our European partners' is about the same as the frequency with which they speak of 'our European competitors'. Further afield, much of the political wrangling over the Kyoto protocols has been about economic competitiveness and unequal burden-sharing that advantages developing countries at the expense of developed ones. One need only consider the way in which culture and ways of life, employment, access to food and water, the demands of a rapidly growing population or of rapidly expanding industry and many other fundaments of life at local and national level can drive environmental degradation – or be affected by international environmental agreements. (One significant by-product of China's booming export economy is that it is set to become the world's largest emitter of carbon dioxide.) Although all of the world's 190 or so nations has sovereign equality under the United Nations, there is no denying huge disparities between them. Not only do some countries lack power and influence in international negotiations; many also lack the ability to enact and enforce environmental standards (whether these are determined at domestic or international level) – and in some cases, they do not possess the ability to ensure the survival of all their citizens. (This can easily generate further rounds of environmental degradation and political tension.) Even in the more developed and prosperous parts of the world, environmental problems affect populations in different ways, at varying speeds and with highly differing rates of personal and practical as well as political consequence. For this reason, some environmental 'problems' are a matter of perception, at least for a time. What for some of the dispossessed is subsistence farming, or logging, is seen by those at a distance as a threat to biodiversity.

In addition, planetary and regional natural systems (the physics and chemistry of the atmosphere; weather; biodiversity and so on) and their interactions with a variety of human systems (cities; the volume of traffic driven by internal combustion engines; agriculture) are staggeringly complex. We have only recently reached near-unanimity on whether or not atmospheric pollution is driving climate change. Even then, determining causation for the purpose of liability or political responsibility can be very difficult, because sometimes causation is diffused, either across countless individual actors/actions, or across a long span of time – or both. That is, it cannot be located in the actions of any one country, or confined to specific periods. While it is true that the build-up of polychlorinated biphenyls (PCBs) in the world's environments was caused by the industrialised nations, this does not make the framing of environmental measures to deal with that and related problems much easier, particularly as much of the rest of the world is industrialising quickly.

It is also difficult to design international environmental agreements so that the empowering/disempowering trade-offs are politically acceptable to all. Preserving certain jungles as conservation areas could be good for tourism (and hence the national economy) and good for biodiversity; but bad for local inhabitants and their way of life; it might also, say, make hydroelectric power generation impossible. The national government involved must try to balance international demands with local interests and pressures – and the latter might not receive a lot of sympathy or support from outside. And finally, because enforcement provisions for international agreements will always be weak and because verification will always be difficult, what is required is a level of trust – or at least, a perception of mutual and balanced interest – which is all too rare in international politics.

The connectivity challenges facing an effective global governance – even sectoral ones on the scale discussed in this chapter – can be summarised in the following thematic points:

The local/global and the individual/international levels are connected but incommensurate.
Whatever the source of global governance, the action required to deal with issues on this scale will be felt where it matters most: at the local level in terms of access to relatively cheap and dependable goods and services; job prospects; and the maintenance of established ways of life. So one of the principal reasons why the international politics of the environment are so difficult and contentious even in urgent, rectificatory modes, let alone preventive ones, is that prohibitive or restrictive measures will be borne by locals, which in political terms means constituents. There is no escape from the biology, chemistry and physics of life, but nor is there any escape from politics. Such is the fabric of a world we describe in shorthand as 'seamless'. The particulars for any other sectoral global governance issue will vary – for example, the kinds of individual acts that combined to form the global

credit crisis of August 2007 entailed were less uniform than, say, the aggregate numbers of car drivers and frequent flyers producing unsustainable levels of carbon emissions. But whether the connectivity is simply additive, or requires intentional accumulation, the global impacts can be considerable. Such dynamics are not reversible; and for the full range of reasons ranging from the personal to the diplomatic, they are not easy to halt, diminish or regulate either.

The difficulty of aligning global governance to individual behaviour and localised activity is not that these separate realms are not connected, but they are connected by intricate lines of causation that, broadly speaking, do not require political consensus beyond what is required for their routine functioning – and often enough through the normal course of life in the developed world, little forethought or afterthought. Fluctuations in the volume of private motorised traffic throughout the world are more likely to be determined by fluctuations in the price of petroleum than by any considerations about the state of the earth's atmosphere – and at present, there seems to be little difference between citizens and their governments on this point.

At the highest level, identified issues are not always sufficiently important or immediate to demand prompt action or concerted effort.
Within the realms of the international politics of the environment, the Montreal Protocol, negotiated to eliminate ozone-depleting CFCs from industrial processes and consumer products, is an anomaly rather than an exemplar. The levels of ozone depletion extant and in prospect were measurable with an unusual degree of certainty; and it was plain that were the situation left to then-existing trends, the prospect for all life on the planet was dire. But most crises that can reasonably be considered global, including environmental ones, pose no immediate threat; and the incentives to act (especially when these involve protracted negotiations) are further diminished in the face of countervailing interests. The fracturing ice sheet that covers most of Greenland signals future risk rather than immediate danger, catastrophic though its collapse would be;[30] and the risk itself is but a manifestation of innumerable dynamics, local and international – the stuff that bedevils the politics of climate change.

Local/personal needs diverge from systemic requirements.
It is the burden of contemporary life that we are (or can be) so knowledgeable about the many ramifications of even our most mundane choices and defaults. We are routinely confronted by campaigning

organisations, if not our own governments, about the 'true cost' or the longer-term consequences of continuing and expanding ways of life that are now broadly recognised to be unsustainable. It is one thing, as the well-known feminist assertion would have it, that 'the personal is political'; and quite another to embrace that fact fully and conscientiously, with due regard to the quality of life of the disenfranchised, let alone of future generations.

For us as individuals, inconsistency, compromise and denial are the commonest form of mitigating these felt pressures, but we can discern much the same in at least some of the policy positions of our governments. The failure of many states to meet their agreed carbon emissions targets as agreed under the Kyoto Protocol is but one example. More instructive are cases from within single states:

> On Wednesday [13 December 2006] the [UK] secretary of state for communities launched a bold plan to make new homes more energy efficient. She claims it will save 7m tonnes of carbon. On Thursday, Douglas Alexander, the transport secretary, announced that he would allow airports to keep growing: by 2030 the number of passengers will increase from 228 million to 465 million. As a result, according to a report commissioned by the Department of the Environment, carbon emissions will rise between 22m and 36m tonnes. So much for joined-up government.[31]

One of the criticisms of the carbon trading (cap-and-trade) scheme set up under the Kyoto Protocol is that, according to the Economist, it is '...a second-best route to a greener world. [Under] cap-and-trade [...] the quantity of emissions is limited (the cap) and the right to emit is distributed through a system of tradable permits. The original Kyoto treaty set up such a mechanism and its signatories are keen to expand it. The main market-based alternative – a carbon tax – has virtually no political support.'[32] Yet despite governments' reluctance to confront their citizens with blunt realities and painful costs, governments do come under pressure to act – and to act more consistently – both from 'below' in the form of concerned citizens and organised campaigns; and from outside – via bilateral and international pressure. In the case of western Europe, the European Union (EU) has assumed the highest-profile leadership role on environmental matters. And returning to the 'all politics is local' perspective, there are already signs that governments at least recognise that they cannot shelter from the political costs of making explicit links between global governance and citizen expectations.

What all politicians would prefer, of course, is to conform to the momentum of changed and/or changing social norms (the subject of Chapter 6), but even then, there is a difference between subsidies for domestic energy saving and higher taxes.

In the case of the global environment at least, might we already be witnessing the beginnings of a more explicit link between global governance (and its chief means of affecting change in this realm, states and the international system) and activities that are local and/or individual? The UK is considering a scheme to oblige all businesses and other organisations above a certain level of energy consumption to face compulsory carbon quotas. And at the end of 2006, the UK minister for the environment expressed interest in the possibility outlined in a commissioned report, that 'Every citizen would be issued with a carbon "credit card" – to be swiped every time they bought petrol, paid an energy utility bill or booked an airline ticket – under a nationwide carbon trading scheme that could come into operation within five years.'[33] Whether in practical terms such a scheme would have what the minister concerned described as 'a simplicity and beauty that would reward carbon thrift', the public airing of the possibility carries with it an implicit endorsement of the proposition with which this chapter begins.

3

The sum of all global governances is not likely to be entirely coherent or to avoid competitive or antagonistic relationships

The use of the term 'governance' is not confined to activities taken to regulate matters at the highest levels or in the most inclusive arenas of human activity – *global* governance. 'Governance' has long been in use to describe the ways in which non-governmental actors, activities and relations combine with the machinery of government to produce social order. Effective government is necessary for the orderly functioning of large and complex societies throughout the developed world, but state and society are not co-extensive; and it would be difficult to imagine a state lacking an extensive civil society that was not also a tyranny of frightening proportions. So there are many forms of order and association which are outside of the remit of government, or outside of its purview; and the lines between public and private are routinely contested. At the same time, when international organisations and donors subject weak states to 'good governance' criteria, they do so on an understanding that an imbalance between forms of order that are regulated/ unregulated, public/private, accountable/unaccountable can be pernicious, as in aptly-named 'kleptocracies'.[1] However benign and inclusive the form of governance in particular states or sub-state polities, we can say that governance '[comprises] patterns that emerge from governing activities of social, political and administrative actors…[Thus], modes of social-political governance are always an outcome of public and private deliberation.'[2]

Applying the term 'governance' to myriad forms of social organisation allows for more nuanced understandings of the ways in which governmental and non-governmental orders are configured – and subject to change. Within states, a good deal of interest has been

34

generated by the decreasing willingness and/or competence of governments to continue to assume a number of burdens that have become familiar over time – notably various kinds of social welfare, the control of key industries and the regulation of certain business practices. Privatisation and deregulation have their ideological proponents, but the pressure of globalising dynamics has also hastened and/or necessitated governments shedding certain roles, or adopting less direct involvement in certain areas.[3] At the same time, as non-state actors of many sorts form allegiances, alliances, partnerships and networks on a global basis, the 'governance without government'[4] phenomenon is both a product of globalising forces and also a means of furtherance and consolidation of it. Indeed, as the facts and mechanisms of globalisation have become more familiar, altered relations and relational possibilities have superseded the physical means that have enabled them (especially telecommunications) as a focus of globalisation studies.[5]

As a preliminary to the study of global governance, it has become a commonplace to note that there is no single, overarching global governance – no single actor, configuration of actors or other form of authority which makes the international system less anarchic. Within the study of International Relations, the condition of anarchy gives rise to the domestic analogy question – that is, 'How beneficial is it from the viewpoint of world order to transfer to the domain of international relations those legal and political principles which sustain order within states?'[6] On first sight, this question, or a variation of it might seem to apply to global governance as much as to interstate relations. But the most commonly cited and drawn-upon definitions of global governance do not characterise it as a scaled-up form of national or international governance, but as a summative phenomenon, including non-state and lower-level forms of governance. This is the understanding of the term that has been in circulation for nearly two decades, notably by the Council of Rome in 1991:

> [The] term governance [is used] to denote the command mechanisms of a social system and its actions that endeavour to provide security, prosperity, coherence, order and continuity to the system...Taken broadly, the concept of governance should not be restricted to the national and international systems but should be used in relation to regional, provincial and local governments as well as to other social systems such as education and

the military, to private enterprises and even to the microcosm of the family.[7]

A similar understanding was adopted by the Commission on Global Governance in 1995, which has gained widespread acceptance:

> Governance is the sum of the many ways individuals and institutions, public and private, manage their common affairs....At the global level, governance has been viewed primarily as intergovernmental relationships, but it must now be understood as also involving non-governmental organizations, citizens' movements, multinational corporations, and the global capital market.[8]

From this it follows that when we employ the term 'global governance' in the singular and without specific reference to any particular arena (such as the global environment) or activity (such as world trade), it is necessarily a summative phenomenon – that is, the overall global governance that results from the order produced by many governances. Clearly, not all governances are equal: lower-level and less inclusive forms of social order are meaningful in human terms, but not determining of the overall organisation of the world, or other large-scale forms of order and stability. (This does not discount the cumulative effects that six and a half billion human beings can produce: climate change is not the outcome of low-frequency, high-impact actions, but of countless individual ones.) But nor is the sum of these many governances merely additive – it is relational: the diverse, powerful and complex dynamics that form the substance of globalisation have left states in an arena that is at once both enlarged and highly interactive: '[T]he contemporary world order is best understood as a highly complex, contested and interconnected order in which the interstate system is increasingly embedded within evolving regional and global political networks. The latter are the basis in and through which political authority and mechanisms of governance are being articulated and rearticulated.'[9] So although there is little disputing the primacy of states or the standing of the international system as the largest, most inclusive and most coherent system for ordering socio-political and socio-economic human affairs, states as agents of governance do not stand above or outside of the dynamics they are impelled to govern: states act, but are also acted upon. This is clear in recent examinations of the structure and performance of the intergovernmental structures that states have created for the purposes of governance – International

Organisations (IOs). For some analysts, global governance is identical with the work of IOs, a perspective framed by the challenges confronting the international system under globalised conditions.[10] Yet the identification of transnational and transgovernmental dynamics has long been a source of interest, not only in respect of what IOs must contend with, but also with respect to how they function.[11]

The global governance through many governances phenomenon entails not only a proliferation of the number of governances, but also a proliferation of kind – the myriad configurations of state and non-state actors linked across borders and boundaries of every kind and their competing, contesting, combining and complementing activities. Depending on the perspective adopted and the example(s) chosen, one can see in this multiplication of governances – (some would say 'fracturing'[12]) – possibilities both benign and malign. The progressive possibilities include a great deal of what has come under the concept of global civil society: advancing, upholding and strengthening norms;[13] possibilities for an extension of 'bottom up' political dynamics, opening out of the space for public participation in politics; giving voice to human solidarity;[14] holding states and IOs to account;[15] and taking advantage of networked forms of communication and action to secure goals.[16] The more worrying possibilities include an increase in private power and authority with a concomitant decrease in public accountability;[17] increased difficulty in achieving consensus; and 'a significant erosion of the boundaries separating what lies inside a government and its administration and what lies outside them'.[18]

The intensification and growing importance of globalising dynamics has obliged states to adapt by incorporating an increasing number of transnational dynamics and intergovernmental relationships into their modes of operation. So it is that states, their institutions, and certain classes of professionals employed by them have formed extensive working relationships with their national counterparts for the accomplishment of key tasks that are essentially domestic, as well as for international ones (to the extent that these two realms are distinct in a number of issue areas – such as the threat of terrorism).[19] The characterisation of this, a variation, perhaps on 'global issues require global solutions', is that 'networked threats require a networked response'[20] – both of which are notable for the way in which states are depicted as being in reactive mode to dynamics that are not entirely of their making or directly within their competence as discreet actors. Whether as a consequence states are becoming 'disaggregated' returns us to questions of authority and accountability and the negative possibilities recounted above.[21]

A very considerable literature has grown around the possibilities of hybrid forms of global governance – combinations of legal, corporate, NGO and government actors working on the basis of prevailing norms and/or shared interests to provide essential oversight in places or over issue areas that are otherwise inadequately governed – in matters ranging from the conservation of natural resources to securing labour standards.[22] But does the emergence of new and/or additional forms of governance that include but extend beyond the familiar machinery of government and intergovernmental cooperation also extend the possibilities for a more comprehensive and effective global governance? Even if a composite global governance is more than the sum of the parts, can the number and diversity of forms of governance that comprise it – and the number, interconnectedness and sheer complexity of the matters that need to be governed – deliver the kinds of order, stability and sustainability that is implicit in the concept of 'global governance'?

The furthest possible extent of a summative global governance that is comprehensive, inclusive and coherent is not within the bounds of reliable estimation, but we can gauge the prospect in outline by examining the features of human life and organisation which currently militate against it, together with a consideration of the extent to which matters that are currently subjects of political contestation could over time be shifted to considerations of a more technical sort (the subject of Chapter 4). The difficulties are already visible when we examine sectoral governances not in terms of the capacity and competence of the agents engaged, but in terms of the larger world of human and natural dynamics and the ways these inform and constrain any particular variety of global governance. The global governance of health is a case in point.

Any form of governance must limit its activities to those matters which are within its cognizance and authoritative reach. In practice, this can mean that a large part of the global governance of certain issue areas will comprise remedial action to deal with the consequences of dynamics that clearly fall within separate areas of governance but which nevertheless can have a considerable bearing on other, distinct but related fields. For example, when we speak of the global governance of health, we include the many actors and mechanisms by which the health of the world's population is monitored, maintained and improved – national health establishments, the WHO, the Global

Effort to eliminate AIDS, malaria and TB, dedicated centres for epidemiology and disease control and so on. Concurrently, we have innumerable systems of governance to regulate matters as diverse as car traffic; the food industry; the use of pesticides; the supply and use of drugs including alcohol and tobacco; the import and export of weapons; and the disposal of industrial wastes. All of these matters and many more besides can and do have a direct impact on human health, yet none fall within what can reasonably be termed the global governance of health.[23] Moreover each of those practices has advocates and each is supported by countervailing claims against health-inspired calls for restrictive or prohibitive governance, ranging from social convenience to the provision of tax revenues. The inadequacies and failures of the global governance of health are by no means merely a matter of shortfalls in funding or poor coordination; and some of the most serious obstacles to improving human health are not microbial but social, political and economic interests and the governance structures we have constructed at national and international levels to pursue them. It is therefore not difficult to argue that on their own, or as presently configured, these many individual facets of health governance are inadequate for the general purpose, or for important aspects of it (say, dealing with malnutrition, or the health effects of its opposite, widespread and worsening obesity.)

There is no overarching global governance; no actor or authority to prioritise, coordinate or reconcile the many forms and levels of governance that together comprise the global governance of the world. Even the most widely-shared and endorsed normative principles and the internationally-sanctioned initiatives they inspire are insufficient for this purpose. The United Nations Millennium Goals,[24] for example, which include the eradication of extreme poverty and hunger; ensuring environmental sustainability; and developing a global partnership for development must contend not only with weak and corrupt governances, but also with strong ones, within states and between them.

Contending governances

Behind the structures and mechanisms of all forms of governance are constituencies with pronounced values and focused interests. The difficulties of framing public policy at all levels of human organisation are particularly vexed in any matter that has a global dimension, because of the number and complexity of the subjects at issue; the number and variety of interested parties; and the problem of abstracting any sectoral governance from nets of relations in distinct but related fields. These themes come into sharp focus when we consider the international politics of the environment. Plainly, if we are to achieve global environmental stability in a populous, heavily industrialised world, we need to achieve a high degree of political consensus around the articulation of goals and the means to achieve them – in short, the determination to conceive and enact a global governance of the environment. The difficulties entailed are clear in the intricacies of almost any set of multilateral environmental negotiations, but all the more striking in a configuration of states as coherent as the European Union (EU).

The EU has a regional character (in terms of physical and political geography) and in some particulars, has supranational status legally and politically – that is, its member states have ceded sovereign control over some aspects of what is elsewhere in the world nationally-determined policy. This gives the EU a rather special place in the international politics of the environment, since it can sign agreements *as* the EU. This certainly strengthens its bargaining position; and at the same time, because it is a Europe-wide organisation, it at least holds the potential of bringing common environmental standards to one of the most developed regions of the world.

In practice, the establishment of EU environmental policies and standards are subject to the same range of problems which beset any other international forum for the same purposes. These include the problems of negotiating around the lowest common denominator; of leverage between sectoral interests (that is, trade-offs between environmental goals and others); of securing compliance with agreed goals; of economic competitors cooperating environmentally; of burden sharing (expressed succinctly: how are the economic and opportunity costs to be allocated and balanced against political costs?); and of balancing the internal political coherence of the EU (or of individual states in any other forum) against external pressures and demands, both environmental and political.

It is therefore important to keep in mind that EU environmental measures are conceived, framed and implemented within a very dense network of other political dynamics and tensions. In one sense, this is as it should be – after all, we cannot talk sensibly about 'sustainability' if we are not prepared to enter into negotiations about carbon emissions, transport or industrial standards. At the same time, the EU is a political organisation and not, in the first instance, or primarily, an environmental one. Environmental politics within the EU, just like environmental politics outside of it, are part of the larger web of international relations – and outside of emergency conditions, very unlikely to drive or dominate them. In any event, the political meaning of environmental problems is not fixed or something that can be measured scientifically. Determining political meaning – and from there, political responsibilities – is often a large part of the substance of environmental negotiations, as well as their necessary prelude. This includes considerations of historical responsibility, equity and justice – all of which underline considerations of quantifiable measures and acceptable costs.

Even a cohesive and competent state with a good-faith determination to enter into multilateral governance arrangements is likely to confront competing internal priorities as well as the contending governance priorities of other states. The latter was certainly the case as EU ministers worked to persuade Russia to sign up to the carbon emissions limitations specified by the Kyoto Protocol – a political initiative essential to bring the protocol into force, given the steadfast refusal of the United States to do so. But within Russia, the threatening implications of climate change were, as elsewhere, gauged against the political and economic costs – and in the case of Russia, against what it considered a more immediately pressing strategic goal: entry into the World Trade Organisation (WTO):

> At a climate change conference in September [2003] [President Putin] said he would not sign Kyoto unless it was altered in favour of Russia's national interests. His leading adviser on the topic, Andrei Illarionov, said [in April 2004] that the protocol would be an 'Auschwitz' for Russian economic development, and [in May 2004] the Russian Academy of Sciences told the Kremlin the treaty would have spurious benefits to Russia's environment and economy.[25]

Suggestions that such pronouncements were a hard bargaining position to assist the Russian leadership in achieving its goal of membership in the WTO appear to have been validated once the appropriate concessions were made, as expressed by President Putin:

> 'The fact that the European Union has met us halfway at the negotiations on membership in the WTO cannot but influence Moscow's positive attitude towards ratification of the Kyoto protocol. We will accelerate our movement towards ratifying this protocol.' Mr Putin [...] said agreements over EU enlargement and the WTO 'lowers the risks for our economy in the midterm and unties our hands to a

certain degree to resolve the problem of joining the Kyoto protocol sooner'.

On any reckoning, halting and reversing climate change will be critical in the range of tasks that come under the heading 'global governance of the environment'. Yet not even planet-threatening circumstances appear to be sufficient to secure an unconditional commitment from all of the states most responsible. And climate change is not unique in this regard. Few imagine that any other pressing and inclusive global governance issue could be fenced off from the human and natural systems that comprise or inform them, or from the material, financial, political and other interests that give shape and meaning to our organisations of human community. Yet to say that global governance cannot be abstracted from politics (and the kinds of interests that shape and propel them) does not make global governance impossible, any more than it does international relations. We do conceive and enact systems of global governance that maintain numerous kinds and varying degrees of order, stability and predictability – hence the characterisation of the work of International Organisations as the global governance of particular fields, or as the largest and most significant aspect of global governance in its entirety. Moreover, given our globalised condition and in the absence of any kind of global political authority, our largest and most extensive forms of global governance are impressive: the art of politics and hard-edged interests can combine to powerful but – a critical qualification – rarely all-inclusive and uniform effect. This is familiar to anyone who has studied International Relations. The advent of the concept of 'human security'[26] would have little purchase were 'international peace and security' – the absence of inter-state war – adequate to address the worst forms of preventable human suffering.

Any consideration of 'inclusive' governance arrangements brings us to the difficulty of coherence. If in a world organised into more than 190 sovereign states we have no prospect of conceiving and initiating a single global government, or any form of centrally ordained and coordinated global governance, we must face the difficulties involved in having governances of many kinds, at many levels, for purposes that are not always compatible and (even when they are accountable) that are rooted in the familiar, competitive postures of politics everywhere. And the coherence problem has international and global dimensions as well as domestic ones – that is, we are as likely to find contending governances as a key difficulty in global governance as in more familiar, nationally-based struggles to frame public policy:

> 'Policy coherence' is [...] clearly an amalgam of several disparate ideas, each of which embodies only one part of the notion of 'governance'. Even if we were to limit the idea of policy coherence to the efficient management of the public sector itself, we would find that it [...] only tells part of the story. This is because:
>
> - Policy *co-ordination* means getting the various institutional and managerial systems of government that formulate policy to work together.
> - Policy *consistency* means ensuring that the individual government policies are not internally contradictory, and avoiding policies that conflict with reaching for a given policy objective.
> - Policy *coherence* goes further – it involves the systematic promotion of mutually reinforcing policy action across government departments and agencies creating synergies towards achieving the defined objective.[27]

At the inter-state and global levels, the number of these challenges is not merely an additive phenomenon – they bring about new orders of complexity. And it would be fanciful to suppose that the span of activities captured by the phrase 'governance without government' will largely or easily complement such coherence as we are able to secure at the highest levels. In the following from an Organisation for Economic Cooperation and Development (OECD) document about its work on governance issues, the framework is certainly broad – 'establishing effective institutional and policy frameworks for markets and society' – and its logic (if not its priorities) is compatible with a great deal of both the descriptive and prescriptive literature on global governance:

> Effective governance requires that governments implement the institutional and policy framework for the efficient operation of markets and societies, based on the rule of law. Governments are partners with business, labour and civil society in the functioning of the individual national economies and the international economy. Business and labour create the national wealth, while government sets the rules and the framework in which all enterprises can operate in a competitive environment. While this framework is above all national, markets have become increasingly linked through

globalisation, vastly expanding the space in which governments need to provide a framework for a level playing field and where borders are open to trade and investment. This expanding need for efficient markets calls for greater attention to governance issues at local, national and international levels.[28]

Yet consider what the document lists as 'the main elements of effective systems of governance':

- an institutional and legal framework which supports the emergence of an enterprise-based economy;
- the development of a competitive environment which enhances the efficient functioning of markets, including effective regulatory policies and strong competition laws and enforcement;
- a good corporate governance framework providing for transparency of corporate structures and operations and the accountability of management;
- a performance-oriented and efficient public sector;
- vigorous action to fight corruption and organised crime;
- sound national policies and institutional frameworks for environmental management;
- government investment in people through sound education and training policies, and
- strengthening social safeguards; and fair, equitable and efficient taxation policies.[29]

A number of these objectives, such as provision for fighting organised crime and establishing systems of equitable taxation are unexceptional. But although the list does make room for 'environmental management' beside the core remits of the OECD – enterprise-based economies and efficient, functioning markets – it does so without any suggestion that these might be difficult to rationalise – or indeed, that they might be incompatible in any quite fundamental way, not least the collision of domestic and foreign market forces which feature as a key antagonism of globalisation. We might get a better sense of the difficulties of trying to coordinate these matters – and produce a more coherent global governance thereby – were the preservation of environmental integrity not reduced here to 'management'. The difficulties are all too plain in the highly contestable notion of 'sustainable economic growth' and in the difficulties of not privileging one set of governance activities over others.

And what is true about the standing of environmental governance beside governance for other purposes (especially economic growth) is also true about the 'poor cousin' standing of global social policies:

> There is a lack [...] of the institutions required to make effective global social policies – and to make such policies effective. A range of organizations, whose primary responsibilities lie elsewhere, dabble in social policy concerns. The IMF advises countries on the design of new social security systems. The World Bank has pronounced on a wide range of social policy issues. Inevitably there are differences of view between different international bodies. The ILO has traditionally been a supporter of state social security and of the earnings-related principle – both of which principles are questioned by the World Bank and the IMF. The WTO is in a position to make a potentially powerful impact on social policy but has been reluctant to link trade with labour standards or with environmental protection.[30]

Further to this, John Ralston has observed

> ...that the Globalization movement has produced myriad market-oriented international binding agreements at the global level and not a single binding agreement in the other areas of human intercourse – work conditions, taxation, child labour, health and so on. The deep imbalance of the movement, however successful in its own terms, cannot help but provoke unexpected forms of disorder.[31]

These forms of disorder – physical and social imbalances, displacements and unexpected costs – can come about either as a direct result of public policy initiatives (grossly inappropriate and/or unsustainable 'development' schemes come readily to mind), or less directly, from combinations of pressures, such as the deleterious effects brought about by mass tourism, or the remaking of urban spaces to accommodate automobile traffic. We can also observe how the cumulative effects of local initiatives can generate unexpected and sometimes quite serious social, environmental and economic consequences well beyond the sphere of any initial cost/benefit analysis – for example, as the International Commission on Dams reported.[32] Globalisation quickens, amplifies and extends these dynamics; and global governance, particularly as practiced by the world's governments and their international organisations, is at least as likely to generate incoherence as to mitigate it, a point which is at the heart of the contention between environmentalists and the World Trade Organisation. The problem of balancing local needs against global opportunities and pressures; and ensuring that policy-making is coherent against a vastly expanded number of considerations is certainly evident at lower-order forms of governance, which we can see in the attention now being devoted to regions and even cities as active and effective agents.

Contestation and coherence

Considered as the overall order of the world – that is, the sum of the world's innumerable governances – 'global governance' suggests comprehensiveness and inclusiveness; and to the extent that the many governances that comprise it combine rather than clash, it can also be regarded as coherent. But when set against the catalogue of the world's ills, both environmental and human, such coherence as we have mustered appears to be 'global' largely in exclusive and functionalist senses. There is little disputing that the largest, institutionalised forms of global governance favour the world's wealthier countries (whatever promise they are said to hold for the less advantaged[33]); and these arrangements also favour a range of non-state actors whose interest in securing the conditions for their activities is congruent with the larger security concerns of states. Yet for all the policy-making that makes globalisation possible (and for a sizeable minority, stunningly advantageous), we are at the same time undermining the basis of planetary sustainability – by action, omission, default and even denial. Doubtless some portion of this can be blamed on the pathologies of international relations, such as a Realist would readily identify. But Realists and non-Realists alike recognise survival as the *sine qua non* of any state's governance initiatives; global environmental degradation is not in anyone's interests and there is widespread recognition – extending to the US Central Intelligence Agency – that climate change 'should be elevated beyond a scientific debate to a US national security concern'.[34] In addition, large swathes of humanity desperate for the fundamentals of a secure life pose a threat to regional if not global order – and the extent to which national and international policy-making exacerbates these conditions is well documented.[35]

Yet policy-making is not entirely or even largely conducted on the basis of zero-sum calculations, or devil-take-the-hindmost attitudes. A recognition of the importance of systemic stability (political, economic and environmental) attends national and international reckoning of both ends and means. Indeed, globalisation has the effect of making such considerations inescapable but also more difficult – as the protracted business of bringing such countries as Australia and the United States into the climate change regime illustrates.[36] And genuine concern for the plight of the least well-off (palliative though it might well be) still animates societies, governments and the international organisations they maintain for the purpose of human betterment. So if neither rationality nor humane decency are in short supply, the sources of incoherence need to be found not only (and perhaps not primarily) in the immediate and exclusive interests of governments, but in the difficulties of framing public policy more generally.

In outline form, the constraints on global-level policy-making are familiar at the level of domestic politics. What is of note is that these limitations and deficiencies do not prevent the establishment of coherent policies or their implementation, at least for some purposes – and by extension, for some constituencies. But what is adequate for some purposes creates imbalances or generates new difficulties in other arenas (such as markets, or our physical environments), or for other forms of human endeavour. Everyone understands that a policy-making framework that includes the abundant particulars of individual and social wellbeing means that a strictly functionalist approach to public policy (as though the satisfaction of human needs and wants were configured in parallel) is impossible. It follows from this that a wholly comprehensive consideration for every new or adjusted mechanism of governance cannot be achieved. In a now-classic article published in 1959, Charles E. Lindblom observed:

> For complex problems, [a fully comprehensive] approach is of course impossible. Although such an approach can be described, it cannot be practiced except for relatively simple problems and even then only in somewhat modified form. It assumes intellectual capacities and sources of information that men simply do not possess, and it is even more absurd as an approach to policy when the time and money that can be allocated to a policy problem is limited, as is always the case. Of particular importance to public administrators is the fact that public agencies are in effect instructed not to practice [a comprehensive approach]. That is to say, their prescribed functions and constraints – the politically or legally possible – restrict their attention to relatively few values and relatively few alternative policies among the countless alternatives that might be imagined.[37]

With this as a framing condition for conceiving and exercising governance, the meaning of politics as 'the art of the possible' takes on another, cognitive, dimension. We can add that globalisation greatly increases the number, variety and dynamism of important variables and possible impacts of any particular exercise of governance; and the world's altered physical systems introduce to human affairs various kinds of unpredictability unprecedented in history. None of these matters makes governance or even global governance (of kinds or in sum) impossible, but it does impart to the largest governance initiatives a considerable gravity and urgency; and they heighten awareness of the ways in which governance at the national and local scales are causally linked to the larger issues besetting humanity (as we saw in Chapter 2). But this awareness, an apprehension of the human condition, has done little to diminish the competition and varieties of antagonism that feature in the framing of public policy either within states or between them. Even planetary-level crises only prioritise and inform political deliberation and bargaining, not dissolve them.

There are several sources of political contention over public policy – and in practical terms, they are often entangled. As we have seen, incompatible and/or incommensurate objectives can arise because of the impossibly large scale and complexity of taking a comprehensive view, but it can also be the result of a failure of coordination, or because alternatives are too costly, financially or politically. In the following, the workings of denial and the logic of short-termism in local agricultural practice apply equally to the full range of behaviours that have inhibited genuine progress in halting climate change: 'The expectation of normal times allows us to ignore the degree to which human intervention itself perverts natural dynamics in ways that play themselves out beyond the manager's time horizon…The overriding temptation of modern human societies is to maximise for a narrow range of values, so that maximum…yield of forest or fishery or rice field forces managers to ignore the importance of long-term successional dynamics, in favour of short-term output.'[38] Sectoral minorities blocking consensus is another source of difficulty, at levels both low and high: 'Well-organised interest groups exert disproportionate power within their states and obtain an equally disproportionate percentage of political and tangible goods, such as lower tax rates, more subsidies, and more favourable legislation. Well-organised or well-financed local governments can also obtain disproportionate influence using similar means. In both cases, suboptimal resource allocation is the unfortunate, albeit logical, result.'[39] And precaution will not easily win out over momentum, particularly as industrialisation spreads and quickens.

International consensus about any form of global governance, for any purpose, is therefore only a beginning – an arena in which the hard contestation of international politics (and domestic political expectations and pressures) can be hammered out. The December 2007 climate change conference in Bali at which US inclusion was hailed as a crucial step, only set out a two-year 'road map' for negotiations that will be concluded in 2009. The incoherence that has brought us to this pass is unlikely to be mitigated in advance of those negotiations – and their outcome will be a critical test of our ability to conceive and enact global governance on the largest scale.

4
Global governance needs to be relational, not merely technocratic

Problems and solutions

Even on the largest scale, life appears to present us with problems for which there are solutions: wars can be fought to a decisive conclusion; epidemic outbreaks can be halted; and global financial crises can be stabilised. Yet describing any dedicated human endeavour as a 'solution' is at the same time a way of characterising the matter to be addressed as limited – that is, as a special set of circumstances, clearly discrete in space and/or time, rather than as a particular manifestation of a more persistent condition. So it is that World War II can be sited with precision, geographically and temporally, but its many legacies persist[1] (as does the propensity for politically-directed violence); we were successful in preventing SARS from becoming a pandemic, but a disease-free human future is not more likely as a result;[2] and the regularity of global financial crises cannot be put down to what the insurance industry terms, 'acts of god'.[3] We must address disasters and grave threats – and we do, often with considerable effectiveness. But human history has a thematic consistency because the fundamentals of the human condition are consistent; and human life is less a matter of problem-solving than of navigating a course through changing circumstances. For example, the goal of maintaining human health, which includes efforts to prevent and cure diseases, presently entails such varied initiatives as health education and safe sex programmes; a call to reduce the indiscriminate use of antimicrobials in order to slow the adaptive processes of pathogens such as the TB bacillus; and monitoring the migratory patterns of birds in the hope of preventing an outbreak of avian flu. Individuals and societies can protect themselves from contracting certain diseases by a variety of means, but human vulnerability to disease, although it might well be described as a 'problem' cannot be cured, or fixed.

We make strenuous efforts to manage our physical and human environments for purposes which can best be described as favourable conditions rather than as end goals. As individuals, we might seek physical security, a sense of community, intimacy, trust, prosperity and a good degree of predictability. At the social level, the striving for equality, justice, safety, stability and sustainability are familiar practically everywhere. All of these are relational qualities and their satisfactory attainment does not require static configurations of human and physical resources, or conditions that can be frozen. That is, in seeking them and/or maintaining them, we must monitor, adjust, adapt, prioritise, compromise – and in the social realm, organise and maintain systems of governance. Few of the most fundamental aspirations of individuals and societies can be achieved fully and finally.

On an historical scale, discernible, even remarkable progress in addressing a number of the worst scourges of humanity reinforces an understanding – and an expectation – of a problem-solving progress. In support of this perception, medical science is often cited, not least the elimination of smallpox in the 1970s. In the decades before, progress was such as to lead US Secretary of State George Marshall to declare in 1948 that the conquest of all infectious diseases was imminent.[4] The reality, with HIV/ AIDS at the forefront, has been quite sobering. In addition to a re-adjusted view of human progress comes an understanding that few of the perils faced by human societies are amenable by scientific or technological resourcefulness alone; and likewise few of our collective needs and wants. These must be articulated and met by cultural and political choices.

> The development of culture is not, as most Westerners thought until a century ago, simply a progressive 'enlightenment', in which Western civilisation has led the way. The growth of knowledge and skill is indeed to some extent cumulative, though the progress is not so smooth, so linear or so comprehensive as we used to think and the corresponding losses are more than we notice. But knowledge and skill are only part of culture. The most basic aspect of culture is its aptness for enabling a society to preserve reliable and acceptable relations, both internally between its members and externally with its milieu. If either fails, the society perishes.[5]

Those external relations include our myriad forms of relatedness with the natural world, from microbial life to atmosphere physics and chemistry.

The dream of physical security, material abundance and of a physical world more directly and immediately amenable to human dreams and designs is something of a hardy perennial which lies at the heart of a good deal of utopian thinking, of which Francis Bacon's *New Atlantis* (1627) is a striking example. The idea that worldwide affluence would obviate the need for politics, or bring about its end, is not confined to fantasy, or to the distant past. A particularly strong form of what is in effect a problem-solving approach to the human condition proceeds from an understanding that politics (and international politics in particular) inhibits the free and creative engagement of peoples everywhere in making the world work for the common good. In our own time, the futurist and inventor R. Buckminster Fuller describes the competitive aspects of life in the form of a diagnosis: 'All the world [is] preoccupied with intercompetitive survival, being spontaneously motivated by the working assumption of the existence of a fundamental inadequacy of life support on our planet.'[6] For Fuller, the essential problem facing a globalising humanity was the persistence of sovereign states, or '"blood clots" imperilling the free inter-flowing of the evolution-producing metals and products recirculation as well as of the popular technical know-how disseminating'.[7]

Not every positive imagining of the human future is one in which riches are so abundant as to not interfere with the realisation of virtue and to render political calculations redundant. Even on Bacon's island of Bensalem, in which scientific knowledge rendered wondrous results, there is a scientific elite, who confide to the narrator, 'We have consultations, which of the inventions and experiences which we have discovered shall be published, and which not; and take an oath of secrecy for the concealing of those which we think fit to keep secret, though some of these we do reveal sometimes to the state, and some not.' In modern terminology, this combination of scientific expertise and elite control would be termed 'technocratic'. So in addition to science and/or technology as a substitute for politics, or its eventual culmination, we also have technocratic practices *as* politics. For the purpose of this discussion, a technocratic approach to governance and to public policy more generally is one grounded in a belief that the fundamentals of human existence and co-existence can be secured by the application of specialist techniques, principally those of science and technology, directed and managed by technical experts. This has a number of strands, all of which re-introduce the 'governance of, by and for whom?' question. This is because technocratic means cannot meaningfully be abstracted from ends – that is, from values and from political choices – even if the end in sight is not a full-scale technocracy. The history of eugenics demonstrates this amply: a scientifically-validated 'solution' for supposed deficiencies of a racial or genetic character – a practice given extensive and long-lived sanction in a number of countries including the United States, where it continued even after the Nuremberg trails for Nazi outrages.[8]

One of the deep appeals of technocratic approaches to governance is (or at least was) premised on their supposed objectivity – scientific facts and judgements thought to be objectively true and hence beyond falsification and beyond the reach of bias and self-serving interests. This is highly questionable on epistemological grounds (with the notion of 'value free science' having attracted particularly close scholarly attention.[9]) The philosophical critique has its counterpart in historical experience: the disastrous experiments with 'scientific socialism' in the former Soviet Union and its satellites; and elsewhere in grand schemes for human betterment founded on scientific principles.[10] But in a world now so highly developed, with a multitude of complex interactions between natural systems and highly engineered, often tightly coupled human systems, the appeal of technical 'fixes' – and the experts who might deliver them – retain a considerable and at times urgent appeal. A recent article on planetary-scale geo-engineering schemes, 'Can science save the world?' begins: 'Endless treaties to cut carbon emissions and halt global warming have failed to turn the tide of pollution. Now scientists want to intervene on a planetary scale, changing the very nature of our seas and skies.'[11] Not only might we consider geo-engineering the planet as a substitute for conceiving ways of living sustainably; we also have a proliferation of weapons of mass destruction, together with plans to counter them with further extensive and cripplingly expensive technologies ('Star Wars' and missile defence shields.)

As human life has become increasingly enmeshed in technologies, there has been no shortage of trenchant social and cultural criticism of the demands that machines make of human life and of a growing subordination of human purpose and human possibility to technology.[12] Writing in 1970, Lewis Mumford presents a technocratic world view that he describes as 'regrettably typical':

> In 'Genetics and the Future of Man,' a social scientist, highly respected as a population expert, has declared that deliberate genetic control is '*bound to occur*,' and once begun, 'it would soon benefit science and technology, which in turn would facilitate further hereditary improvement, which in turn would extend science, and so on in a

self-enforcing spiral without limit.' He concludes that 'when man has conquered his own biological evolution, he will have laid the basis for conquering everything else. The Universe will be his, at last.'[13]

Unfortunately, as we shall see below, 'the notion that human development itself can be equated with the unconditional support of science and technology'[14] has not disappeared. The promise of profound and wide-scale human betterment through scientific and technological innovations combines with a diminishing public capacity for considering their fitness and their risks and costs, with the result that many aspects of our governances are becoming increasingly technocratic.

Technology, technocracy and governance

It is certainly the case that the participation of the scientific community in Nazi Germany did much to discredit the idea of value-free science;[15] and one might suppose that we have come a considerable distance from the views of the great twentieth century French mathematician Henri Poincaré: 'Ethics and science have their own domains, which touch but do not interpenetrate. The one shows us what goal we should aspire, the other, given the goal, teaches us how to attain it. So they never conflict since they never meet. There can be no more immoral science than there can be scientific morals.'[16] Yet such views, or variations on them, persist into the present: Marvin Minsky, co-founder of the Artificial Intelligence Lab at the Massachusetts Institute of Technology, opposes regulating the development of new technologies on the grounds that 'Scientists shouldn't have ethical responsibility for their inventions, they should be able to do what they want. You shouldn't ask them to have the same values as other people.'[17] Minsky's 'other people' are citizens – and in democratic countries, at least in principle, they are the source of deliberation for decision-making on the purposes and means of governance. Leaving aside the matter of ethical exceptionalism, it remains the case that expertise in invention easily becomes expertise in diagnosing problems – and at least on occasion, prescribing 'solutions' which are outside of popular understanding – or indeed, even beyond serious legislative reckoning. An early example of this can be seen in the development that led from the design and construction of the first nuclear weapons to the development of nuclear strategy. As Hans J. Morgenthau pointed out, 'The great issues of nuclear strategy cannot even be the subject of meaningful debate, whether in Congress or among the people at large, because there can be no competent judgement without meaningful knowledge. Thus the great national decisions of life and death are rendered by technological elites.'[18]

In subsequent years, the shift from informed public deliberation to exclusive forms of expert advice and direction has gathered pace and extended to other areas of public policy-making, but it is in the areas and issues created or informed by scientific advance and technological development that the trend toward technocracy is most clear. The political sanction, funding and advocacy for converging technologies illustrates this clearly.

The convergence of technologies (CT) refers to a politically supported merging of nanotechnology, biotechnology, robotics, information science and cognitive science into what its proponents hope will be a 'single engineering paradigm'. On a practical level, CT has been facilitated by advances in nanotechnology, which makes it possible to manipulate matter at the molecular and even the atomic scale. The possibilities this opens up, for good and for ill, are breathtaking.[19] For our purposes, what is most notable is the way in which at least some of the advocacy has a strongly technocratic character. Three examples will suffice, all from the principal US report on converging technologies, produced jointly by the US National Science Foundation and the US Department of Commerce.

> Science and technology will increasingly dominate the world, as population, resource exploitation, and potential social conflict grow. Therefore, the success of this convergent technologies priority area is essential for the future of humanity.[20]

The technocratic assumptions embedded in this assertion are remarkable. It is not made clear why advances in science and technology cannot presently assist in preventing or diminishing the dissolution of world order, or why, given the downward trajectory, their furtherance will be essential; and there is no suggestion that science and technology might in any way be causally related to social fracturing and environmental degradation. More important is the agentless quality of the 'domination' of science and technology. 'Domination by whom?' would of course open up the question, 'for what purposes?' Given the range of considerations and interests (ethical, biomedical and economic) generated by any single new technological advance, such as the medical use of human stem cells, the prospect of 'science and technology

...dominat[ing] the world' hardly seems something that any society would freely choose to subject itself to. Yet we are told that this development is 'essential'.

The second example is also strikingly technocratic:

> Technological convergence may be the best hope for the preservation of the natural environment, because it integrates humanity with nature across the widest range of endeavours, based on systematic knowledge for wise stewardship of the planet.[21]

This is an astonishing assertion. The preservation of the environment is fundamentally a matter of human relations, not technology. Humanity is already integrated with nature: this is fundamental to any understanding of life and life processes, together with a rudimentary understanding of open, complex systems. Human integration with nature 'across the full range of human endeavours' is one of the meanings of environmental degradation through the accumulation of countless mundane human acts (car driving, home heating, jet travel). Moreover, there is nothing in any body of knowledge that immediately or necessarily opens out on wisdom: our systematic knowledge of biology can be turned to finding a cure for HIV/AIDS, or to making biological weapons. Wisdom does not inhere in data bases or scientific textbooks. In addition, the ideas of human 'stewardship' of the planet might be attractive, but it is a contestable notion. 'Wise stewardship' – or whatever passes for it – is not going to take place outside of political arenas. That is why, despite the extent of the scientific evidence demonstrating climate change, the international politics around the topic remain quite contentious.[22]

The final passage explicitly looks forward to the integration of hoped-for technological advances and governance:

> It may be possible to develop a predictive science of society and to apply advanced cognitive actions, based on the convergence ideas of NBIC [nanotechnology, biotechnology, information technology, cognitive science]. Human culture and human physiology may undergo rapid evolution, intertwining like the twin strands of DNA, hopefully guided by analytic science and traditional wisdom.[23]

What is most of note here is not the fantastic, muddled notion of human biology and culture rapidly 'evolving', but the 'guidance of analytic science' – again, an apparently agentless and presumably disinterested force for human betterment. This is clearly a technocratic dream; and a 'predictive science of society' a technocratic utopia – but for those subjected to its governance, in all likelihood a dystopia.

It is difficult to read the advocacy and prognostication for technological convergence and not see in it the trajectory toward what Jacques Ellul termed, 'technical autonomy' – 'The complete separation of the goal from the mechanism, the limitation of the problem to the means, and the refusal to interfere in any way with efficiency...'[24] But the government of the United States is by no means alone in pursuing technological convergence. The EU also has a CT programme; and its principal report on CT, 'Converging Technologies – Shaping the Future of European Societies' does at least acknowledge the range and seriousness of possible disruptions that converging technologies might introduce: 'Each [of the likely characteristics of CT applications] presents an opportunity to solve societal problems, to benefit individuals, and to generate wealth. Each of these also poses threats to culture and tradition, to human integrity and autonomy, perhaps to political and economic stability.'[25] Yet the report recommends a European-wide research and funding programme; a 'widening of the circles of convergence'; and urges the European Commission to establish a CT dimension to the EU internal market in science and technology, the European Research Area. These initiatives appear to be underwritten by the fact that public anxieties will only have an airing within an arena in which the direction and momentum of CT is already a settled matter:

> Tremendous transformative potential comes with tremendous anxieties. These anxieties need to be taken into account. When they are, converging technologies can develop in a supportive climate. *To the extent that public concerns are included in the process*, researchers and investors can proceed without fear of finding their work over-regulated or rejected.[26]

Fencing off or limiting public deliberation (occasionally reduced to 'public anxieties') over what CT advocates themselves term the 'transformative' potential of their plans is at the very least a firm foundation for technocracy. But while the public and private interests involved in CT add considerably to the prospect of more technocratic forms of governance, accountable deliberation has already been undermined in other ways, both directly and indirectly. This is despite the fact that in the aftermath of World War II and in response to the growing importance and highly specialised nature of scientific and technological advances, the United States and other countries in the developed world established technology assessment centres to enable informed deliberation and debate within democratically accountable legislatures. So for example, over a period of 24 years the US Congressional Office of Technology Assessment (OTA) produced some 750 reports on a remarkably wide range of subjects. Then for partisan and highly ideological reasons, the OTA was disbanded.[27] 'When the US Congress did away with OTA in 1995, other nations were stunned. "That the leading technological state in the world, a democracy like us, should have abolished its own main means of democratic assessment left us aghast," wrote Lord Kennet, who created an umbrella group of mini-OTAs called the European Parliamentary Technology Assessment network.'[28] Now, as scientific advancements and their technological applications pose ever more numerous and considerable governance challenges, in themselves and in respect of their possible outcomes and uses, the strain on our systems of governance is becoming clear, firstly if not principally because of our relatively weak means of ensuring accountable deliberation about them and about the balance of benefits weighed against costs and risks. In addition, our deliberative systems – social, ethical and legal – are necessarily slow-moving, while the sheer scale and pace of innovation and change and the interests of national security, national competitiveness and private investment create incentives for bypassing them.[29] Even our more technical forms of deliberation are now under pressure: patent offices are struggling to deal with innovations, most notably the tools and processes of bioinformatics, that can machine-generate patentable information. For example, 'Incyte and similar companies have filed thousands of provisional patent applications with the United States Patent and Trademark Office (USPTO) for ESTs [gene fragments known as expressed-sequence tags] in hopes that, they will someday be able to find the "usefulness" of the sequence.'[30] This is placing the patenting authorities under enormous strain. 'In 1999 alone, 289,448 patent applications were filed in […] bioinformatics[s] and the USPTO has created working groups to deal with the influx of bioinformatics applications.'[31]

Similar pressures apply to large-scale public works projects no less than to leading-edge endeavours that embed or employ novel scientific techniques. For example, a number of public works initiatives have been proposed as a 'solution' or part-solution for climate change: nuclear power generation; cleaner coal-burning power; the development and deployment of alternative forms of energy generation (solar, wind, tidal, geo-thermal) and agricultural policies that will enhance the production of biofuels. But even once we agree about the relative importance of its many causal factors, what kind of a problem is climate change? Is it a thorny complex of relational issues which might best (or at least initially) be addressed politically, or in social and economic terms? Is the amount of power generated (and the quantity of fuels imported or exported) in any country deemed a fundamental necessity – and if so, is it sustainable environmentally? Does it create unacceptable vulnerabilities or costs? These matters are not open to technical solutions, since they deal with shared ways of life in some quite fundamental ways; and they can only be overridden at some cost to fairness, prudence and (where it applies) to democratic transparency. Bringing these and other matters to open, public debate and working through to a consensus might then entail a close examination of technical approaches – if the nature of the problem so warrants. So '...it is important to develop a planning process that is less concerned with technical solutions and information about these, and has more focus in the early stages on the requirements with respect to the economic performance, environmental sustainability and safety performance required of the project. The objective is to reach, as far as possible, consensus on these particular issues. [...] It is not until these basic parameters of the planning process have been established that it is really meaningful to start to identify the technical solutions that would be able to meet these requirements.'[32]

An increasing number of issues, projects and planned developments entail a degree of complexity and scientific or technical detail that force both citizens and legislatures back onto expert advice to the extent that 'An uncritical and theoretically uninformed discourse of expertise has fostered both an instrumental attitude toward experts on the part of government and relatively weak demands for accountability from citizens...Expertise has legitimacy only when it is exercised in ways that make clear its contingent, negotiated character and leave the door open to critical discussion.'[33] In addition, there has been an astonishing growth in the expert/technical input into a great many of our deliberative processes. For example, 'expert testimony' is now an established field, for private consultancies, large law firms, insurance companies and others. What results is not only a considerable narrowing of the purposes and range of critiques of leading-edge science and technology, but also the facilitation of more general technocratic forms of governance.

[There is] evidence of a broader swing back toward a technocratic model of governance in the United States. Expressions of this shift include: a rise during the past decade in official discourses of 'risk assessment,' 'sound science' and 'evidence-based decision-making'; a retreat from precautionary approaches to regulation; an attempt to cut back on citizen participation in environmental decisions; and, in the court system, a partial displacement of jury trials by judicial pre-screening of scientific and technical evidence.[34]

In the twenty-first century we have made for ourselves a world in which the tools and processes of science and technology can be useful in the many activities that comprise governance (computerised data analysis; and techniques and devices for monitoring environmental quality, for example), but science and technology must themselves be extensively governed in matters such as the release of genetically modified organisms into the environment, the control and disposal of fissile material and the uses to which we might put advances in human embryology and genetic engineering. There now exist fourteen international organisations to regulate biotechnology alone.[35] Moreover, we can already trace the way in which the introduction of new technologies into our social and political arenas generate innumerable impacts on established forms of human relatedness, on a global basis, in realms such as identity,[36] privacy,[37] financial stability[38] – and our national and international governance arrangements.[39] What has come to be known as the 'digital divide'[40] is fundamentally a matter of human relatedness – development, equality, education and access to information – not computers, *per se*.

The human condition as nets of relations

In recent years, a considerable increase in the number and variety of concepts denoting significant extensions of human relations have gradually entered the vocabulary of the social sciences, even outside the literature which generally comprises studies of global governance: the concept of individual and collective 'carbon footprints'; global ethics; global civil society – and perhaps most notably, significant increases in the application of human rights to situations and behaviours. These matters (and others) are grounded not only in shared, practical concerns but also in felt senses of moral responsibility. Yet as Zygmunt Bauman observes, 'Morality which we inherited from pre-modern times – the only morality we have – is a morality of proximity, and as such woefully inadequate in a society in which all important action is an action on distance.'[41] He goes on to argue, 'The cancelling of spatial distance as measured by the reach of human action [...] has not been matched by the cancellation of moral distance, measured by the reach of moral responsibility; but it should be so matched. The question is, how can this be done, if at all.'[42] Myriad forms of global governance need not be explicitly ethical in terms of either ends or means any more than the forms of governance exercised by governments. But many instances of both require adjustments to shared ways of life, occasioned by claims of responsibility, culpability, equity, fairness, justice and the like. And on an individual basis, one of the many outcomes of globalisation is to make us acutely conscious of the impacts of our ways of life on 'distant others'. So the moral substance of our goal-setting and policy-making is usually discernible, even through our occasional studied indifference.[43] Technocratic and narrowly focused problem-solving approaches to governance exacerbate these linkages, albeit not frequently to politically significant degrees. Indeed, Bauman argues that organised counter-movements, particularly in the form of single-issue social movements, broadly conform to technocratic ways of understanding and responding to the world:

> Contemporary social movements, like all organizations in the technologically structured society, are as a rule dedicated to the pursuit of a single task (undertaking such auxiliary tasks only as may be reasonably hoped to strengthen the chances of the main one); they are, more often than not, 'single issue' movements. By the very fact of being single-issue, they confirm the principle of singularity and the assumption of autonomy or the self-containment of issues. Obliquely and inadvertently, they corroborate the image of the world as composed of issues that can be pursued and resolved in separation – one at a time, and one independently of the other. Willy-nilly, they co-operate in keeping the *totality* of the actor and of the world out of focus, and consequently also in the substitution of efficiency standards for ethical norms, and technical procedure for moral responsibility.[44]

The 'actor-world totality' – the human condition – comprises the complex interaction of human and natural systems: a world increasingly shaped by human designs and by the unanticipated or disregarded consequences of our ways of life. But the animate and inanimate foundation of human life is not a static backdrop. It is an intricate web of complex exchanges.

Governing relations on a global scale

Governance is an art, not a science: there is very little in the fundamentals of human affairs that can be satisfactorily ordered with scientific exactitude, for all that we might in certain instances apply scientific means to do so. Similarly, non-Realist and popular understandings of the purpose of law is to serve the interests of justice – the particulars of which vary across cultures and time. For most of human history, governance largely comprised adjustments to individual and group relations against largely stable (if not unchanging) human and natural settings. In the twenty-first century, through the advancement of scientific and industrial prowess and the progress of globalisation, all forms of human relatedness have multiplied beyond reckoning – certainly beyond the cognizance of any individual. Yet we find ourselves having to exercise forms of governance to adjust the relations of six and a half billion human beings to planetary ecosystems. In making a global arena for human activity (or perhaps, having made of the planet increasingly subject to the impacts of human activity), we have also extended the necessary reach of our governance – hence, global governance. To be sure, we cannot manage the world as though from outside, or above – instead, we are faced with the difficult and intensely political business of governing ourselves and our activities with a keen awareness of our power – and of the kind of damage we can wreak to our life support systems, even inadvertently. What is entailed in the task of governing relations on a global scale can be grasped by by an appreciation of Geoffrey Vicker's characterisation of policy-making *within* states:

> The policy-maker is expected not merely to balance but to optimize, to achieve, within the limits of the practicable, some state chosen as most desirable or least repugnant. The mere existence of policy-making attests the will to impose on the flux of event some form other than that which the interplay of forces would give it. Whatever scientists, as scientists, may say, men as political animals expect from their policy-makers – at least in our present society – not merely balance but artistry; the realization of social form, in redesigning cities, in enfranchising minorities, in many not necessarily consistent ways. These demand consensus focused and sustained for decades [...] if they are ever to be reflected in changes in the actual state of the milieu.[45]

This is not the stuff of problem-solving, as Vickers also argued:

> As all policy makers know from experience, policy does not consist in prescribing one goal or even one series of goals; but in regulating

a system over time in such a way as to optimize the realization of many conflicting relations without wrecking the system in the process. Thus the dominance of technology has infected policy-making with three bogus simplifications, just admissible in the workshop but lethal in the council chamber. One of these is the habit of accepting goals – states to be attained once and for all – rather than norms to be held through time, as the typical object of policy. The second is the further reduction of multiple objectives to a single goal, yielding a single criterion of success. The third is the acceptance of effectiveness as the sole criterion by which to choose between alternative operations which can be regarded as a means to one desired end. The combined effect of these three has been to dehumanize and distort beyond measure the high human function of government – that is, regulation – at all levels.'[46]

Nations cannot escape the generation of new and complex forms of relatedness – with each other, as ever, but also with human groups and human activity at sub-state levels, and with the natural environment. As we enhance our technical means for managing some of the ensuing issues, the appeal of technocratic approaches to public policy might well continue to sharpen. But '...[W]e need to revitalise our idea of "international governance" more radically. Governance is what we contest as political but there is very little we are not *also* able to see as a "mere" problem of technical management, and vice versa...[P]oliticians now speak the language of background experts. The terms of professional expertise increasingly provide the frame for political debates and decisions. The media has become adept at educating its audience into the nuances of what had been technical disputes.'[47] The political meaning of this does not end with a recognition that there are no purely technical solutions to the problems of human relations, but extends to the quality of our systems of governance, for 'Although our world is densely governed, we have only the thinnest experience of participating in global politics. We remain subjects of an invisible hand – not that of the market, but of expertise which denies its politics.'[48] The path to common security – the condition to which an inclusive global governance aspires – is one of hard choices, not quick fixes. It is not difficult to substantiate the assertion that 'Stability...is a special case of change, not the natural order of things'[49] – a tenet that policy-makers, both national and international, have long endured, but in respect of global governance, one they must now learn to embrace.

5

Although global governance arrangements concern state behaviours to some degree and rely on state compliance and furtherance, the regimes are not only about states

What is global about the human condition cannot wholly be contained or directed from within the international system, despite the fact that many of the empowering aspects of globalisation have been set in place by states themselves. This is partly a matter of the complex interaction of human and natural systems, which generally need to assume crisis proportions in order to achieve political visibility. But the limits of states and the international system to exercise a fully comprehensive global governance (whatever that might comprise) also arise because states are enmeshed in nets of relations which not only impact on them in functional ways, but which also constitute the larger order in which states themselves operate. An acknowledgement of this does not entail an evasion of the long-standing structure/agency debate in International Relations theorising, which as one author contends, can help us to confront notions of globalisation as akin to a force of nature:

> [I]t is important that we acknowledge the strategic use made of the rhetoric of globalisation. For, as a process without a subject, seeming to operate above the heads of elected officials it provides, or is capable of providing, a most convenient scapegoat for the imposition of unpopular and unpalatable measures. By restoring active and strategic subjects to the process of globalisation we can not only contribute to the demystification of this process without a subject, we can also contribute to the repoliticisation of political and economic debate.[1]

But there are clearly many human and natural orders that fall outside of direct national and or international oversight but which nevertheless impact on states (and on human security more generally) in important ways. For that reason, the predominance of international organisation (as a form of action) and of International Organisations in the global governance literature is striking.[2] So typically within global governance studies, a question of the sort, 'What would an adequate global governance be the governance *of*?' does not arise: the '*of*, *by* and *for whom*?' of global governance are defined in terms that are not radically different from the familiar activities of states and international organisations. On such an understanding, the qualities of issues requiring *global* governance – unusual and challenging kinds and degrees of extensiveness, inclusiveness and seriousness – are matters which various combinations of national and international actors and mechanisms can engage. If one accepts that the sum of globalising dynamics does not offer systemic challenges to the international system, global governance can be characterised as 'Government, management and administration capabilities of the United Nations, World Bank and other international organizations, various regimes, coalitions of interested nations and individual nations when they act globally to address various issues that emerge beyond national borders, such as development, the environment, human rights, infectious diseases and international terrorism.'[3] A similar view is captured in the following: 'Global governance is governing, without sovereign authority, relationships that transcend national frontiers. Global governance is doing internationally what governments do at home.'[4]

In many other characterisations of global governance, the 'by whom?' question is addressed by extending significant governance activities to a range of non-state actors, configured in a wide variety of ways, both alone and in concert with states: 'The complex of formal and informal institutions, mechanisms, relationships and processes between and among states, markets, citizens and organisations – both intergovernmental and non-governmental – through which collective interests are articulated, rights and obligations established and differences are mediated.'[5] As useful abstractions these 'institutions, mechanisms, relationships and processes' have a precision and discreteness that shape rather than erase the multitude of ways in which we can understand the complexities of our world. Here, for example, is a depiction of markets as structures of governance (and seemingly, as agents, too) in particularly strong form:

> Our political thought should start by understanding that markets do not make government unnecessary; markets are a type of government.

> Governance is an unavoidable task, an activity that takes place within any group of humans, including the far flung band of people who more or less participate in the processes we call globalization. Markets are the institutional devices such people, we, have chosen to govern a wide range of matters. Mechanisms of governance, [including] capital markets, are important because such mechanisms are literally constitutional, they inform the character of the society they govern, and so human lives.[6]

However, we should not confuse the creation and maintenance of order for instrumental purposes (whether for private actors or for states) – that is, governance which makes immediately self-interested behaviours possible – with ordering and regulatory activity at systemic levels. Although markets can credibly be described in terms of governance activities (as above), markets themselves are also subjected to governance, both within and between states. The 'of, by and for whom' of all forms and levels of governance cannot be satisfied either in strictly structural or functional terms, because governance arrangements and acts of governance are both outcomes of political deliberation and contention. Indeed, contention extends to differences that arise between the many kinds and levels of governance which are generally thought to comprise global governance, the most notable example of which is the tension between the free trade provisions of the World Trade Organisation and national environmental legislation.[7]

The belated, rectificatory governance of markets and market-based institutions in times of crisis also reveals the very considerable complexity of relations and transactions that can be packaged, converted and transferred at speeds that outpace our deliberative mechanisms. The liquidy crisis in the global financial system from Augsut 2007 (with particularly egregious effects in some countries and industries) occasioned concerted action by the federal banks of several governments, both singly and in concert. And even as they struggled to address the immediate and secondary effects of the turmoil, the underlying vulnerabilities of the global financial system began to become apparent:

> The demand for liquidity is not just driven by the need to take a given known value of off-balance sheet assets onto the banks' balance sheets. It is also driven by pervasive uncertainty about who owns what and who owes what and to whom. Massive losses have been incurred on a wide range of asset-backed securities (not only

subprime mortgage-backed) that have not yet been recognised by the owners of these assets, revealed and reflected in balance sheets and profit and loss accounts. Hundreds of billions of US dollars worth of capital losses are still 'missing in action.'[8]

Given the potential of global financial turbulence to affect the stability of even the world's strongest economies, with everything that implies in terms of both national and international security, the weaknesses of this aspect of global governance are clear, particularly in view of the legitimacy and deployable power of states. As one well-known commentator expresses the matter, '...the combination of the fragility of the financial system with the huge rewards it generates for insiders will destroy [...] the political legitimacy of the market economy itself – across the globe. So it is time to start thinking radical thoughts about how to fix the problems.'[9] However, there is a good deal of evidence to suggest that the 'problems' are systemic rather than accidental or anomalous – outcomes of the myriad forms of governance in place for these systems – and that governance 'fixes' could worsen rather than alleviate the incidence of serious financial turbulence:

> Just because you can turn some cash flow into a tradable asset doesn't mean that you should; just because you can create a swap or forward contract to trade on some state variable doesn't mean that it makes sense to do so. Well, in the efficient market paradigm it does, because nirvana there is attained when a position can be taken against every possible state of nature. But in the world of normal accidents and primal risk, limitless trading possibilities might cause more harm than good. Each innovation adds layers of increasing complexity and tight coupling. And these cannot be easily disarmed through oversight or regulation. If anything, attempts at regulating a complex system just makes matters worse. Furthermore, if innovation is predicated on behaviour predicted by efficient markets theory, then things might not operate as advertised: People just don't behave that way. The point is that these innovations have externalities for the entire financial system that are hard to measure but dominate their apparent value. Rather than adding complexity and then trying to manage its consequences with regulation, we should rein in the sources of complexity at the outset.[10]

Whatever proposals might address that call, such as the establishment of a World Financial Authority,[11] states and the international system will remain at the centre of ensuring systemic stability – or what passes for it. Certainly, the degree to which 'markets are a kind of government' is exposed once things go awry and governments feel themselves obliged to bail out financial institutions and/or to stabilise markets:

> The world has witnessed well over 100 significant banking crises over the past three decades. The authorities have even had to rescue important parts of the US financial system – on most counts, the world's most sophisticated – four times during the same period: from the developing country debt and 'savings and loan' crises of the 1980s to the commercial property crisis of the early 1990s and now the subprime and securitised-credit crisis of 2007–08. No industry has a comparable talent for privatising gains and socialising losses. Participants in no other industry get as self-righteously angry when public officials – particularly, central bankers – fail to come at once to their rescue when they get into (well-deserved) trouble. Yet they are right to expect rescue. They know that as long as they make the same mistakes together – as 'sound bankers' do – the official sector must ride to the rescue. Bankers are able to take the economy and so the voting public hostage. Governments have no choice but to respond.[12]

Public bail-outs of large financial institutions can reasonably be termed acts of rectificatory governance, but it is less easy in this case – and in many others – to give a definitive answer to the question, 'of, by and for whom?' There is no clear hierarchy of power, so such actions can hardly be described as top-down; a sense of high-stakes urgency dampens or at least postpones more fundamental, systemic considerations; and the way remains open for the full range of actors and interests to benefit from what passes for global governance without necessarily being subject to its strictures. One hedge fund trader explained his investment strategy in the wake of the uncertainties generated by 9/11: 'As soon as it happened, I liquidated everything and bought Swiss Francs. It's a classic fascist trade. Money went to stability and that was Switzerland. You know the Swiss won't come under attack because everybody dirty in the world has their money there. Nobody is going to burn their own money.'[13]

None of this diminishes the importance of international organisation, but it does contextualise it – or rather, sites it in a field of complex relations that cannot entirely be rendered down to forms of manageable interdependence, or abstracted from the sub-national actors and dynamics that also shape our world. The most prominent features of the systemic quality of relations between states – the international system – are the formal, intergovernmental mechanisms we have established for communication, negotiation, and exchange. But as David Kennedy points out, 'Any so-called "realism" that attends only to overt acts of national sovereigns is no longer realistic. In our world, power lies in the capillaries of social and economic life. Myriad networks of citizens, commercial interests, civil organizations and government officials are more significant than interstate diplomacy. Statesmen and stateswomen act against a background fabric of expectations – the legitimating or de-legitimating gaze of world public opinion – and they act in the shadow of all manner of public and private norms.'[14] For all of the extent and depth of this 'background fabric' of sub-state human values, interests, activities and organisation, much of it directly or indirectly depends on, or coalesces in (or around) states. So the number of conditions, issues and threats impinging on both state and non-state interests requiring the coordinated international organisation are considerable. Thematically these include governance initiatives that are preventive (arms control; the Geneva Conventions; the Antarctica Treaty); stabilising (the IMF/World Bank, at least in principle); facilitating (WTO); and rectificatory (some environmental negotiations and agreements.) Of course, whatever their legal basis and technical machinery, these arrangements are politically inspired and maintained, since historically and presently, what counts as stability in the international system need not necessarily accommodate the security and stability of many of its weaker members, especially to the degree that such distress works to the advantage of other, more powerful states. The economic and social damage wrought by the application of the 'Washington Consensus' in many parts of the developing world only remained a consensus in respect of the powerful state and private interests driving it.[15]

States can and do act on their own behalf, but in anything that might reasonably count as a global governance initiative undertaken either singly or in concert with other states, they cannot abstract their interests from non-state actors and related but sometimes unconsidered conditions, structures and dynamics (even were they disposed to do so.) Whether or not one believes that states are 'unitary actors', their operating environments are highly dynamic; their borders porous; and innumerable human realities and natural forces either condition or drive their actions – and these react or adjust accordingly.

The definitional and analytical clarity we can assign to states and state actors, their arenas and roles, is but rarely so neat in practice, particularly if we regard the term 'global governance' not only as the orders established and maintained by national and international initiative (International Organisations most notably), but also as a summative phenomenon – an 'everything that is the case' order of orders. Seen in this way, neither the power nor the importance of states is discounted, but they are placed in a context which is richer and more intensely relational than the kinds of hierarchies that predominate in debates about hegemony,[16] polarity and state security more generally. The capacity of, say, the Bretton Woods institutions – and the power of the political interests driving them – remain considerable; and any general account of global governance must surely take account of them, but it is also notable how much of nationally and internationally directed global governance is reactive: anti-terrorist action; currency, liquidity and market stabilisation measures; dealing with infectious diseases and their consequences; coping with global environmental crises.

The deployable power of states and International Organisations has global reach, at least for some purposes, but their operating environments – the many orders on which states themselves depend – are both more extensive and more fundamental than is commonly acknowledged. The conditions as well as the purposes of global governance indicate fields of relations that comprise something more akin to ecology than functional interdependence. Geoffrey Underhill asks,

> Can one really claim a meaningfully and empirically verifiable distinction between political authority and the market? If so, where does one place authoritative political decisions on environmental regulation, trade law, or competition law, all of which have huge implications for transaction costs in market-based economic competition, both within and across borders? Are these very political matters in the public domain of politics and states, or the private domain of the market (and one should note that these policies are heavily influenced by the interests they affect)? How would one answer such a question? It is argued that one cannot, if one attempts to maintain a distinction between states and markets for other than occasional analytical purposes.[17]

So although hierarchies of power have little analytical use for delineating global governance either as a condition (in summative form) or as an activity, power in its many forms remains central: the 'of, by and for whom?' question is always present. Perhaps the pole around which there is the greatest contestation is between public and private authority – matters intensified and given weight by globalising forces. Outbreaks of antagonism arising from the exercise of private power and/or authority are not confined to states: much of what comes within the sphere of 'global civil society' movements contends with the activities of private actors such as transnational corporations.[18] However, in practice – and particularly in the practice of global governance – the public/private polarity is not always so stark. Many of the most widely-cited definitions of global governance are quite explicit on the matter of the importance of both state and non-state actors; and the role of non-state actors is clearly implicit in the concept of 'governance without government': '[T]he concept of governance without government is especially conducive to the study of world politics inasmuch as centralized authority is conspicuously absent from this domain of human affairs, even though it is equally obvious that a modicum of order, or routinized arrangements, is normally present in the conduct of global life.'[19] But many of these orders are tensioned when not actually contested; and the very considerable accruals of power now open to private groups and even individuals has sharpened interest in how public/private balances are formed and adjusted. Indeed, questions of public and private authority are not always a negotiable matter of who should exercise global governance for any particular purpose (or have the largest say in its formulation and enactment) – often, they are key sites of contestation in the continuous business of making and re-making global order. Yet states and the world's larger non-state actors cooperate to considerable degrees to ensure forms of stability and predictability that are mutually beneficial to both, which still allows room for antagonism over regulatory particulars.

Moreover, non-state actors can undertake governance activities on their own initiative – legally, but without the explicit consent of their states, and sometimes in outright opposition to their policies. A particularly striking instance of this is the coalition of US states and cities agreeing to adhere to the carbon emissions standards of the Kyoto Treaty, in defiance of the federal government's refusal to ratify it.[20] The state of California has concluded an agreement with the UK on global warming;[21] and several US states have used their powers to pursue funding in stem cell research for their companies and universities – again, which the federal government has refused to provide, and which the states concerned believe to be important for their international scientific, industrial and commercial standing.[22] And the billionaire mayor of New York City has donated 100 million dollars to Johns Hopkins University for the same purpose.[23] The power – and at least on occasion, and for some purposes – the willingness of private actors to shape their larger milieu for more than narrowly self-interested purposes is a clear illustration of the way in which governance and global governance has never been a wholly one-way, top-down Realist expression of state power. Recently, three of the largest banks on Wall Street, produced a document, *The Carbon Principles*, which requires power companies seeking finance for new fossil fuel plants to take account of their effects on climate. Their consultation with energy companies themselves and environmental NGOs makes this all the more noteworthy:

> The Principles were developed in partnership by Citi, JPMorgan Chase and Morgan Stanley, and in consultation with leading power companies – American Electric Power, CMS Energy, DTE Energy, NRG Energy, PSEG, Sempra and Southern Company. Environmental Defense and the Natural Resources Defense Council, environmental non-governmental organisations, also advised on the creation of the Principles. This effort is the first time a group of banks has come together and consulted with power companies and environmental groups to develop a process for understanding carbon risk around power sector investments needed to meet future economic growth and the needs of consumers for reliable and affordable energy. The consortium has developed an Enhanced Diligence framework to help lenders better understand and evaluate the potential carbon risks associated with coal plant investments.[24]

This and similar developments might hold more promise than substance, at least in view of the nature and scale of what have come to be regarded as global issues; nevertheless, they indicate the ways in which global governance is not monolithic or uni-directional. But if '...the overwhelming majority of challenges facing the world can be met only by constantly renewed cooperation between public and private actors on an international scale'[25] and if 'By definition, global governance implies that individuals take charge of matters that concern them by sharing the management and responsibility for them with public authorities',[26] are we entering an era of 'multilateralism from below', or of a balanced mix of governance by, with and without government, or of 'hybrid governance'? The evidence for such a state of affairs, even in nascent form, is mixed – and such conceptualisations share the stage with many others – some related, as in much of the 'global civil society' literature, while others discern less heartening patterns emerging from the same dynamics.[27]

The ways in which the numerous kinds, sizes and orientation of private actors operate independently of public authorities – or oppose them, or combine with them, can be conceptualised in many ways and for many purposes. The point on which most analysts concur is that there has been an explosion in the facilitating conditions that make an extension in the forms of governance necessary or possible. Many concepts have been coined or appropriated to describe the shifting conditions that have impacted established modes of governance and other forms of human relatedness: de-territorialisation; disaggregation; spheres of authority – unsurpisingly, terms that are also familiar in the globalisation literature.[28] Other phenomena, themselves connected to globalising forces, have added further impetus: privatisation; self-regulation; the growing power and importance of the corporate sector; the ease of the movement of global capital.

The phrase now commonly used to depict novel arrangements of governance actors and activities is 'hybrid governance'. The phrase has been in use in a wide variety of non-international or sub-global contexts, especially in respect of the governance of relations between firms or within markets more generally, in large part because markets are non-hierarchical organisational forms; and even to the extent that they are regulated politically and/or legally, there has long been fascination with the distributed forms of order and stability they display. Broadly, these are 'Form[s of] industrial organization [in] intensive long-term customer-supplier relations in industrial markets, [which] while [the firms] engaged in these relationships formally remain independent, they cooperate in ways not easily reconciled with the conventional concept of arm's-length market interaction. This cooperation often comprises areas like production, logistics, quality assurance, and research and development. These intensive long-term customer-supplier relationships are often referred to as *hybrids,* because they seem to combine characteristics of hierarchical governance with characteristics of market governance, as far as duration, adjustment mechanisms, and the nature of commitments are concerned.'[29] Much the same general depiction was subsequently applied to other forms of governance – and global governance. Note how in the following characterisation of governance, state 'adaptation' does not necessarily connote a re-assertion of hierarchical dominance:

> [O]n one hand [governance] refers to the empirical manifestations of state adaptation to its external environment as it emerges in the late twentieth century. On the other hand, governance also denotes

a conceptual or theoretical representation of coordination of social systems and, for the most part, the role of states in that process.[30]

Implicit in the recognition of coodination-as-governance are degrees of common interest between disparate actors, or at least incentives for the accommodation of differences for a shared purpose. In this sense, 'hybrid governance' does not readily imply merger, or fixed organisational form – after all, 'coordination' requires discrete actors: it is the activity – the exercise of governance – that is hybrid.

Hybrid governance

Of course, not everything that can be counted as global governance can be characterised as hybrid – a great deal of the work of International Organisations most clearly; and when global governance is defined as a summative phenomenon, what is most often evoked are the outcomes of separate, multi-actor and multi-level governances, and such compatibility as they have is not a matter of explicit coordination.

   A recent surge in interest in hybrid forms of governance is not surprising: the phenomenon touches on many of the fundamentals of theorising about states and the international system under globalising conditions: the relative standing of actors; the important influences on the framing of public policy; appropriate and effective organisational forms for dealing with global public goods (and bads); whether what counts as global civil society can shape the larger contours of international life; and not least, the possibilities and limitations of global governance. A key area of investigation is the organisational and/or perhaps relational forms that various actors assume in order to produce hybrid forms of governance. A primary source (and what could be regarded as an antecedent) for studies in hybrid global governance was research on the conduct of national and even local governments as they underwent various pressures to reduce state-provided welfare systems, to privatise and to conform to a more general 'hollowing out of the state'. In the case of the UK, this 'refers to the loss of functions upwards to the European Union, downwards to special-purpose bodies and outwards to agencies'.[31] As these trends, pressures and opportunities have multiplied and extended, hybrid governance has 'gone global'.

At the same time, the facilitating, empowering aspects of globalisation engendered a literature not only on the role and performance of non-state actors in international politics,[32] but also on the dynamics of their relationships and their (often hybrid) modes of operation – networks (such as The Third World Network); coalitions (Oxfam International); and campaigns (Jubilee 2000) of startling variety and extensive transnational reach.[33] A great deal of attention has been devoted to the possibilities these developments hold for progressive politics, but much as globalisation has its many darker possibilities, the condition of being 'connected' carries with it no guarantee of orientation and requires no benign commitments. And to the extent that these hybrid groupings can exercise governance, or exert considerable influence on governance-making, 'governance without government' is not always a welcome prospect.[34]

However, the extension of connectedness, reach and deployable power cuts in every direction. To the extent that states find themselves on the receiving end of threatening dynamics so generated or enhanced (presently, international terrorism features routinely), they can and do employ networked forms of organisation and action. 'Government networks' can be regarded as something wider than a form of enhanced multilateralism, since the use of the term extends to include non-state actors.

> Each of these [government] networks has specific aims and activities, depending on its subject area, membership and history, but taken together, they also perform certain common functions. They expand regulatory reach, allowing national government officials to keep up with corporations, civic organisations, and criminals. They build trust and establish relationships among their participants that then create incentives to establish a good reputation or avoid a bad one. [...] They exchange regular information about their own activities and develop data bases of best practices, or, in the judicial case, different approaches to common legal issues. They offer technical assistance and professional socialisation to members from less developed nations, whether regulators, judges, or legislators. [...] Understood as a form of global governance, government networks meet [the] needs [of nations operating under global conditions].[35]

Whatever its merits, the assertion that 'a world of government networks would be a more effective and potentially more just world order than either what we have today or a world in which a set of global institutions perched above nation-state enforced global rules',[36] implicitly acknowledges that it is the quality of states' relationships – (some of them hybrid) – not their fixed standing in hierarchies of power that is likely to secure their interests. International relations are but one facet of the relations that states must contract in a milieu which also includes the forms and dynamics of global politics. But hybrid actors – and more significantly, the kinds of hybrid governance they might deploy – open up a wider range of possibilities than large-scale outcomes that might be 'more effective' and 'potentially' more just. The effects of shifting patterns of relations can enable the accrual of power and influence which is not legitimate or accountable.[37] Unsanctioned forms of public means and private ends are also possible. And for all that such arrangements might be authoritative, a substantial increase in hybrid governance is likely to make it more technocratic, more subject to expert rule – ushering in 'governance without government' when the latter stands for transparency and accountability.

Concerns about legitimacy and accountability are more than expressions of a generalised anxiety, since forms of hybrid governance can offer constitutional and legal challenges – or less directly, bring about undeliberated, gradual shifts in the political orders that make them possible in the first place:

Hybridization engenders constitutionally relevant costs. It weakens the democratic legitimation of governance and judicial control. It loosens the protection of minorities and individuals. It circumvents organisational and procedural checks and balances. It results in a less clear separation between law and politics, which in turn leads to partial de-differentiation. Hybrid bodies usually have narrowly limited authority. They can become single-issue constituencies. It becomes difficult to link issues. Veto positions are harder to overcome. Social conflict is more likely. Disintegration is possible. [...] Once hybrid governance is accepted in principle, interested actors can strategically increase the degree of such governance. All this can be addressed as partial de-constitutionalisation. The constitution loses control over governance activities. The distinction between the ordinary and the constitutional level of law gets partially blurred. In the extreme case, governance boils down to what the governance body can do without running the risk of being overthrown.[38]

One might want to stop short of suggesting that hybrid governance runs the risk of becoming like art for Andy Warhol: 'anything you can get away with'. But nor is it clear that hybrid global governance cannot (or should not) help create the conditions for a more secure human future, or that it will be less resourceful and engaging than other forms of political contestation, bargaining and compromise. When expressed in generic form (above) the risks of hybrid governance are far from negligible, but we might best regard these as cautionary rather than forbidding. And the accomplishments of hybrid, state/non-state cooperation, particularly in the legal field, should not be overlooked: perhaps the most high-profile of which was the 'Ottawa process' that led to the ban on land mines.[39]

The perils and promise of hybrid governance are both likely to increase, but in conjunction with these developments, we can also expect to see a greater awareness of the need for what has been termed, 'the normative legitimacy of global governance institutions'.[40] As for the hybrid governance developments themselves, the centre of attention might soon move from the work of NGOs with a liberal orientation toward actor configurations with a good deal more in the way of power and resources:

> Some of the largest institutional investors in the world yesterday called on the US Congress to introduce a mandatory national policy to reduce greenhouse gas emissions by up to 90 per cent below 1990 levels by 2050. It is the latest move that underlines the way business leaders have dramatically seized the environmental agenda and are now pushing politicians to tackle global warming. The group of forty investors which [...] controls 1.5 trillion dollars worth of funds, also wants the financial regulator, the Securities and Exchange Commission, to insist that companies listed in new York and elsewhere disclose their exposure to climate change risk.[41]

As part of our larger, summative global governance hybrid governance actors (and the arrangements they put into place) are unlikely to decline in number and importance any more than the complex issues they are useful for addressing, or the kinds of networked relations that are open to practically any form of purposeful action. The larger point is that states, too, are unlikely to lose their central place in maintaining either bounded orders or global governance, not by dint of raw power and command, but by the quality of the relationships they contract and deploy.

6
Global governance will rely on normative acceptance rather than lego-political enforcement

Norms and laws in the international system

The concept of 'anarchy' in International Relations theorising is not disputed: in those contexts, the term means that states exist in a world in which there is no overarching authority, no global government. Realist emphasis on this point gives anarchy the quality of an arena in which states contend with each other quite sharply and directly, because in the absence of any supranational authority, war and violent conflict are inevitable; and states are thrown back onto self-help, with the prospects for trust and cooperation limited and generally short-lived. But is the absence of any authority that can exercise power over states so determining? It is perhaps more helpful – and more 'realistic' – to consider anarchy not as an arena but as one of many conditions informing state interaction. This is easier to grasp if we 'scale down' to sub-state levels. In law-abiding societies, most people do not eschew acts of law-breaking because they fear arrest, but because they see it as in their interests. After a period of civil unrest, violent conflict or other form of social dissolution, one is likely to hear calls for the establishment or re-establishment of 'law and order' – a phrase that can convey an understanding that law imposes and maintains social order. But it is more often the case that law arises from order, which is why the imposition of martial law is an emergency measure, not a viable and sustainable form of governance. Few would care to live under conditions in which laws (however just) needed to be routinely enforced.

One of the curiosities of Realist conceptions of international relations is that although the behaviour of states is thought to scale up from an essentially self-interested, selfish and aggressive human nature, little room is made for the moral substance of human life and interaction.

How many of us, Realists included, would want to deny that we are moral beings? Moral cognizance – the capacity to discern morally significant relations and actions, and to exercise moral judgements accordingly – is generally taken to be a fundamental of full human capacity. We do not put children on trial; we protect the mentally infirm; and most legal systems recognise acts of criminal insanity. For all that we differ in terms of the content of our moral codes and the degree to which we adhere to them, we are moral beings. The life that tens of millions of people enjoy cannot be put down to material abundance alone – the substance of which cannot protect us from a life 'nasty, brutish and short' if the ordinary conduct of daily life is not at least civil.[1] Peoples everywhere establish and maintain forms of behaviour and ways of life that allow for un-coerced social cohesion – norms.

It is adherence to social norms that makes societies law-abiding, not fear of legal enforcement. This is the case because by and large, laws consolidate and formalise norms. As we reviewed in Chapter 1, laws can be implemented contrary to social norms, or in advance of them, but within democracies this requires political courage – and sometimes, a good measure of enforcement, too. The norms/laws dynamic works in both directions: organised violations of domestic law are sometimes carried out in the name of justice – that is, on an understanding that a prevailing social norm and the laws that formalise and require it ought to change. The campaigns against female disenfranchisement and against apartheid government in South Africa are obvious examples. Although those cases have historical prominence, they indicate the more general ways in which the relationships between laws and norms are more complex and dynamic and more richly textured than is commonly apparent. After all, large, standard-setting or standard-altering laws do not arise by chance, or unbidden. Sometimes, they represent the outcome of years or decades of concerted effort by individuals and groups to so alter normative expectation that a change in the law essentially validates rather than initiates change. Campaigns of this kind extend back at least as far as the movement to abolish slavery in the UK (which was accomplished in 1807, and in its colonies in 1833); and more recently, the term 'norm entrepreneurs' has been coined to describe this kind of initiative:

> Political actors might be able to exploit private dissatisfaction with existing norms in order to bring about large-scale change. In fact many political participants can be described as *norm entrepreneurs* […] Norm entrepreneurs can alert people to the existence of a

shared complaint and can suggest a collective solution. Thus political actors, whether public or private, can exploit widespread dissatisfaction with existing norms by (a) signalling their own commitment to change, (b) creating coalitions, (c) making defiance of the norms seem or be less costly, and (d) making compliance with new norms seem or be more beneficial. We might say that the intrinsic value of some option is held constant, but the reputational and self-conception values may shift dramatically. Thus there can be a 'tipping point' when norms start to push in new directions.[2]

While it is true that functioning democratic states with their police and judiciaries are hardly anarchic in the IR sense, neither are they stable and orderly by dint of constant surveillance or the application of coercive force. Individuals and communities share many interests which they can best pursue in conditions that promise a good measure of safety, stability, predictability – and trust. Much the same applies at the international level: even in anarchic conditions, most states obey most international laws most of the time, because it is in their interests to do so: the cost/benefit calculus of defying legal restrictions set against what a law-based order provides routinely favours conformity with the law. This is not a surprise: international law is made by states, for states. International law codifies and makes explicit what states themselves have come to regard or choose to specify as 'normal' behaviour in any given issue area:

> Importantly, international law provides a normative framework, an essential ingredient for the successful operation of any large and complex social arrangement. By providing a reasonably clear guide as to what is the done thing and what is not in any given set of circumstances, of what can be expected and what not, and what will be tolerated and what will likely be met with a disapproving, perhaps vociferous, perhaps even violent, response, law helps to reduce the degree of unpredictability in international affairs.[3]

But shared expectations both within communities and between states cannot be reduced to rational calculations of practical advantage: '[I]t is also true – despite the inattentions of most international relations scholars – that moral and emotional factors related to neither political nor economic advantage but instead involving religious beliefs, humanitarian sentiments, faith in universalism, compassion, conscience, paternalism, fear, prejudice, and the compulsion to proselytize can and do play important roles in the creation and evolution of international regimes.'[4] Moreover, morally-infused belief and sentiment has always traversed political borders – and never more easily than under our present, globalised conditions. Although international proselytising was a feature of the anti-slavery movement in the eighteenth and nineteenth centuries, what has come to be known as 'transnational norm entrepreneurs' have now become much more familiar – indeed, on some reckoning, they are key actors and important catalysts in the making of a global civil society. Ethan A. Nadelmann's characterisation of the techniques adopted by transnational norm entrepreneurs in trying to construct global prohibition regimes is also more widely applicable: 'These groups mobilize popular opinion and political support both within their host country and abroad; they stimulate and assist in the creation of like-minded organizations in other countries; and they play a significant role in elevating their objective beyond its identification with the national interests of the government. Indeed, their efforts are often directed toward persuading foreign audiences, especially foreign elites, that a particular prohibition regime reflects a widely shared or even universal moral sense, rather than a particular moral code of one society.'[5]

Laws and norms exist in a tensioned balance – never static, but as an ideal, mutually reinforcing, to the degree that enforcement is exceptional. Within the international system, the quality of norms is of particular significance because international law has no general enforcement mechanisms; and those agreed within specific treaties are generally very limited in scope. Even at the level of maintaining what the UN Charter terms 'international peace and security', the Security Council's enforcement provisions are such that two of its permanent members, the US and the UK, could not be prevented from launching a war against Iraq in 2003. Nevertheless, the attempts of both states to receive Security Council sanction and their strenuous efforts to advance legal and political justifications in other forums indicate the strength of the international norm against intervention, since we can '...regard a norm as settled where it is generally recognised that any argument denying the norm (or which appears to override the norm) requires special justification'.[6]

At crisis-ridden junctures it can appear that international laws and norms are epiphenomenal to the structure of the international system, but their place in its routine functioning is much deeper and more fundamental than dramatic acts of law-breaking might seem to indicate. As a scholarly undertaking, the task of delineating these relationships has been hampered by a decades-long gulf between international law and the study of international relations.[7] This gap has recently begun to show signs of being bridged, driven in part by developments and events that cannot satisfactorily be grasped within inflexible disciplinary boundaries. The following is indicative:

> International law, like philosophy and ethics, has been ignored by IR scholars for decades, yet customary international law *is* norms, and empirical research in IR is [...] demonstrating that these legal norms have powerful behavioural effects. Legal norms are also bound up inextricably with the workings of international institutions, which have been the central focus of virtually all types of IR research in recent years. Further, these legal norms are structured and channel behaviour in ways that create precisely the types of patterns political scientists seek to explain. Understanding which norms will become law ('soft' law as well as 'hard' law) and how, exactly, compliance with those laws comes about would seem, again, to be a crucial topic of inquiry that lies at the nexus of law and IR.[8]

One might well consider the absence of vertical authority in the international system to be a puzzle when set against its considerable order and predictability; and there persists some scepticism about the capacity of international law to inform, let alone constrain certain state behaviours. But there can be little doubt that certain state behaviours are widely and strongly deemed unacceptable by the majority of other states, for systemic as well as self-interested reasons, either formally (in law), or because they are contrary both to established state practice and to broadly shared expectation – which is the meaning of customary international law. Although the term 'rogue state' lacks precision, its use hardly conveys a sense in which the fact of anarchy is the predominant characteristic of inter-state relations; and when the term is applied, it would carry little weight were it only a term of abuse. So in order for state behaviour to be 'rogue' there must be a normative expectation against which the term derives its meaning in specific cases. Indeed, norms are one of the chief characteristics of any social system; and '[A]lthough it is possible [for a norm] to be sanctioned by a single social actor, it is only when most social actors sanction [a] behaviour that we can say a norm exists. [...] Adherence to norms is, then, in part an unintentional result of the acceptance of a larger social system as a frame of reference.'[9]

Perhaps one consequence of the now extensive literature on norm entrepreneurs and the influence wielded by non-state actors is to cast states typically as defenders of status-quo norms and resistant or reluctant in the face of norm creation and norm change. Of course, such a disposition is hardly uncommon – again, as when apartheid South Africa came under normative pressure not only from within, but also from other states, from international organisations and a variety of other transnational actors.[10] One key indicator of the importance of norms in inter-state relations is the efforts states devote to UN General Assembly resolutions – and in particular, avoidance of condemnatory ones. Although General Assembly resolutions are not binding on states, they are regarded as authoritative by dint of their inclusiveness, as a result of which they are also 'a rich source of evidence about the development of customary law'.[11] Although campaigning NGOs and international NGOs have now received a good deal of scholarly attention,[12] norm entrepreneurship is not an exclusive province: states are not only capable of accommodating changing norms, they can also initiate and facilitate them – and there are remarkably extensive nets of political, legal and bureaucratic mechanisms for doing so. Uncovering these helps us to understand how it is that despite the lack of supranational authority or of international legal enforcement mechanisms, we can still speak meaningfully of a summative global governance.

In addition to transnational norm entrepreneurs, Harold Hongju Koh has identified 'six key agents in the transnational legal process' by which states negotiate, create, amplify, promulgate and consolidate norms: through governments acting as norm sponsors; by exerting their influence within transnational issue networks; through the work of interpretive communities and law-declaring fora; by the establishment of bureaucratic compliance procedures; and by enabling issue linkages.[13] Each of these can be briefly illustrated. The best-known recent example of a state acting as a norm sponsor was the Canadian government's sponsorship of the movement to ban landmines; and the 'Ottawa process' engaged a wide variety of non-state actors as well as Canadian diplomats.[14] States' engagement with transnational issue networks is extensive (human rights; climate change; HIV/AIDS) and often fundamental to the positions they adopt or advocate, as well as in the more general framing of certain developments or situations as shared political matters. Koh illustrates 'interpretive and law-declaring fora' by listing the variety of actors engaged in ensuring that the Genocide Convention as a norm of the international community finds expression – for example, with respect to atrocities in Bosnia these include 'the UN General Assembly, the UN Security Council, the World Court, the International Criminal Tribunal for the Former Yugoslavia and Rwanda; numerous scholarly groups, human rights organizations, as well as both the Congress of the United States and a US federal appellate court'.[15] The work undertaken by the majority of the bodies in this case was not direct enforcement of the Genocide Convention but intersecting initiatives enabling the pursuit of justice through clarification and reinforcement of the norm. Bureaucracies, particularly those at international level, serve a more fundamental role than the construction and enactment of compliance mechanisms; in fact, as Michael Barnett and Martha Finnemore argue, 'we can better understand the power of International Organizations wield by viewing them as bureaucracies [...] [because] they use their knowledge and authority not only to regulate what currently exists but also to constitute the world, creating new interests, actors and social activities'.[16] It is in bureaucracies that we can see the importance of norms in constitutive roles as much as in their regulative and evaluative or prescriptive ones:[17]

> [T]o say the world is covered in law is also to say we are increasingly governed by experts. Not by the American empire, not by 'global capital' – but by experts. These experts – quite often lawyers – make decisions that affect the wealth, status and power of other people. They do so by interpreting and enforcing the background norms and institutions which structure activity in the market, in the state, in the family. Their routine work establishes and refurbishes this complex transboundary legal and institutional milieu. Across the globe, experts communicate with one another in common vernaculars, their significance in every national system enhanced at the expense of conventional politicians by the processes we so often refer to as 'globalisation'.[18]

Finally (and also constitutively) is Koh's identification of issue linkages: 'Because international legal obligations tend to be closely interconnected, deviation from international commitments in one area tends to lead to noncompliant nations into vicious cycles of treaty violations. To avoid such cascading violations, domestic bureaucracies develop "institutional habits" that lead them into default patterns of compliance.'[19]

Each of Koh's six mechanisms offers insight into the intricate skein of norms that condition state behaviours and inform their relationships, not only with each other but increasingly with non-state subjects and with the global environment. In his terms, norms 'bring international law home' but they also serve as a means for states to recognise and to begin to articulate acceptable limits about matters for which there is no codified legal provision but which cannot long remain a free-for-all. The large-scale environmental consequences of rapid, extensive industrialisation and globalization are a case in point – and by no means a twenty-first century novelty. In 1971, 'the [US] Secretary of State declared that "…perhaps it is time for the international community to begin moving toward a consensus that nations have a right to be consulted before actions are taken which could affect their environment or the international environment at large. This implies, of course, that nations contemplating such actions would be expected to consult in advance other states which could be affected." […] The very suggestion by a United States Secretary of State that the international community move toward consensus in requiring consultations, much of the burden of which would fall on the United States, constitutes a significant step in the direction of building a new binding norm.'[20]

In sum, norms permeate international relations; and instances of state conformity to specific norms are made routine by an ethos in which the existence of a great many norms tempers the stark fact of anarchy. The behaviour of most states is not held in check by fear of coercion or retaliation by other states, but by a recognition of kinds and degrees of interdependence, and an acknowledgement of the importance of systemic stability. Indeed, conformity to international law is itself a norm of international politics. At the same time, however, norms and laws alike are negotiated relations around key interests. Because they are compromises, they are also tensioned – subject to changing conditions, both political and material. And although state non-conformity to any given law or norm is likely to entail negative consequences, these can sometimes be accommodated in a cost-benefit calculation. So if laws and norms are equivalent in terms of required adherence, what then is the case for asserting that global governance will rely on normative acceptance rather than lego-political enforcement?

Norms and global governance

To appreciate the importance of norms in the framing and exercise of global governance either summatively or in issue-specific terms, it is necessary to understand it as something more extensive than intergovernmental arrangements, central though these are likely to be. Many of our larger and more vexed global issues are not low-frequency/high-impact events, of the sort that are driven by state-level policy and which can most directly be dealt with by negotiations in an international forum. Atmospheric nuclear testing is an example of the kinds of issues that are generated by states and negotiated between them. However, our highly globalised condition now means that high-frequency/low-impact actions – in other words, the ways of life of many millions of people – have dramatic impact on our physical and political environments. Climate change, widespread biodiversity loss and ozone layer depletion are not the objectives of any state; and although it is not difficult to trace the connections between those conditions and state-determined policies for energy generation, commodities exploitation, economic development and trade policy, the lines of causation are neither simple nor unidirectional. Cheap energy, largely unrestricted, worldwide travel opportunities, falling commodities prices and cheap imports or booming export industries are not self-evident global public goods, but they are much prized by the majority of those who enjoy or aspire to a middle-class life. These expectations have normative force – and states, especially democratic ones, are sensitive to it. The absence of immediate and visible crises and of high-impact consequences adds force and momentum to the current pace of resource extraction, industrialisation and consumerism – international climate change negotiations notwithstanding. This is not to suggest that states are hapless in the face of the well-marshalled human wants of their citizens. Behind the astonishing pace of Chinese industrialisation and its impacts on the energy market, on trade and currency valuations and on the environment both within its borders and beyond, is a strategic drive to re-position China in the hierarchy of states. Neither its ends nor its means is unique.[21] If for democratic governments what might answer to 'leadership by example' in the international politics of climate change could amount to electoral suicide, for all states it would also carry serious strategic considerations – reasoning of the kinds advanced at various stages by China, Russia, Australia and the United States in respect of the Kyoto carbon emissions targets.

Through the Intergovernmental Panel on Climate Change (IPCC) and the Kyoto Protocol, states have at least made carbon emissions a political issue and agreed on the necessity of quantified reductions (much though these are widely regarded as inadequate to the scale of the problem). The most important states in this matter have the legislative, enactment and enforcement mechanisms to see through any changes they agree to implement. (The speed and efficiency with which the manufacture and sale of ozone-damaging CFCs were phased out in line with the provisions of the Montreal Protocol makes this plain.)

The preamble to the Montreal Protocol could, with a few obvious substitutions, stand as a declaration of intent by the states negotiating climate change: '...recognizing that world-wide emissions of certain substances can significantly deplete and otherwise modify the ozone layer in a manner that is likely to result in adverse effects on human health and the environment [...] Determined to protect the ozone layer by taking precautionary measures to control equitably total global emissions of substances that deplete it, with the ultimate objective of their elimination on the basis of developments in scientific knowledge [...] Acknowledging that special provision is required to meet the needs of developing countries....'[22] So, even allowing for tough negotiating positions on carbon emissions, why are the international politics of climate change so vexed – and why has progress been so tentative? One important answer to that question is that one must not mistake the rhetorical force of a statement of intent for something with normative force. Within the international system, in matters that are not subject to relatively fast change or fundamental challenge (the parameters of diplomatic exchanges, for example), the gap between norms and laws is quite narrow, and in the ordinary course of things, neither has to be invoked. But issue-based matters, either in respect of existing conventions or in the form of novel challenges, bring to the fore questions of how agreements can best be forged and obligations determined that are likely to meet with routine compliance. (In the ozone depletion case, the science was incontrovertible and inaction threatened planetary rather than localised disaster.) Negotiating a treaty to address a challenge that affects key interests of all or most of the world's states is difficult enough, but it would be naïve to suppose that, once a treaty is signed and ratified by the states concerned, an inter-state normative expectation will have been created that will suffice for immediate and thorough-going enactment. Rather, in such cases the law is created on the basis of common interests – but that is not the same as normative consensus of the kind that ensures enactment. Because most international law lacks any enforcement mechanism, the full range of possible reasons (and motivations) for non-compliance is open. These include strong, countervailing interests, 'free riding', anxieties about relative advantage – and about cheating; and neglect of implementation, or lack of capacity to do so, whether because of poor governance, lack of knowledge or lack of resources.

The comparison between action taken to reverse ozone layer depletion and the intense state wrangling over the specifics of reducing carbon emissions has another, fundamental difference: while manufacturers and users of CFC-based aerosols, refrigerants and the like could be compelled to phase them out and/or supported to find substitutes, carbon emitting behaviours are deeply entrenched in established ways of life. Many of the most extravagant such as private car use and trans-continental leisure flights have the force of normative expectation, while other large sources of carbon emissions provide the electricity generation, commodities and finished products that are no less woven into the fabric of individual and community life throughout the developed and – increasingly – the developing world. The formal, inter-state recognition of the facts and likely trajectories of climate change does not as yet have complementary normative adherence in populations throughout the world, at least of a size and coherence to drive political action forwards. A recent, nine-country survey of attitudes found that 'Climate change is the number one concern in the developing economies surveyed. It is the number three concern in Europe and the joint fourth with another issue in the US. India (60%), Mexico (59%) and Brazil (58%) have the highest levels of concern about climate change, with the lowest being the UK (22%) and Germany (26%).' And yet, 'Overall confidence is low. China (46%) and Hong Kong SAR (38%) have the highest confidence, with the UK (5%), Germany (6%) and France (7%) the lowest. In Germany, the UK and China, more than a third of people think we should not be individually trying to fix the problem.'[23] The survey concludes that:

> Consumers are giving governments a clear mandate for leadership in every one of the [nine] economies surveyed. If governments are waiting for consumer action first to ensure their regulatory interventions have popular legitimacy, then consumers are waiting for government action first to ensure their individual interventions have sufficient scale to be effective. Even in India, where belief in the collective power of individual actions is strongest and where there is least tendency to delegate to the government, 59% of people think that the government should be playing the leading role, compared with only 27% for individuals.[24]

But is it really the case that citizens are waiting for law to make obligatory what judgement and conscience indicate; or that governments are hesitant to use their law-making powers except in response to considerable normative changes? Or might we instead have constructed means to clothe reluctance, interest and denial in the form of the as-yet weak normative commitment of others, or of our governments? We have known for some time that the planet will not support developed-world levels of consumption and pollution greatly in excess of current numbers, but worrying trends are given their momentum by an interlocking of individual aspiration, community interests, the pursuits of public and private bodies and the strategic calculations of governments – in other words, by a normative consensus against which campaigning dispositions struggle even now. The following projection from the International Energy Agency is indicative:

> If governments around the world stick with existing policies [...] the world's energy needs would be well over 50% higher in 2030 than today. China and India together account for 45% of the increase in global primary energy demand in this scenario. Both countries' energy use is set to more than double between 2005 and 2030. Worldwide, fossil fuels – oil, gas and coal – continue to dominate the fuel mix. Among them, coal is set to grow most rapidly, driven largely by power-sector demand in China and India. These trends lead to continued growth in global energy-related emissions of carbon-dioxide [...] – a rise of 57%. China is expected to overtake the United States to become the world's biggest emitter in 2007, while India becomes the third-biggest emitter by around 2015. China's per-capita emissions almost reach those of OECD Europe by 2030.[25]

It seems clear that the global governance of the environment, for which a substantial decrease in carbon emissions is all but a *sine qua non*, is going to require normative change on a commensurate – that is, global – scale. Whether the principal impetus is top-down or bottom-up, it seems unlikely that changes in our ways of life on the scale required could be brought about by legal means alone, even were this an immediate prospect.

For all that the scale and implications of climate change give it a unique status, the normative qualities of human life and organisation apply no less to the many other forms of global governance, both established and nascent. In generic terms, what Jan Kooiman defines as 'governing' can be applied directly to 'governance' – and to global governance: '...[T]he totality of interactions, in which public as well as private actors participate, aimed at solving societal problems or creating societal opportunities; attending to the institutions as context for these governing interactions; and establishing a normative found-ation for all those activities.'[26] Global governance, as with any other level of governance, is concerned with adjustments to prevailing conditions which provide for the establishment or maintenance of broadly agreed conditions and relations – norms. Normative change occurs when those conditions or relations come to be widely regarded as unsatisfactory or unsustainable. What is both instructive and encouraging is that our globalised condition has made normative challenges, appeals and diffusion a substantial current of international and, increasingly, domestic politics.

> Implementing international norms is a core aspect of global gover-nance. It raises the central question of whether, and through which mechanisms, developments at the international level can influence domestic policymaking. Scholars of global governance have placed much emphasis on processes of multilateral negotiating within international regimes and unilateral coercion by individual states or international organisations to explain how international agendas reach the domestic level. [But] cross-national diffusion constitutes a third and distinct mode of global governance which has not received due attention so far.[27]

Moreover, the articulation and coalescence of norms, across borders and boundaries of every kind, has helped to bring about a global pol-itics in which power, authority and legitimacy does not reside with governments by default. James Rosenau has coined the phrase 'spheres of authority' (SOAs) to describe emergent forms of order in an increas-ingly disaggregated world. Note how in this description, the formation of SOAs is issue-driven:

> And whose needs delineate the size and scope of SOAs? The answer is obvious: the needs of the individuals and groups encompassed by its jurisdiction as these are defined by its politically effective leaders – by those whose resources, followership, knowledge, or legal status provides them with the capacity to speak and act on behalf of the individuals and groups affected by the issues out of which SOAs legitimacy is constructed.[28]

Without necessarily crediting the existence of a coherent 'global civil society', we can nevertheless identify an emerging global public domain, an 'increasingly institutionalised transnational arena of discourse, contestation, and action concerning the production of global public goods, involving public as well as private actors'.[29] There is considerably more to this contestation than the politics of protest: 'Non-state market driven systems have proliferated to address: global problems such as fisheries depletion; deleterious environmental impacts from forestry, food production, tourism and mining; rural and community poverty; and inhumane working conditions.'[30] At the same time, however, private actors can exert their power and influence for exclusive purposes detached from any conception of public good – and as necessary, by their own forms of norm entrepreneurship. And to the extent that normative consensus provides the basis for the exercise of power (including moral pressure), questions of legitimacy are certain to arise – not least in light of the encompassing normative expectations of democracy and accountability.

As norms become the common currency of global politics, clear hierarchies of actors and well-defined actor arenas are losing a portion of the practical force they once had: domestic and international politics continue to be shaped by familiar actors in familiar modes, but also by NGO-corporate partnerships;[31] the UN's 'Global Compact';[32] forms of industrial and commercial self-regulation;[33] and non-coercive forms of public and private norm convergence.[34] None of this diminishes the fractiousness that so often accompanies competition, but it takes a good deal of cooperation to organise competitive relationships that are not a force-based free-for-all. And if our present, globalised conditions make this much more difficult by dint of the number of actors and variables to be taken into account, it also makes it a more pressing need – and for the already powerful most of all. The growing appeal of norms – and appeals to them – has the effect of emphasising organising principles over actors, the full range of causal relations over formal authorities, and common interests in the fundamentals of systemic stability. The development of a global politics in which non-legal as well legal norms and non-state as well as state actors can have some standing (at least in principle) is far from unproblematic but still more likely to advance the conditions for peaceful order and sustainability than a global governance confined to international legal agreements and multilateral cooperation, important though these are likely to remain. This is because 'Global governance is not so much a label for a high degree of integration and order as it is a summary term for highly complex and widely disparate activities that culminate in a modicum of worldwide coherence.'[35] In our plural and highly inequitable world, the enactment of laws *for* the world is going to require local and/or cultural mediation – that is, a degree of normative coherence between norm communities. After all,

> It is [...] difficult to visualise how the notion of a centralised global environmental governance structure would square with the general need for local solutions to environmental problems. The notion of 'free trade' has universal appeal; the notion of 'uniform environmental responses' does not. [Multilateral environmental agreements] can establish general guidelines for action, but local environmental conditions vary, making the global application of such guidelines problematic in most cases (except for truly global environmental problems, such as climate change.)[36]

If changing social norms are the catalyst for changes in domestic and international law, we can expect that the lego-political enforcement of global governance measures which run contrary to established norms will meet with resistance – and/or failure.

> [T]he challenge for global governance in heavily contested areas... remains how to forge globally valid norms of global governance that can take account of diversity, not just scientific but also economic, moral and cultural. Even if some predictability in international relations is a driving motivation and legitimate goal of global governance, the route to such predictability cannot lie in the denial of deep differences. Nor can it...lie in the effort to impose precise and objective scientific standards on enterprises that are uncertain and politically charged. Instead, legitimizing the use of science in governance requires evolution of the institutions that can confer legitimacy on scientific input into decision making, especially in areas of heightened controversy.[37]

We might best consider how this prescription applies to the kinds of recalcitrance in the developed world that have bedevilled concerted action to reverse climate change. Surely what we face is not merely a challenge to enact and enforce stringent laws aimed at, say, private transportation and energy use, but a change in normative expectation and behaviours that would make such laws viable?

This is not to gloss over the importance of law, its enactment and, when necessary, its enforcement – and this will also apply where global governance arrangements are codified. Unanimity is not a basis for governance except on the very smallest scale of human organisation:

on occasion and when the stakes are high, the law must instruct the norm.

For no complex problem of policy is any society wholly agreed on criteria for choosing a solution. A society may give a great deal of lip service to ideals such as liberty and equality, but it will not agree on just which liberties in what circumstances should be observed or how far which of many possible equalities should be pursued. Even if it agrees on some more concrete objective such as educating the young, it will not agree wholly on the curriculum, or on the budget, tax burden or management of the school system. For at least 2,500 years, philosophers – others too – have sought formulae for deciding such questions, but we are still far short of agreement. Given disagreements, no cognitive or intellectual solution is possible. By that I mean that no reasoned policy choice satisfies everyone and that, consequently, any policy choice made will have to be somehow imposed over the reasoned objections of advocates of alternative policies. Every choice requires imposition, power and politics. Reason alone will not do.[38]

7
Global governance systems must deal with or be able to accommodate large-scale violations/disruptions

How comprehensively and thoroughly must something be governed in order for the governance in question to be fully meaningful? The governance of any large human system can comprise a staggering number of component sub-systems and variables, many of which can have negative, though not usually systemically threatening consequences. States, for example, can experience a variety of economic, social and political crises which might unseat a government but leave the general integrity of the state unscathed. Even the routine business of hard budgetary choices can affect the quality of some aspects of state governance as much as instances of managerial incompetence or the impact of unanticipated events. And although weak, failed and 'quasi states' are a source of practical concern and of scholarly interest,[1] the terms themselves are not free of ambiguity; and a determination of these conditions is a matter of judgement, not precise measurement against agreed criteria. Yet when a state is unable or unwilling to halt widespread violence, human rights abuses, or other sources of large-scale human suffering within its sovereign bounds, definitional precision is moot. Indeed, the report of the International Commission on Intervention and State Sovereignty argued that sovereign immunity from humanitarian intervention should be regarded as conditional on a state's ability and willingness to protect its citizens from catastrophe, not a legal absolute.[2]

However, the 'responsibility' of states to intervene in places where governance has failed is not an imperative: the record clearly indicates that neither a governance vacuum nor human suffering on their own are sufficient to prompt states to act. It is when events pose a threat to neighbouring states, to regional security or to larger, shared interests that states will intervene. If it matters sufficiently, they will do so even in defiance of international law, as was the case with the North

Atlantic Treaty Organisation (NATO) intervention in Kosovo in 1999. In contrast, the international community stood by as Rwanda descended into genocide in 1994. As a prompt to action, what mattered in both cases were not internal dynamics but external implications. A post-Dayton outbreak of the running sore of violence in the Balkans, with its regional impacts including refugee flows was confronted forcefully. The appalling violence in Rwanda posed no serious threat to the powers best able to intervene; and the subsequent violence that has persisted in the Great Lakes region of Africa is much less likely to pose a challenge to the systemic stability of the international system. It would appear that what the UN Charter terms 'international peace and security' can withstand a good deal of sub-systemic disruption.

This relational framework is not unique to the inter-state relations. Our larger systems of governance (and anything that could reasonably be described as global governance) comprise many governance sub-systems. The extensive nets of arrangements and relations that make our globalised world possible require interleaved governance arrangements of many kinds. But a failure of governance in one or more of these sub-systems, even a catastrophic one, will not necessarily trigger a rectificatory response from other related systems or from the larger system or systems of which it is a part. So, for example, even quite large firms can fail without disrupting overall business confidence – the collapse Enron in the United States in 2002 is a well-known case.[3] But in 2008, in the midst of months of global financial turmoil and a shortage of liquidity in the banking industry, the immanent collapse of Bear Stearns, the fifth largest bank in the United States, brought the intervention of the US Federal Reserve. The Fed effectively underwrote an emergency sale to its rival, JP Morgan, because it feared that a bank collapse of that size – and in those circumstances – could have had a serious effect not only on the wider banking industry but also on the global economy. The sum of thirty billion US dollars was provided to guarantee Bear Stearn's non-liquid assets.[4] Throughout the same period, concerted action was also taken by five federal banks to inject more liquidity into the highly stressed system of global banking. By October of the same year, the US government part-nationalised nine major US banks with a US\$250 billion bail-out;[5] and many other governments around the world were soon obliged to take similar action.

As a matter of course we do not expect our systems of governance – themselves human systems – to exhibit degrees of virtue or levels of precision and consistency greatly beyond the cultural norm. We do, however, construct and maintain them in the expectation of preventing or at worst, mitigating catastrophe. We might then best regard the broad purposes of governance as the avoidance of threats rather than the attainment of goals. In the case of the governance of states, these include survival; meeting competition of various sorts on a sound footing; the maintenance of continuity through change (that is, the avoidance of change so large or sudden that it cannot be mediated); stability within broadly agreed parameters; and the minimisation of harm or damage (the purposes of health systems and defence establishments respectively.) Of course, such requisites do not exhaust either hope or expectation: a society cannot long remain viable if the largest part of its energies are devoted to survival; and firms cannot function well or for long on the verge of bankruptcy. A great many of our systems of governance are devoted to maintaining and improving the quality of human life, not merely securing its structural foundations – clear enough in the health, education and welfare provisions of states; and at the international level, the UN's specialised agencies, funds and programmes comprise an impressive roster of public goods, including global public goods, to be enhanced and furthered.

Nevertheless, the importance assigned to the viability, security or stability of any human system is gauged not only in terms of its intrinsic worth, but also, and at times solely, against larger factors that feature significantly in the operating environment of other, not necessarily competitive enterprises. We cannot account for the inconsistency of humanitarian interventions by any other means: the stark truth is that there was no intervention in Rwanda in 1994 because it was not sufficiently important for those in a position to act that they should shoulder the costs and risks. Much the same applies to Darfur more recently. Similarly, the Bretton Woods institutions were established in 1944 on a clear understanding that economic stability and international security were highly interdependent. Then and subsequently, both international organisations and individual states are more likely to respond to economic crises that affect their own, immediate interests, or the conditions on which all or most depend, than to relatively isolated or systemically minor instances, however severe. One hundred thousand per cent inflation in Zimbabwe[6] has had terrible human consequences, but it is hardly a surprise that political attention has been galvanised instead by the potential dislocations of a global credit crunch occurring at the same time. In contrast, the centrality of oil to the working of the world's economies is a near-constant of world politics – its availability; the actors and conditions that affect its price; increasing competition even as world supplies are thought to be at or past their peak; the periodic search for energy efficiency and alternatives. Similarly, members of The Climate Group, which describes itself as 'highly influential world leading companies, cities and states that are committed to: improving their operational performance; best practice and leadership within their sectors and developing and implementing solutions for a low carbon economy' have a common interest in trying to secure environmental stability. Their website expresses the matter quite starkly: 'If nothing is done to stop climate change, economic losses from extreme weather will be larger than GDP by 2065.'[7] It is small wonder that the reinsurance industry in particular has taken such a strong position on halting climate change, since it will bear the financial brunt of its effects.[8]

Action and accommodation in global governance

In law-based systems, some allowance is often made for unusual and/or unanticipated circumstances – and for this reason, some discretion is often shown by law enforcement and judicial officials, even if it is not formally sanctioned. Social norms, difficult cases and the appeal of natural justice can moderate the application of the law to good effect. It is because justice 'must be seen to be done', not in spite of it, that we are able to distinguish the letter of the law and its spirit. Some instances of wrongdoing or lapses in conduct can, under the right circumstances, be accommodated without offering a fundamental challenge to the rule of law. Beyond that, few sets of civil and criminal statutes are ever comprehensively enacted; and enforcement is not always successful. For some, crime does pay – and this ranges from petty theft to international cartels smuggling drugs and weapons or trafficking people. To the extent that these crimes do not upset the overall, routine functioning of our various social orders, they are accommodated – not in the sense that one might turn a blind eye to miscreant behaviour, or apply the law only loosely; and not acknowledged as acceptable after the fact, but absorbed, or recognised as the 'friction' of imperfect human systems. Our globalised systems of trade, currency exchange, international travel and communications facilitate criminal activity that is effectively parasitical upon them. Like a pathogen which infects but does not kill its host, certain forms and levels of criminal activity can elude systems of regulation and governance, much though they are indirectly reliant on them. And although there will be costs to the host system (lost revenue; counterfeited goods; fraud; corruption), it is still able to function satisfactorily. We can say of a good deal or organised crime that it is not tolerated, but where it cannot be prevented or detected, it is nevertheless accommodated. Terrorism is another matter because it is a challenge *to* our governance systems, not primarily an attempt to achieve illicit ends through them.

At the level of global governance, challenges do not always have the quality of deliberate infringement; and nor is 'accommodation' always an outcome of judgement. The first reason for this is because many of our forms of global governance are networks of many related governances, in all their plurality: sited in diverse political settings; with varying degrees of legitimacy and competence; operating at different levels; and dealing with diverse if complementary sub-themes. For example, although the World Health Organisation is probably the most important and certainly the highest-profile expression of the commitment by states to global health, it lacks commanding oversight and resources, let alone the authority to direct states and communities in health-related matters (bar state reporting requirements for plague, cholera and yellow fever.) So despite the considerable success of the WHO's GOARN (Global Outbreak and Alert Response Network) in halting the SARS outbreak, '...surveillance and/or reporting mechanisms remain patchy and unreliable in the Southern China influenza basin. More generally, establishing and maintaining a transparent and reliable network of sentinels in otherwise rural, low-resource settings, compounded by an opaque political regime, have always been a challenge in infectious disease control.'⁹ The preparations under way for an anticipated return of an avian flu pandemic clearly signal that a disease outbreak of that kind and on that scale cannot be met with resignation by any state. But pandemics are not all alike. It would be morally odious to say that AIDS in much of Africa has been 'accommodated' in a deliberated sense either by the countries affected or by the world at large, but for a variety of reasons not susceptible to direction from any one source of governance or global governance,¹⁰ the AIDS pandemic in Africa persists – and it co-exists with a system of systems that can still with some justice be regarded as the global governance of health.

The second reason why the 'accommodation' of infringements of global governance regimes is not always a deliberative one is because sometimes there are no options for any of the significant players to act otherwise. The 2003 invasion of Iraq by the US and UK was a clear violation of Article 2(4) of the UN Charter – the legal basis for the post-World War II international system. But short of opposing one or both countries militarily, none of the states who opposed the war could prevent it. Whatever long-term damage to the standing of the UN, to the Charter or to international law more generally might eventually result, this violation of the law was 'accommodated' at least to the extent that the essentials of law-based inter-state conduct have not as yet been seriously undermined in the subsequent years.

A third reason is that our systems of global governance sometimes lack 'reach' – that is, they cannot easily exercise surveillance, regulation and control in respect of every actor or actor arena that might have a bearing, directly and/or cumulatively, on the purposes of the governance in question. Since global governance is a summative phenomenon (the outcome of many related governances), the delegation of authority 'downward' to align local practice with international agreements mitigates this in certain instances – and will certainly be necessary to ensure that agreed carbon emission reduction targets in the developed world are met. But one of the many outcomes of globalisation is that it has enabled quite low level actors to act in ways which pose significant systemic challenges from within human enterprises that are legitimate, by using skills acquired for politically sanctioned purposes: pernicious applications of the life sciences, rogue traders and computer hackers are obvious examples.[11] We can predict such behaviours in outline, but in the cases above preventative action by more restrictive governance measures are limited by the need to maintain biotechnology industries and our extensive and highly interconnected computer networks. This has clear parallels with the workings of the world economy and those who criminally profit from its regulated structures and activities, but with the difference that in some large-scale systems, single individuals can create very considerable dislocations or turbulence – and until such time as they do, they are likely to remain 'below the radar' of global governance.

But in the context of global governance, 'accommodation' has an additional meaning. There are many aspects of globalisation that create or amplify quite large and significant dynamics without immediate, dramatic effect but, occasionally and crucially, these occur outside of our established deliberative systems, including our systems of governance. Here, for example, an experienced trader in the currency markets describes the change that crept over that industry over three decades:

> Computers have changed the game. In foreign exchange back in the late 1970s, banks would get a call to see a billion dollars and were given two weeks to get back with the fill. Now it's a push of a button and it goes down so smooth. It shows you just how vast the markets are and how many people are playing today. I could walk down onto the floor right now and sell a billion dollars of anything. It will

make some noise but it will get done quickly. That's a phenomenal change from the old psyche.[12]

It is also a phenomenal change from the old systems that once pre-vailed in global finance – unhurried, deliberate and painstaking – qual-ities that are difficult to divorce from an understanding of 'governance' in any of its forms.

> Money used to flow via bank loans, which is an insignificant game now. If there has been a major change it's that hedge funds have taken over the role of global financing. Where banks are methodical and slow, hedge funds are fast. Hedge funds don't get themselves invested with clients by doing weeks of credit work, committee meetings, cross-selling and so on. For them, it's just a question of in or out, then a push of the button.[13]

And in anticipation of the global financial turbulence that ensued only a year later, the same trader asked,

> The real question is what banks actually do in the world today – finance hedge funds? If that is indeed the answer, it means that you and I, the taxpayers, will bear the brunt of any fallout. Every one of those institutions is too big to fail, as we saw with Long-Term Capital Management. And LTCM was a drop in the bucket com-pared to some of the positions that exist out there today.[14]

And so it proved, first with Bear Stearns in the United States; and with the Northern Rock Building Society in the UK;[15] and by the end of 2008, in many other countries. An accommodation of new actors, dynamics, modes of integration and speeds of operation brought us not only enlarged and speedier financial systems, but an altogether larger and more complex system of systems, with potentials and vul-nerabilities few grasped; and over which no one exercised a truly global governance before the quakes reached the foundations. When a crisis of global governance arises (or a crisis requiring governance initiatives on anything that could reasonably be termed a global scale) we can see that sometimes, what can be accommodated as routine within our social, political and economic systems – and even within our systems of governance – can still offer surprises of a kind and on a scale that cannot be accommodated. Whether or not the coordinated action of five central banks to pump liquidity into the global financial system[16] on two occasions qualifies as an act of global governance, it most certainly signifies a considerable gap in the systems that are generally considered to comprise the 'global governance of finance'.[17]

Violations and disruptions

An important measure of the importance we attach to any law or norm is in the resources we devote to ensuring compliance – and the penalties we often exact for non-compliance. The human systems that comprise forms of global governance are considerably larger, more sophisticated and more consequential than those devised for, say, regulating urban traffic, but they are little less vulnerable to violations and disruptions. 'Violations' and 'disruptions' indicate a difference between breaches of governance that are deliberated – that is, in defiance of a prevailing norm or law – from those which come about by accident, mishap or by natural causes. Legal regimes and most systems of governance are premised in part on an anticipation of breaches, which is why forms of adjudication and/or specified penalties are integral to them. In cases where the law is enforceable, we do so in the hope that the disruption caused by an illegal act does not facilitate a broader disruption of legal and/or normative adherence – the other, hard-edged reason why 'justice must be seen to be done'.

Within legal systems, infringements and concomitant penalties are not difficult to scale up. Indeed, many penal codes delineate offences and commensurate penalties on a scale or seriousness – say, from petty theft to grand larceny to corporate fraud. But there is no global governance criminal code; and the enforcement capacities of international law are neither numerous nor strong; and international law is without any centralised authority. So the proposition that global governance systems must be able to deal with large-scale violations/disruptions immediately runs up against the problem of agency.

The particular difficulty is that although global governance is a summative phenomenon – related systems of regulation and control variously coordinated, or with combined effect – breaches of global governance do not always manifest themselves in ways that allow for an obvious distribution of responsibilities to deal with them. It is not only that there is no 'governor' to do so, but that systems-level disruptions can be outside the competence and even cognizance of any of the actors responsible for routine maintenance of the component subsystems. After all, none of the nations affected by the 2007–08 banking crisis is without regulatory systems for that industry and nor is there any shortage of international agreements to ensure the stable functioning of global finance.[18] The case of climate change is similar. Until the creation of the Intergovernmental Panel on Climate Change (IPCC), no actor or group of actors had responsibility for addressing the implications for global climate of aggregate carbon emissions, or at least for making it a matter of practical politics. Before this essential of global governance can be exercised, the actors, their responsibilities and agreed timelines must be clarified and agreed to. In other words, 'dealing with' climate change first requires that a dedicated global regime be created. Pending arrangements sufficiently comprehensive and functional, the problem persists – and worsens; and by default it is in some senses accommodated. This is the meaning of studies in many fields about the adjustment of human systems to climate change.[19] But the worsening of climate change is not merely a matter of the pace of international bureaucracy versus the speed of atmosphere physics: it is also a problem of the pursuit of other, countervailing interests, many of them competitive – and nearly all of them short-term.

There are likely to be limits to the number and severity of disruptions to global governance systems committed in a deliberate fashion by any of the principal actors that comprise them (most often states and the organisations and regimes they create) for the same reason that there are relatively few infringements of international law. In the absence of credible enforcement, the maintenance of global governance in any particular arena, like adherence to law, is also an act of accommodation; a balancing of the large gains that come from systemic stability against the smaller gains of tactical and sometimes even strategic advantage. Even in the case of the 2002 US National Security Strategy – the so-called 'Bush Doctrine' of pre-emptive self-defence – the document maintains a concern to present its own asserted right as an exception to a law that should continue to apply to other states for the continued purpose of maintaining international peace and security: 'nations should not use pre-emption as a pretext for aggression'[20] On the same note, other nations are offered the reassurance that when in the future the US acts pre-emptively, 'the reasons for our actions will be clear, the force measured and the cause just'.[21]

A gain-loss calculus is operative not only for actors that consider contravening global governance arrangements, but also for those responsible for preventing or mitigating such acts. At times, overall systemic stability will not be impacted, so there is not a strong incentive to act; and activating or strengthening governance arrangements might be incompatible with the interests and/or values of some of the key actors. In short, the global governance *of* any sphere is crucially conditioned on the basis of 'by and for whom?' considerations. There are numerous humanitarian, economic, environmental and other crises that are sidelined, overlooked and forgotten, in part because the ways in which they are meaningful are not systemic. Not every crisis that could at least potentially be dealt with by global governance mechanisms is a crisis *of* global governance.

However, there are systemic-level disruptions caused inadvertently or in unforeseen ways rather than through direct violations of existing governance provisions. The worldwide market stresses triggered by the collapse of the US subprime mortgage market is particularly revealing of the extent to which systems that were functionally adequate for short-term profit expanded and grew beyond the cognizance (and hence, the effective governance) of either the financial institutions themselves, or their regulators. The following is a self diagnosis of the crisis by the Global Association of Financial Institutions, The International Institute for Finance:

> The areas of weakness revealed include deteriorating lending standards by certain originators of credit prior to summer 2007; a decline of underwriting standards both with respect to the packaging of structured products and leveraged loans; excessive reliance on poorly understood, poorly performing, and less than adequate ratings of structured products; valuation difficulties as assets shifted quickly from liquid to illiquid; purchase of structured products without full appreciation of the risks; liquidity risk and reputational risk exposure of conduits and structured investment vehicles with major adverse implications for sponsoring banks; and difficulties in identifying where exposures reside in a world of widely dispersed risks.[22]

This is a breathtaking catalogue of ill-considered and even unconsidered risk on a momentous scale, which makes the Institute's expressed hope that a 'suite of best practices to be embraced voluntarily' appear absurdly inadequate. The economic fallout from the crisis and its impacts on governments throughout the world, together with a recognition of systemic risk to the world economy might well render the hope of voluntary standards within the industry to be a forlorn one. While it is true that political and competitive interests might prevent or complicate a more restrictive, comprehensive regulatory regime for financial institutions, the primary lines of causation of the crisis are sector-specific and already subject to governance arrangements that can be extended and/or more strictly monitored and enforced. But global crises can arise from more diffuse sources – and even as a combinational outcome of already governed activities that in themselves accommodate the interests of large and/or powerful constituencies. Crises that can neither be accommodated nor dealt with directly and effectively by existing means of global governance require us to reconsider the span of activities, relations and conditions over which we will be required to conceive and enact new or more extensive forms of governance – and failing that, to consider what 'accommodation' might mean in such circumstances.

Governances and the global food crisis

There is no shortage of preventable human suffering arising from dysfunctional and corrupt governance, but the moral disquiet that accompanies our comprehension of the world's larger injustices is all the more sharp when they occur, worsen or persist as a direct or indirect outcome of governance initiatives. Campaigning organisations bring instances of these to our attention with numbing regularity, when the orders we create for a sector of activity, for a nation or region have unwanted (and sometimes unforeseen) consequences in other sectors – and for other regions and peoples. One need not read far into the globalisation literature or conduct an extensive review of the statistical indicators of human security to appreciate that accommodations of environmental degradation and human impoverishment of practically every kind are neither minor nor incidental to global governance as presently constituted. After all, a substantial decrease in aggregate carbon emissions would entail radical changes to the governance arrangements which serve the established ways of life of those most responsible. Likewise, the extensively governed conditions of world trade have not prevented a lengthy catalogue of social, economic and environmental ills listed alongside its intended benefits; and free trade in particular is frequently cited for its negative impacts, both systemic and local.[23] These are controversial matters because ascribing clear lines of causation in complex interactions of human and natural systems is very difficult and the burden of proof rests with advocates of change; because (it is argued) we should extend and adjust such governance arrangements rather than abandon them;[24] and, not least, because powerful interests, aspirations and ways of life are well served by such arrangements.

The moral implications of accommodating and even mitigating (rather than preventing) human suffering have long featured in the philosophical literature[25] as well as in humanitarian and political campaigns. Although it can appear that our largely unvoiced desire for an accommodation of costs largely borne by others drives and indeed necessitates a good deal of political theatre, the extent to which our governance fixtures accommodate morally awful outcomes is not entirely 'out of sight, out of mind', much though our national and international efforts to mitigate large and/or widespread negative outcomes are something of an attempt to have things both ways:

> At the 1996 World Food Summit, governments agreed on the goal of reducing hunger by fifty percent by the year 2015. By stating a numerical goal – the product of negotiations among parties with different viewpoints, using cost/benefit arguments – 'success' in the fight against hunger was defined as a world where 'only' 400 million people continue to go without sufficient food. Cuban President Fidel Castro was the only world leader to point out that 400 million hungry people is a disgraceful goal for humanity to set.[26]

Eliminating malnutrition and starvation has remained on the international agenda, but not to the extent of marked progress overall. In fact, as at 2006, the Food and Agriculture Organisation (FAO) estimated the number of malnourished people to be 850 million. Despite the efforts of the FAO, WFP and many sophisticated humanitarian and lobbying efforts, cycles of poverty, hunger and conflict persist in many parts of the world. But more recently, a global food crisis has emerged, a 'perfect storm' of factors, the majority of which are not of an unpredictable and catastrophic quality, but which are outcomes of our governances.

The rocketing cost of basic foodstuffs is a worldwide phenomenon. Although the effects are most immediate and severe amongst the poor (who as a matter of course spend a much larger proportion of their income on food than the better-off), the shockwaves are being felt everywhere. 'Since 2000, the average price of food around the world has nearly doubled. In the UK, food prices are rising at three times the rate of inflation. In the US, the price of eggs has risen by 40 per cent in the past year alone, while rice in Thailand and tortillas in Mexico have shot up in price, in some places trebling. [In 2008] the soaring cost of food has triggered street demonstrations in 30 countries, some of which tipped over into riots.'[27] In Egypt, the army and police have been drafted in to bake two and a half million loaves of bread a day, while the government has had to use foreign currency reserves to buy wheat on the international market. It has also increased the acreage of wheat by a third.[28] India, Bangladesh, Cambodia, Thailand and Madagascar all introduced at least partial bans on the export of rice, prompting the Philippines, the world's largest rice importer, to urge the UN to use 'moral persuasion' on those nations to lift the bans.[29]

The unfolding food crisis is global not only in its extent, but also in its sources. Throughout the world, practically every aspect of agricultural production is closely bound up with other globalised conditions (climate change; trading regimes; the credit crunch) or systems of exchange (the price of oil; currency fluctuations; shifting demands of world markets; domestic food supply versus export cash crops). There is little new in the fact of most of these particulars, but the coincidence of several in particularly stressed configurations, together with longer-standing deficiencies of global governance have brought about a condition that threatens to imperil millions of people, even beyond those we have accustomed ourselves to over decades. According to the FAO, '...many factors have contributed to these events, though it is difficult to quantify their contributions. Among the most important factors it is possible to list are the strengthening of linkages among different agricultural commodity markets (i.e. grains, oilseeds and livestock products) as a result of rapid economic and population growth in many emerging countries; the strengthening of linkages among agricultural commodity markets and others, such as those of fossil fuels; biofuels and financial instruments that influence not only the costs of production of agricultural commodities but also the demand for them; and the depreciation of the US dollar against many currencies.'[30] What is striking about this list of causal factors is that several of them are indirect, unintended consequences of initiatives mounted to counter other crises of governance. The biofuels initiative is particularly instructive in this regard.

What many regard as the largest and most vexed global governance issue, climate change, was to have been addressed by a switch from fossil fuels to biofuels. The practical development of oil alternatives had been growing for some years, but the 2007 US State of the Union Address placed biofuel development at the centre of the US government's plan for energy security as well as environmental protection.[31] The European Union also introduced subsidies for the energy crop sector, which was soon over-subscribed.[32] The logic was compelling: an April 2006 press release by the FAO outlined the expected benefits:

> Under the pressure of soaring oil prices and growing environmental constraints, momentum is gathering for a major international

switch from fossil fuels to renewable bioenergy, according to FAO. [...] Factors pushing for such a momentous change in the world energy market include environmental constraints – increased global warming and the Kyoto Protocol's curbs on emissions of carbon dioxide and other greenhouse gasses – and a growing perception by governments of the risks of dependence on oil. [...] FAO's interest in bioenergy stems from the positive impact that energy crops are expected to have on rural economies and from the opportunity offered countries to diversify their energy sources. 'At the very least it could mean a new lease of life for commodities like sugar whose international prices have plummeted,' noted Gustavo Best, FAO's Senior Energy Coordinator.[33]

But in highly globalised conditions, few human systems of any size run in parallel. The consequences of a widespread shift from food crops to biofuel crops were swift.

Since the FAO's report [...] tens of thousands of farmers have switched from food to fuel production to reduce US dependence on foreign oil. Spurred by generous subsidies and an EU committed to increase the increase of biofuels to counter climate change, at least eight million hectares (20 million acres) of maize, wheat, soya and other crops which once provided animal feed and food have been taken out of production in the US. In addition, large areas of Brazil, Argentina, Canada and eastern Europe are diverting sugar cane, palm oil and soybean crops to biofuels.[34]

And stressed lines of supply and demand in basic foodstuffs set off further dynamics, many of which serve only to intensify shortages or soaring costs:

...[M]ore fundamental is the effect of speculation in food as a commodity—like oil and precious metals. It has become a haven for financial investors fleeing from paper assets tainted by subprime mortgages and other toxic credit products. The influx of buyers drives prices and makes food unaffordable for the world's poor. 'Fund money flowing into agriculture has boosted prices,' Standard Chartered Bank food commodities analyst Abah Ofon told the media. 'It's fashionable. This is the year of agricultural commodities.'[35]

Of course, what counts as a commodity for investors is sustenance for the poor. In Ethiopia, according to the Director of the World Food

Programme, 'We are seeing more urban hunger than ever before. Often we are seeing food on the shelves but people being unable to afford it.'[36]

Numerous other primary and/or contributing factors driving the global food crisis have been advanced: the weakness of the US dollar;[37] the accelerating price of oil;[38] years of under-investment in agriculture;[39] a move to meat-intensive diets;[40] and climate change[41] amongst them. The ways in which national and/or international actors deal with these issues are never fully comprehensive of all of the direct and indirect costs. This is only partly a matter of sheer complexity. In the first instance, it is a matter of well-defined national interests, pursued with particular tenacity in difficult and worsening operating environments. So it was that the June 2008 UN Food Summit in Rome failed to secure an agreement beyond generalities. 'In the face of US and Brazilian opposition to any review of ethanol production, there were only vague references to "the challenges and opportunities posed by biofuels." The declaration from the summit [...] said: "We are convinced that in-depth studies are necessary to ensure that production and use of biofuels is sustainable".'[42] Such weak rhetorical devices are often regarded as instances of a 'lack of political will' but quite the opposite was on show in this case. The outcome of the Rome Summit could fairly be described as a failure of global governance to prioritise human security over economic and other national considerations, but it is global governance nonetheless: hugely complex, multi-sectoral, intensely political and shot through with the kinds of compromises that are in fact accommodations of a sort that we profess to deplore. According to one report, corn prices rose in the final hours of the Rome Summit; and food aid levels have sunk to their lowest level in almost 50 years.[43]

Accommodation and the ends of governance

The imperfections and inefficiencies of governance mechanisms, together with relatively fast-changing conditions and the vagaries of both willful violation and natural disruption mean that our systems of global governance most often entail coping – that is, avoiding the worst rather than achieving or maintaining an optimum. This in turn means bearing with conditions or outcomes that many if not most would prefer to eliminate or adjust. But the determination of ends, whether they are regarded as the best achievable or the least worst option, return us to the 'of, by and for whom?' of global governance. The histories of pollution and of colonialism are replete with examples of accommodation – as disregarded externalities; as cost/benefit calculations; and as unintended or regrettable outcomes which were relegated to means, insufficient to challenge the ends in view. The post-1945 international legal order saw an eventual end to colonialism and there is now no shortage of national and international environmental legislation, but world-threatening pollution and pervasive human suffering and insecurity persist. In short, global governance as presently constituted – the sum total of the orders of our world – accommodates a great deal of preventable environmental degradation and human impoverishment. It is small wonder then that for some theorists, the 'of, by and for whom?' question opens out onto perspectives less directly concerned with the politics of organisation and coordination, or with issue-specific matters. For these theorists (and for some political campaigners, particularly those most strongly opposed to globalisation[44]), what passes for global governance can instead be understood as a continuance of elite domination, variously depicted as liberal hegemony,[45] the creation or maintenance of empire and the self-interested hardening of core-periphery relations.[46]

These perspectives might impute to global governance (both as an aggregate phenomenon and in its sector-specific forms) more coherence, more focus and a greater concentration of political authority than is warranted. Much the same can be said about globalisation: its structural transformations have also worked largely to the benefit of the already prosperous and powerful and not without terrible costs, borne by the environment and by the excluded. But its drivers are both diverse and diffuse; and the least well off, whom globalisation advocates argue will continue to benefit from its continuing advance,[47] will in turn make their own accommodations, human and environmental, as we have already seen in China.[48]

The extent to which systems of global governance accommodate unwanted or otherwise undesirable outcomes is only partly a matter of deliberation in the face of options so narrow as to constitute a dilemma, or so poor as to nullify meaningful choice. More often, accommodations demonstrate a certain willingness after the fact – policy decisions and defaults adhered to in pursuit of short-term goals (often based on perceptions of national interest) rather than for any longer-term, inclusive and sustainable forms of global governance. The international politics of climate change, beset by denial, prevarication, hedging and manoeuvering for relative advantage make the point clearly. And although considerable evidence can be marshalled against global governance as a form of structural injustice and against particular international organisations (typically the IMF and/or World Bank) or nations, global governance is far from monolithic. Nor can its ends entirely be reduced to the predatory impulses of the powerful. After all, extensions and amplifications of globalising dynamics of many kinds (in which popular 'pull' factors work in tandem with high-level 'push' factors) require commensurate regulatory measures, where the accommodations of millions of individuals are consolidated and formalised.

Global governance as presently constituted is the aggregate of our human orders; and if the majority of these are, as some would argue, constrained by hegemony, even hegemonic orders must be adaptable to changing circumstances and responsive to challenges if they are to persist. This is unlikely to be a mater of incremental adjustments since, even now, the social and political orders that comprise global governance struggle to come to a full reckoning of climate change – essentially, that the planetary ecosphere cannot accommodate our unaltered ways of life.

8
Global governance must be highly adaptive in respect of changing human circumstances

For the largest part of human history the environmental and material circumstances of human groups everywhere were subject only to incremental change, much of it generated and mediated locally.[1] '[I]t took 99.4 per cent of economic history to reach the wealth levels of [the hunter-gatherer], 0.59 per cent to double that level by 1750 and then just 0.01 per cent for global wealth to leap to the levels of the modern world...[in other words], over 97 per cent of humanity's wealth was created in the last 0.01 per cent of our history.'[2] With that wealth has come the dislocations, uncertainties, impacted problems and the governance challenges of our globalised world. Certainly in a world less comprehensively globalised, less populous and less industrially advanced, *global* governance would not be necessary. In fact, it would scarcely be possible.

The centuries-old mainstays of human circumstances persist, albeit under globalised conditions. Now that half of the world's population lives in urban areas,[3] what counts as human circumstances are less directly and immediately a matter of environmental happenstance and the vagaries of nature than of the short- and long-term consequences of human activity. In the twenty-first century, 'human circumstances' are not merely the features of life common to all but to a degree unprecedented in history, features of life that are *shared*. 'Shared' in this sense need not entail equality or even willing participation, but instead denotes a dense network of relations that defy, erode or supplant boundaries and the once sheltering effects of distance. This is the blunt fact of globalisation, but its implications for the number, kind and scale of governance arrangements necessary for any form of stable and sustainable continuance is difficult to grasp even now. There are a number of reasons for this, the least becoming of which is that the further enrichment of the already prosperous through globalisation has occasioned us little in the way of immediate or direct costs (and certainly nothing commensurate with the considerable gains.) Even climate change can appear a distant and as yet uncertain threat; and there has been little to demonstrate irrefutably that our existing modes of governance cannot be adapted to deal with the political tensions and environmental impacts of accelerating globalisation. Many views of globalisation still tend to approach it more in terms of outcomes rather than processes; from the perspective of structures rather than dynamics; and in terms of the familiar gain/loss calculus of economic and political interests.

For the purpose of considering the global governance challenges brought about by globalisation and the dynamics now readily associated with it, it is helpful to regard our globalised world as an arena in which even many of the small particulars of physical and human environments everywhere are informed if not determined by our highly stressed planetary environment, by webs of complex inter-dependencies, by the exercise of powerful and sometimes remote interests and by means of exchange open to an ever-increasing number of people. As a consequence, even freak weather incidents that have always wreaked various kinds of havoc on a highly localised basis now often have a 'cascading' effect, extending across a wide variety of social, political and economic concerns. For example, the hurricanes of 2005 destroyed 109 oil platforms and five drilling rigs in the Gulf of Mexico, paralysing 90 per cent of crude oil production and 72 per cent of natural gas output in the region. A surge in world oil prices followed, as did calls for a programme of refinery building, a matter that has been politically contentious for many years.[4] Human populations have always had to be adaptable in the face of unusual weather patterns and extreme weather events, but their impacts can now easily be more widespread, costly and disruptive to a range of human endeavour – including carefully deliberated governance initiatives which are themselves adaptations to changing circumstances. The recent political initiative to promote ethanol as a fuel in order to decrease dependence on oil and to reduce carbon emissions is a notable instance:

> The record storms and floods that swept through the Midwest [US in June 2008] struck at the heart of America's corn region, drowning fields and dashing hopes of a bumper crop. They also brought into sharp relief a new economic hazard. As America grows more reliant

on corn for its fuel supply, it is becoming vulnerable to the many hazards that can damage crops, ranging from droughts to plagues and storms. [...] [The share of ethanol fuel] is expected to rise to at least 20 per cent in the coming decades. Experts fear that a future crop failure could take so much fuel out of the market that it would send prices soaring at the pump. Eventually, the cost of filling America's gas tanks could be influenced as much by hail in Iowa as by the bombing of an oil pipeline in Nigeria.[5]

In addition, a World Bank study is reported to have found that biofuels 'have forced up food prices by 75 per cent'.[6] It would appear that an important and large-scale attempt at adaptation has substituted one form of vulnerability for another – and in the process, greatly intensified the disparate global dynamics in the unfolding global food crisis.[7] The scale of the unintended consequences in this case might be unusual, but the dynamics underlying it are not. This is because we cannot abstract ourselves from the complex interaction of human and natural systems; because these systems are now deeply integrated in highly dynamic ways; and because the aggregate effects of human activity mean that one of the truisms of the globalisation literature – that rates of change in both the human and natural world are accelerating – also applies to global governance as adaptation.

The complex interaction of human and natural systems

Although we can divide the physical world between animate and inanimate and break it down to the molecular and atomic levels, reductions of that kind distance us from an appreciation of life and life processes in their organised form, as systems. 'Systems are nets of *relations* which are sustained through time. The processes by which they are sustained are the process of *regulation*. The limits within which they can be sustained are the conditions of their *stability*.'[8] There are few systems, human or natural, that are not open and adaptive – that is, in quite fundamental relations of response and exchange with the other systems that comprise their environment:

> A system is a set of interrelated elements which interacts dynamic- ally with its environment. For any given system, an environment is the full set of all elements outside the system whose attributes affect the system, and also whose attributes are changed by the behaviour of the system. What is considered to be a system as distinct from its

environment depends upon the level of analysis and the problem at hand.[9]

So the environment of a parasite is an organism; the environment of the organism might be a woodland; and the environment for the woodland is the larger ecology within which it functions as an active constituent. But systems relations of all kinds, within and between those both animate and inanimate, are not a matter of simple hierarchy and nor are they limited to linear exchanges. The biological foundations of human life understood in these terms is quite stark:

> Like all other forms of life, humankind remains inextricably entangled in flows of matter and energy that result from eating and being eaten. However clever we have been in finding niches in that system, the enveloping microparasitic-macroparasitic balances limiting human access to food and energy have not been abolished, and never will be.[10]

Such is the human condition; and for all the differences between the subsistence living that characterised the largest part of human history and today's global food and energy crises, those differences are more a matter of scale than of kind. In the twenty-first century, the particulars of our human circumstances take forms that include vastly complex exchanges between human and natural systems which, though the most considerable are on a global scale, are conditioned by the place of humanity within, rather than at the pinnacle of natural systems. The distinction between natural systems and human systems – those that we have consciously created, built and sustained – is in one sense a matter of straightforward observation, but there is little in history[11] or contemporary international politics (the international politics of the environment most notably) that can adequately be grasped without recognising the extent to which their interactions can be hugely determining. Human and natural systems are more pervasively and continuously interactive than formal distinctions and routine observations might lead us to believe; and with these interactions come forms of complexity that pose very considerable challenges for our ability to fully comprehend and govern the world we have made.[12]

Of course, we are capable of introducing changes to the way our large human systems (and configurations of them) operate and interact – seemingly within the bounds of our governance capabilities, if not our pre-existing governance systems. By such means has computerised trading gradually come to be at the centre of the global economy, albeit with implications that were not widely appreciated before crises of governance began to erupt. If global governance is a summative phenomenon, then timely, competent oversight should suffice for the fundamentals of systemic stability, whatever the fate of many connected sub-systems not crucial for the system as a whole. But what if any system over which we exercise global governance is more than the sum of the parts? That is, what if our human systems (the largest of which are in fact systems of systems) display system-level behaviours? The potential for systems-level behaviour has long been clear in the physical sciences:

> The idea that there exists unpredictable 'emergent' order in natural processes did not originate in biology. It is, for example, well understood in physics. Take the properties of the elements hydrogen and oxygen. These are thoroughly understood in themselves. Yet nobody has ever succeeded in predicting the properties of water from a knowledge of its constituent elements. Trying to explain why water spirals down a plughole simply from a knowledge of atoms is an impossible task. What's missing is a knowledge of fluids – a whole level of order above that of individual atoms.[13]

The 'missing knowledge' problem can also extend to large human systems:

> [W]hatever the set of equations are that might be divined to govern the financial world, they are not simple, and, furthermore, they are not deterministic. There are random shocks from political and economic events and from the shifting preferences and attitudes of the participants. If we cannot hope to know the course of the deterministic systems like fluid mechanics, then no level of detail will allow us to forecast the long-term course of the financial world, buffeted as it is by the vagaries of the economy and the whims of psychology.[14]

The social sciences are only gradually coming to a reckoning with systems behaviours.[15] The following clarification offered by Robert Jervis in 1997 has wide applicability: 'We cannot understand systems by summing up the characteristics of the parts of the bilateral relations between pairs of them. This is not to say that such operations are never legitimate, but only that when they are, we are not dealing with a system.'[16]

To illustrate: one of the most important points to note about the 2007–08 crisis in global banking is that the same interconnections that made possible risky forms of lending and related financial transactions between institutions also made possible a system-wide contagion, not precipitated by illegal transactions or by any single actor or action. On an understanding of relatedness familiar to ecologists, years of innumerable trades and deals not only changed relations between the actors involved, they also changed the system within which they were performed – not without notice, but largely without alarm, until the global financial system reached a 'tipping point'. Or as ecologists succinctly express matters: when you add or subtract a species from an ecosystem, the result is not the same ecosystem plus or minus one species, but a reconfiguration of relations within it – that is, a changed ecosystem.

The link with ecology is more than metaphorical, since for practical purposes our human systems cannot be separated from natural systems – and this is the reason why our globalised relations extend a trail of primary and secondary consequences over considerable distances and extended periods.[17] Coal extracted from mines in Australia and exported to China for steel production entails the coordination of numerous human systems (mining, trade, transport, industrial production; communications, law, banking), while environmental impacts will be spread across land in both countries, the sea between them and atmospheric quality, not only in both locales, but also in respect of a contribution to climate change. These dynamics then return to our human systems through environmental degradation and their impacts on human health.

This complex interaction of human and natural systems is coming to characterise the meaning of a great deal of human activity. As discussed in Chapter 2, the full extent of what needs to be governed in order to have *global* governance of certain kinds is likely to extend to local levels, but the nature of globalised interconnectedness does not merely increase the number of significant governance actors, or the number of variables they must contend with. Forms of human activity are now of a number, kind and intensity that they can create forms of relatedness both within and between human and natural systems that are unintended – and at times, ungrasped until they manifest themselves in the form of unwanted outcomes. This point is not a speculative one: data indicating that human activity had created a hole in the ozone layer was twice regarded as faulty because it was not regarded as plausible.[18]

Even at organisational levels that do not display system behaviours, the intricate and dynamic interconnectedness of the human systems that comprise our ways of life throughout the industrialised world might be a good deal less robust than they appear. As the following example of interconnectedness in the fuel/electricity generation nexus demonstrates, the kinds of interconnectedness on which we have come to rely carry serious vulnerabilities:

> And what if the power goes off? This is where complex interdependencies could prove disastrous. Refineries make diesel fuel not only for trucks but also for the trains that deliver coal to electricity generators, which usually have only 20 days' reserve supply [...] Coal-fired plants supply 30 per cent of the UK's electricity, 50 per cent of the US's and 85 per cent of Australia's. The coal mines need electricity to keep working. Pumping oil through pipelines and water through mains also requires electricity. Making electricity largely depends on coal; getting coal depends on electricity; they all need refineries and key people; the people need transport, food and clean water. If one part of the system starts to fail, the whole lot could go.[19]

Another feature of some human systems is 'tight coupling', characterised as a condition of interconnectedness which 'causes a system to be hard to understand and change because changes in one place will require changes somewhere *else*. Requiring changes to be made in more than one place is problematic since it is time-consuming to find the different places that need changing, and it is likely that errors will be made; [and] a network of interdependencies makes it hard to see at a glance how some component works.'[20]

The abiding feature of the workings of large human systems and of the interactions between human and natural systems is complexity, a quality that Joseph Tainter has described as 'one of the wonderful dilemmas of human history' because 'As societies rise in complexity, more networks are created among individuals, more hierarchical controls are created to regulate these networks, more information is processed, there is more centralisation of information flow, there is increasing need to support specialists not directly involved in resource production and the like.'[21] All of these are features of our systems of governance and global governance: forms of complexity as responses to complexity. Nevertheless,

> [m]ost of the time, complexity works. It is a fundamental problem-solving tool. [...] Confronted with challenges, we often respond by

strategies such as developing more complex technologies, adding more elements to an institution (specialists, bureaucratic levels, controls, etc), increasing organisation or regulation of transactions, or gathering and processing more information. Each such action represents increasing complexity. Their effectiveness comes in part because changes in these dimensions can be enacted rapidly. While humans may be complexity averse when we personally bear the cost, our problem-solving institutions can be powerful complexity generators. All that is needed for growth of complexity is a problem that requires it. Since problems always arise, complexity seems to grow inexorably.[22]

Hence what Tainter characterises as a dilemma:

As the highest-return ways to produce resources, conduct transactions, process information, and organise society are progressively implemented, adaptive problems must be addressed by more costly and less effective responses. As the costs of solutions grow, the point is reached where further investments in complexity do not give a proportionate return. Increments of investment begin to yield smaller and smaller increments of return. The *marginal* return (that is, the return per extra unit of investment) declines. This is the central problem: diminishing returns to complexity. Carried far enough it brings on economic stagnation and ineffective problem solving. [...] A prolonged period of diminishing returns to complexity in problem solving is a major part of what makes societies unsustainable.[23]

In our time, the extent and magnitude of human systems has transformed our world – a point most frequently noted with reference to the debilitation and decreased resilience of even the largest of the world's ecosystems, including the earth's atmosphere. This is a profound change in human circumstances, not only as a register of largely irreversible loss and damage, but also because it increases by orders of magnitude the number of relations that must as far as possible be regulated – neatly summarised if not always wholly appreciated in the phrase, 'global governance'. Throughout the world and particularly in our urban areas, there is little in the physical environment which can be taken as a given of the natural world, but instead must be regarded as elements in socio-technical systems,[24] which entails both the 'control of nature' and the regulation of behaviours – pollution controls, fishing quotas, carbon emissions limitations and the like. In their form as global governance mechanisms, these regulations and controls are adaptations to the alterations we have brought about to human circumstances. But there are no conditions or problems requiring anything that amounts to global governance that can be reduced to linear causality, so global governance is an exercise *in* complexity as well as an attempt to deal with problematic manifestations of it. As a result, our problem-solving, particularly under conditions of intense political pressure, is often reduced to a matter of coping rather than finding 'solutions'.

Global governance as adaptation: to, by and for what purpose?

Governance and global governance are forms of action intended to shape the world to human purposes, to deal with conditions or dynamics that impede our goals or threaten our security. The determination to conceive and enact governance mechanisms, particularly at the largest scales, is political in character, even though they might be legal or technical in substance. But as a form of political action, it is notable how much of what requires global governance – or more comprehensive and effective forms of it – are matters of urgency, often entailing deeply impacted relations of human and natural systems on a global scale – 'dead zones' in the world's oceans growing in number and size;[25] biodiversity loss; climate change; and a multi-causal world food crisis, to list but a few. As a rule, although we expect our governments and various governance arrangements to be able to deal with crises, the measure of effective governance is how successful we are in avoiding them, not mitigating them after the fact. The circumstances conditioning any way of life or activity have never been static, so as a matter of course we expect our mechanisms of governance to be adaptable to changing conditions as well as prepared for adversity or turbulence. However, as the complex and accelerating dynamics of globalisation become important variables in human circumstances throughout the world, our adaptability – and the adaptability of global governance – is becoming more stressed, even as it is becoming more important. We can see this in the ways that the natural world also adapts to changing circumstances in response to the aggregate effects of human activity,[26] and even to our adaptations, important examples of which are the mutations of disease-causing bacteria brought about by the routine use of antibiotics;[27] and the preparations we are obliged to make against the possible return of an avian flu pandemic.[28] Within governance contexts, 'adaptive' suggests an approach to problem-solving that differs fundamentally from the non-deliberated varieties that inform ecological balance; and it connotes considerably more than crisis management. But because the creation and exercise of global governance mechanisms is a political activity, its adaptability either in general or on a sectoral basis cannot be reduced to an essentially technical and readily agreed responsiveness. To assert that global governance must be highly adaptive in respect of changing human circumstances is in one sense obvious, but a variation on the 'of, by and for whom?' question that applies to political initiatives of all kinds applies no less to this. What is key is not so much the fact of adaptability as its quality – and in global governance, this is largely conditioned by political factors. The characterisation of problems – indeed, what *counts* as a problem – is in large measure politically driven.

Adaptability as a cost/benefit calculus

A global governance cost/benefit calculus is unavoidable, for two reasons. The first is that at any scale larger than the inter-personal, the exercise of legitimate authority is never an expression of unanimity. Any exercise in global governance is an expression of values; and in none of its many forms will it necessarily be implemented with a view to justice, equity, inclusiveness or sustainability – evident in the ire directed towards the international organisations and private companies that provide the benefits as well as some of the more serious costs of globalisation. The second reason is that because complexity is a feature of large-scale human problem-solving as well as of the problems to be addressed, the direct and indirect consequences of any global governance initiative are unlikely to be narrow in scope or short in duration. Even that most benign expression of what might fairly be regarded as global governance intent, the UN's Millennium Goals,[29] must confront cost/benefit trade-offs not only and most obviously in political terms, but also in terms of practical implementation. Neither eliminating poverty and hunger nor achieving environmental sustainability (both key Millennium Goals) can be advanced, let alone achieved, with initiatives in one arena not affecting the other – and in ways that can pose quite stark cost/benefit choices. For example, in the developed world, the kinds and degree of environmental impacts brought about by farming are conditioned by subsidies in ways that make their elimination a matter of some consequence environmentally[30] as well as politically. Moreover, the complex ways in which agricultural subsidies feature in local, regional and global interactions of human and natural systems does not end there.

Complexity does not prevent an adjustment in the conditions of agricultural trade to the benefit of the underdeveloped world but it does ensure that we will be faced with managing rather than solving the problem – and that includes managing cost/benefit options and consequences.

Adaptability as least common denominator compromise

International responses to global threats or crises require a considerable degree of consensus and cooperation, and the adaptive postures of states in these situations extend to the practical requirements of acting in concert. Once states agree to begin negotiating on a certain topic, there is at least an implicit recognition of a shared problem – and a shared interest in addressing it. In the case of climate change, years of difficult negotiations can be regarded as a form of adaptation to a pressing reality, by the majority of states, resulting in the Framework Convention on Climate Change.[31] But given the refusal of the United States during the largest part of the administrations of George W. Bush to acknowledge the reality of climate change, and that Russia and Australia did not accede to the Kyoto Protocol until 2004 and 2007 respectively, we might be hard-pressed over what comprises the subject in the assertion that 'global governance must be highly adaptive to changing circumstances'.

In international negotiations as inclusive as those to address climate change, the recognition of a problem is not a platform for cooperation – only a pre-condition. The interests of states in this case (and in many others, particularly in respect of the planetary environment) are sharpened, not lessened by a framework agreement to act. The charge of 'least common denominator' has been a frequent criticism of the Kyoto Protocol,[32] as states predictably sought to maximise benefits while minimising their own costs. But at the Bali negotiations in 2007, the 'least common denominator' charge had an added dimension as delegate nations sought to adapt themselves – and the negotiation of serious carbon emissions reductions – to the recalcitrance of the United States:

> The Delegates and observers said the tenor of the talks was pointing toward a least-common-denominator outcome: a vague plan to negotiate by 2009 a new deal on emissions cutbacks, replacing Kyoto Protocol. 'Everyone wants the United States in so badly that they will be willing to accept some level of ambiguity in the negotiations,' said Greenpeace energy expert John Coequyt. 'Our

worry is that we will end up with a deal that is unacceptable from an environmental perspective'.[33]

Not all forms of global governance are conceived, negotiated and enacted by states and the international system, but it is difficult to imagine a global governance of sufficient span and coherence in which their commanding, organising and regulative capacity will not be central, or at least formative. Decreased environmental resilience; expanding and accelerating industrialisation and consumerism; increased competition for resources (especially non-renewable ones); and the very rapid movement of peoples, goods and services around the world mean that the international politics of the environment is likely to become more complex; the issue areas will grow in number and expand; and in all likelihood, some issues will become matters of urgency. The international system will need to engage the global order that sustains states and peoples alike more routinely, with greater speed, efficiency and common purpose than ever before. In the absence of concerted effort at the international level, ordering complex interactions of human and natural systems on the largest scale will be outside of human ability to control; but our ability to affect them negatively – albeit often by default – will continue to grow. Human adaptability to the changed circumstances we ourselves have brought about is not a logical necessity.

Adaptability as an accommodation of special/powerful interests

The history of international environmental negotiations makes it plain that forging common political cause around any global issue is typically protracted and difficult. Beyond that point, further political and practical complexities await. The Framework Convention on Climate Change, for example, only provides the lego-political arena in which states and a range of powerful non-state actors work to ensure that any agreed global governance-as-adjustment to threatening conditions is also as far as possible adjusted to their own interests.[34] The complexities that are a fixture of large-scale scientific and practical issues ensure that there are rarely unambiguously clear approaches to dealing with them; and powerful interests ensure that there are few disinterested ones.

So although there is little if any political disagreement about the moral awfulness of widespread hunger and malnutrition, consensus on this point only sharpens interests across the full range of public and private fixtures that give the term 'global agriculture' its meaning. In this example, as in so many other matters that are the subject of global governance, we are then posed questions such as whether the plight of some 800 million malnourished human beings is something that can only be addressed with GM crops – a second 'green revolution' – or whether instead we need a fresh look at development and a more culturally-attuned way of thinking about worldwide agricultural production? The suspicions of those opposed to GM crops is that they are a solution in search of a problem – in particular, that such a 'solution' abstracts the problem of hunger from other complex human realities and reduces it to one open to a technical fix, albeit one with an additional, entirely self-interested agenda:

> Increasingly restrictive global intellectual property laws, which are a precondition for commercial GM crop technology, further weaken the bargaining power of poor and hungry. They create a massive market distortion in the global food system in favour of multinational companies that already enjoy near-monopoly positions. Most worrying, according to aid agencies, is that the GM lobby is almost entirely ignorant about how and why people actually go hungry, and how to change it.[35]

But the 'problem in search of a solution' accusation can be flung in any direction. Even sustainable development has been so characterised.[36] Ideology is often a feature of these debates, but what makes many of them so difficult to resolve is the complexity underlying them and a desire by the relatively weak no less than the most powerful to balance the cost of means against the worth of desired outcomes. Do we need to build many more dams, coal-fired and nuclear power stations and secure still greater quantities of oil in order to meet rising electricity demand – or should we instead think about energy conservation, and about environmentally-friendly pricing strategies such as taxing aviation fuel? As approaches to development and environmental security, what are such approaches adaptations *to* and *by*?

Adaptability as responsiveness to, or conditioned by the power of non-state actors does not necessarily take the form of narrow self-interest and enrichment at the expense of others. Indeed, there is a sizeable literature demonstrating the ways in which civil society organisations of many kinds, often in coordinated arrangements, have advanced progressive agendas, practical as well as normative.[37] And the larger global governance literature has at its root a recognition that world orders cannot wholly be accounted for without a detailed understanding of the 'governance without government' phenomenon.[38]

Any form of global governance will entail contestation at every stage, before and afterwards: issue definition; who or what has – or should have – voice and standing; framework and protocol negotiations; the allocation of costs and responsibilities; enactment and enforcement; and modes of resistance after the fact. The particulars will vary considerably from case to case, but it matters little whether the global governance under discussion is established by international treaty, bureaucratic networking or what James Rosenau has termed, 'systems of rule [that] can be maintained and their controls successfully exerted even in the absence of established legal and political authority'.[39] Without some degree of adaptation to powerful interests, no effective, truly global governance would be possible – as the reluctance of a number of highly industrialised states to sign up to the Kyoto Protocol demonstrates. At the same time, the requirement for minimal consensus also leaves space for 'norm entrepreneurs' whose numbers include those most concerned for human welfare under globalised conditions.[40]

With so much emphasis given to the global governance functions of international organisations and the 'architecture' of global governance, it is easy to lose sight of global governance as highly dynamic forms of political engagement on a scale that are historically novel. Whether present or proposed adjustments to our circumstances or to our means of regulating and controlling them are deemed appropriate, just, inclusive or sustainable is the stuff of politics at every level.

Adaptation as a failure or incapacity of global governance

The website of the UK's Department for Environment, Food and Rural Affairs introduces a discussion of adaptation and climate change with the following:

> The Intergovernmental Panel on Climate Change (IPCC) defined adaptation as 'any adjustment in natural or human systems in response to actual or expected climatic stimuli or their effects, which moderates harm or exploits beneficial opportunities.' The earlier we start adapting, the better equipped we will be to cope with higher temperatures, increased rainfall and the other potential

changes. That might mean ensuring homes, buildings and transport links are protected against flooding or heatwaves.

One could hardly dispute that these kinds of preparations are rational, responsible and forward-looking, but at the same time they are second-order adaptations – that is, they are an implicit acknowledgement that at best, we will not be able to forestall serious impacts arising from climate change. In other words, these adaptations to our ways of life will address the consequences rather than the causes of climate change. Neither in this nor in other issues is global governance shown to be a lost cause, but as we adapt our global governance initiatives to social, cultural and economic 'realities', driving them toward least common denominators, there will be consequences which in turn require adaptations. As with treating only the symptoms of disease, these cannot indefinitely postpone changes in human circumstances to which we might not be able to adapt at all.

9

However extensive the coverage, global governance arrangements will remain aspirational to some degree

No part of the world remains unaffected by human activity: we have created or conditioned the fundamentals of human circumstances around the globe. For both good and ill, the world as it is – 'everything that is the case' – is an outcome of our values and the aspirations they inspire. Acknowledging this does not nullify plurality as a fact or as an ideal, nor does it lessen the importance of contention and resistance to dominant forms of social, political and economic organisation[1] – in fact, quite the opposite. As discussed in Chapter 1, our globalised condition has left few aspirations innocent – that is, without far-reaching and sometimes undesirable consequences; and at least in the developed world we have become acutely conscious that aspirations in organised, social forms entail costs and outcomes that not even the most scrupulous democratic procedures can obviate. The extent of globalisation means that 'we the people' is no longer merely an expression of inclusion within a bounded culture or polity, but is now also the expression of a common human fate. So for example, there is a good deal about large-scale carbon emitting behaviours such as power generation, mass transportation and international tourism and their impact on distant peoples and environments that we could reasonably characterise as 'collateral damage'. Yet all of these activities are subject to national and international controls of various kinds; indeed, even internationally agreed mechanisms of global governance such as the Bretton Woods institutions and the World Trade Organisation are routinely castigated for what critics see as their unacceptable costs.

Under these conditions, human aspirations take surprising forms – and at times, they assume surprising proportions. Consider the way in which a variety of large and small aspirations combined to bring us the credit crunch of 2007 and, one year later, a delayed but still more extensive and destructive wave of global financial turbulence. In a matter of weeks in September 2008, some of the world's largest and best-established investment banks failed or were rescued from bankruptcy by buy-outs or government interventions; central banks pumped a further 180 billion dollars of liquidity into the highly stressed commercial banking sector; and the US government organised bail-out of US banks to provide against what came to be known as 'toxic' mortgage assets. The extent of the dynamic interconnectedness between the esoteric derivatives markets of investment banks and the lives of ordinary US citizens (and others around the world) was captured by US Treasury Secretary Hank Paulson, who argued that his bank bail-out plan would 'avoid a series of financial institution failures and frozen credit markets that threaten American families' financial well-being, the viability of businesses both small and large and the very health of our economy'.[2]

The spectacle was also unnerving from a governance perspective. After all, the same US administration had confronted a similar (albeit less immediately threatening) crisis before. In February 2002, '[t]he crisis of th[e] moment was the implosion of Enron, Global Crossing and other companies. Along with conflicts of interest and criminally creative bookkeeping, the culprit was often a combination of financial complexity and insanely expensive compensation packages.' Alan Greenspan, then Chairman of the US Federal Reserve, 'Speaking with a hard-edged frankness rarely heard in public — and seeing that [other US government economic advisers] were not sharing his outrage — [...] slapped the table. "There's been too much gaming of the system," he thundered. "Capitalism is not working! There's been a corrupting of the system of capitalism".'[3] But on that occasion, the day was carried by those who sided with senior White House economic adviser Lawrence Lindsey: 'There's always the option of doing nothing', and that the markets were 'already discounting the stocks in companies that show[ed] accounting irregularities'.[4]

One need not review the fall of civilisations to wonder over the robustness and predictive capacity of governance systems and their ability to discern and effectively regulate pertinent, complex dynamics. Indeed, as one analyst asserted, 'If this is the death of Wall Street as we know it, the tombstone will read: killed by complexity.'[5] But our systems of financial governance had had sufficient health warnings:

> Clearly, with current International Monetary Fund estimates of the costs of the 2007–2008 subprime crisis, the banking system seems to have lost more on risk taking (from the failures of quantitative risk

management) than every penny banks *ever* earned taking risks. But it was easy to see from the past that the pilot did not have the qualifications to fly the plane and was using the wrong navigation tools: The same happened in 1983 with money center banks losing cumulatively every penny ever made, and in 1991–1992 when the Savings and Loans industry became history.[...] [T]he current patching by the banking establishment worldwide is akin to using the same doctor to cure the patient when the doctor has a track record of systematically killing them.[6]

Perhaps, as Ross Ashby once remarked, 'Every system changes its mind by breaking.' Unfortunately, the change need not be either timely or correct; and there is no single, authoritative and sufficiently knowledgeable actor – no metaphorical pilot or doctor – to discern hugely complex causal relations, align conflicting interests and minimise risk. Of course, looming financial catastrophe sharply narrows aspiration and concentrates minds, but it does not guarantee political or any other kind of unanimity; and the US legislators engaged in this belated exercise of governance were quick to distinguish emergency provision and the kinds of structures and behaviours that had necessitated it. After all, de-regulation, sanctioned trade in derivatives on a global scale and faith in the ability of markets to self-regulate were themselves governance positions.[7] And although the United States was the epicentre of what became widely known as a 'financial contagion' the global implications of the viability of the US dollar were not lost on anyone. To the extent that the frantic efforts in Washington in September 2008 to stabilise financial institutions, rescue the housing market and free up liquidity can be described as governance at all, it was also a matter of *global* governance, or at the very least, governance of truly global import:

> Today's dollar [...] is faith-based. Since 1971, nothing has stood behind it except the world's good opinion of the United States. And now, watching the largest American financial institutions quake, and the administration fly from one emergency stopgap to the next, the world is changing its mind. [...] At the end of 2007, no less than $9.4 trillion in dollar-denominated securities were sitting in the vaults of foreign investors. Not a few of these trillions were the property of Asian central banks.[8]

In a fevered political atmosphere, uncovering causative factors and apportioning blame are sometimes difficult to distinguish, but as we have seen, globalised interconnectedness often makes the additive and cumulative impacts of human behaviours and human systems considerable – and at times beyond reckoning. (In July 2007, the Chairman of the US Federal Reserve, Ben Bernanke, estimated the cost of the subprime collapse at 100 billion dollars. Fourteen months later, Dominique Strauss, the Managing Director of the IMF, estimated the cost at 1.3 trillion dollars.[9]) Forms of global connectedness mean that the full span of human aspirations, both blameless and avaricious, often become bound up together. In this case, matters as small-scale as ill-advised mortgage agreements and investors seeking a good return on their capital contributed to and combined with electronically conveyed financial abstractions and eons-old hubris backed by the latest mathematical modelling. The resulting mess imperilled matters that are generally well-governed at various levels; and the aftershocks, although difficult to predict, are likely to be felt for some time in debates over the parameters, conduct and effectiveness of our more deliberated forms of global governance. In the current climate, it appears that the '...rise of fully privatized and self-sustaining markets of global scale [will] be highly unlikely...'[10] but it is not at all clear how the relationship between market authority and political authority can be adjusted in a way that accommodates so many diverse and sometimes powerful aspirations, or how our necessarily slow-moving deliberative and regulative bodies will keep pace with actors capable of bringing about enormous changes in the 'real world' economy electronically and continuously.

Appropriate humility is in short supply when Wall Street firms pay out 62 billion dollars in bonuses in a single year; but even in more chastened times, human aspiration in all its variety and with the full force of its pressing demands is going to present regulative challenges of a kind or on a scale for which we have made little provision and/or for which we have little in the way of precedent to guide us. There are further reasons why global governance will remain aspirational, summarised in the thematic points below.

Global governance is itself an aspiration: it cannot get above the kinds of aspiration that drive politics.
Global governance arrangements are aspirations because they are largely regulative rather than prohibitive; because the principal governance actors – states – are interested parties, not detached overseers; and because the dynamism of human systems and their impacts on natural systems ensure that we will have an endless frontier of challenges, not only to our practical and technical capacities but also to

our willingness and ability to summon and enact the necessary consensus for meaningful action on the largest scale. The opening of the Northwest passage in the summer of 2007 might well help to stimulate international efforts to halt climate change and to incorporate the Arctic region more fully in global environmental governance. But it has also greatly stimulated a range of fundamental national interests and concerns, most notably around the prospect of exploitable energy resources and with them, likely geopolitical challenges.[11]

Several chapters of this book carry the argument that the fundamentals of global governance begin with claims and bargaining positions that cannot be fully and openly addressed except through the 'of, by and for whom?' question. This perspective is useful for opening out the rather bland generalisations first offered by the Commission of Global Governance. It defined governance as 'the sum of the many ways individuals and institutions, public and private, manage their common affairs'; and global governance as 'a broad, dynamic, complex process of inter-active decision making that is constantly evolving and responding to changing circumstances'.[12] Global governance considered as the summative order of the world is logically inclusive but also has the effect of glossing over the largest part of the world's incoherence; and 'interactive decision-making' masks the disparities of power that account for a good deal of it. A further difficulty is that not all world orders are the outcome of coordinated deliberation; instead, many forms of global governance can comprise a loose but functional patchwork of mechanisms that are both formal and informal, state and non-state.[13]

The inevitability of clashes of aspirations is the grounds for politics in all its guises and at every level, up to and including global governance. Of course, our aspirations – individual and collective, large and small scale – exhibit a fundamental tension between order and freedom. Human freedom can find little positive expression in the absence of the means to create and maintain order, stability and/or a modicum of predictability; and at the same time, repressive order seldom works to the advancement and fulfilment of the aspirations of the many. At the global level, this basic tension plays out in remarkably complex ways because under globalised conditions the number and variety of human aspirations – and the means to fulfil them – are increasing, so the concomitant ordering/governing responses are more difficult to negotiate and enact. Because opportunities to engage in activities disruptive to established social, political and environmental orders are now distributed globally, ranging from individual criminal and terrorist acts to the aggregate and cumulative effects of industrialisation and consumerism, many effective preventive and/or rectificatory measures are conceived within a global context that necessitates and informs them.

Besides, not every form or combination of ordering mechanisms that could be described as global governance is intended to address a worrisome issue in a detached, inclusive manner. Global governance initiatives themselves can and do express aspirations that are self-interested, or are negotiated with a view to accommodate the countervailing concerns of powerful actors.[14] 'Whose aspirations?' applies to global governance no less than to large-scale development projects or multilateral trade agreements. This reinforces the idea of global governance as an arena of contention – or at the very least, it de-emphasises the degree to which global governance can be regarded as a technocratic exercise. In addition, one of the richer sub-themes in the global governance literature is the study of how various kinds of private authority shape important aspects of world order, both licitly and illicitly.[15] Frequently posed against such interests are the many aspirations of individuals, peoples and organisations rooted in need and argued in terms of justice. It is hardly surprising that the global civil society literature has run in parallel with that devoted to global governance.

Governance initiatives regulate relations, they do not homogenise behaviours. On the largest scale, the order-creating purposes of governance mechanisms facilitate the pursuit of aspirations, many of them both state-based and highly competitive. Much as we see in sport, where players' adherence to rules is for the largest part enacted rather than enforced because it is mutually beneficial to compete in a bounded arena rather than a free-for all, norms and laws create sufficient stability and predictability in international arenas to allow the pursuit of aspirations. Even those regarded as dangerous or potentially threatening (the trade in fissile materials, or the acquisition of certain weapons or weapons systems) can be regulated in this way, at least to an extent. Routine conformity with international laws and norms is as likely to indicate competitive disposition and standing as its opposite; and it is not necessarily an indicator of future behaviour, particularly when key interests are felt to be at stake. In international affairs, there is rogue behaviour as well as rogue states.

No system of relations can persist if a critical mass of their members are (or regard themselves) as 'free agents' for all purposes; and at the same time, the substance of relatedness requires continual adjustment and responsiveness to others and to environmental changes. The most important forms of sectoral global governance – of trade, the physical environment, global finance – are not goal-oriented, but are constituted so as to allow the pursuit of goals by the actors (in this case, states), who subscribe to them. Hence

> ...the recognition of policy-making as the regulation of *relations* stresses that the standards by which these relations are judged are not goals to be attained once and for all but, like the mariner's course, must constantly be sought anew. [...] [H]uman regulatory behaviour cannot be reduced to goal-seeking without masking the essential element which makes it different from the behaviour of rats in mazes [...] [M]ost regulative behaviour is negative, the avoidance of some relation which has been deemed unacceptable. Even the most positive aspirations of governments may so be regarded. The welfare legislation [of the UK] is based on a report which identified 'five giant evils'. The whole of human progress may be convincingly described as successive redefinings of the unacceptable.[16]

The global governance of any sector of human activity entails the mediation of human aspirations in their innumerable configurations. These not only combine and collide within sectors, but also between them; and they find sanction (and sometimes active stimulus) by states. The sum of human aspirations cannot be narrowed or directed by fiat, but at the same time they are expressions of values – and sometimes, of quite fundamental needs. The ways in which environmental degradation force us to review some of our individual and collective aspirations – to some degree, and at least occasionally – is a key indicator of the likelihood of substantial progress in this fundamental of global governance.

In their larger social and political forms, aspirations are expressions of relative power.
Aspirations also have considerable inertia, particularly as expressions of social orientation or as determined political ends. The point is not only that powerful actors make serious demands, or force large compromises as a matter of course, but that even the requirements for the most important and fundamental kinds of global governance will not necessarily supersede them. The wrangling over the Kyoto Protocol demonstrates this; and the tensions and occasional contradictions between our expressed values and deliberated actions give us what some claim to be the oxymoronic quality of the 'sustainable development' concept.[17]

Order-creating aspirations of one kind, or in one part of the world, frequently generate disorder in the form of human and environmental costs in others – and this applies to governance and global governance initiatives no less than to more narrowly focused activities such as resource extraction. For this reason, even the most marginalised increasingly recognise that in order to secure the fundamentals of a decent life, they need to have global governance arrangements work in their favour – or at least, not against their fundamental aspirations.

Yet the 'global' quality of global governance can for many purposes be conceived in less than inclusive ways; and this has its antecedents and perhaps some part of its logic in the history of political philosophy.

> In the history of thought, the great minds have, with few exceptions, cast the study of social order – how people can live with each other – as a problem of curbing the potential subversion of the mass against the elite. The great philosophers from Plato on, as members of elites or candidates for membership, have been self-serving in assuming that order is possible only with unilateral rather than multilateral controls; and, of course, for much of history military power has joined with religious authority to insist on mass docility as a requisite of social order. Among very few others, Montesquieu toyed with the possibility of order through mutual adjustment, as did Mandeville and Adam Ferguson. Not until Adam Smith, however, does anyone achieve a comprehensive and explicit statement of the possibilities of order through mutual adjustment. Even so, Smith did not generalise from the market system to other arenas of social organisation, with the result that today these possibilities are slighted. No, not only slighted: also feared. Even in our day, elites of power and intellects still fear masses as sources of disorder and are consequently still disposed to prescribe unilateral rather than multilateral controls.[18]

A following, post-Cold War analysis is indicative:

> The key to understanding the real world order is to separate the world intotwo parts. One part is zones of peace, wealth, and democracy. The otherpart is zones of turmoil, war, and development. There are useful things tosay about the zones of peace; and there are useful things to say about thezones of turmoil; but if you try to

talk about the world as a whole all youcan get is falsehoods or platitudes.[19]

One might also reasonably query the prospects for global governance when a senior British diplomat can assert the following, even when writing in a private capacity:

The challenge to the postmodern world is to get used to the idea of double standards. Among ourselves, we operate on the basis of laws and open cooperative security. But when dealing with more old-fashioned kinds of states outside the postmodern continent of Europe, we need to revert to the rougher methods of an earlier era – force, pre-emptive attack, deception, whatever is necessary to deal with those who still live in the nineteenth century world of every state for itself. Among ourselves, we keep the law but when we are operating in the jungle, we must also use the laws of the jungle.[20]

Within the compass of the global governance literature itself there have also been critiques of global governance as essentially a Western exercise in maintaining an inequitable, even iniquitous international *status quo.*[21] While we might look to global governance as a way of resolving clashes of aspiration, it can also be configured to ensure that any resolutions will not significantly disadvantage the already powerful.

Our deliberative systems have already been outpaced in some important matters.
Social, ethical and legal deliberation maintain the coherence of societies, enabling them to adjust to changing circumstances in accord with their values. In any society, the most important and often the most heated debates at least implicitly address the question, 'What kind of a society do we want?' And for both individuals and societies, globalising dynamics now frequently pose the question, 'What kind of world do we want?' – with all of the complications and few of the commonalities that the phrase 'global society' might suggest. The lively debate about the use of human stem cells for research and medical purposes is highly contentious in ethical terms; competitive standing in scientific and commercial terms also feature in the arguments; and, where it is deemed acceptable for some purposes and under certain conditions, the use of human stem cells requires careful incorporation into legal systems.

But our deliberative systems are struggling to keep pace with recent advances in science and technology that have serious and far-ranging implications.[22] Quite fundamental scientific breakthroughs and wide-ranging technological applications generate entire ranges of issues that have already begun to appear as practical problems, rather than weighty prospects – in other words, outside of, or at best, in advance of wide-ranging social deliberation. Synthetic biology – 'the synthesis of complex, biologically based (or inspired) systems which display functions that do not exist in nature...'[23] – is already established, but there is little evidence of any serious, wide-ranging public deliberation about a science which, amongst other things, can now synthesise a virus in a fortnight.[24] Still more remarkable is the drive in the United States and the European Union toward technological convergence – the hope that a 'single engineering paradigm' can be created, joining together nanotechnology, biotechnology, robotics, information technology and cognitive science (discussed in Chapter 4.)[25] It is not difficult to appreciate the enthusiasm of advocates for advances which could deliver wondrous improvements in materials science, biomedicine, electronics, computing and pharmaceuticals, to list but a few. At the same time, however, both American and European advocates recognise that their desire to 'transform' their societies carries serious and incalculable risks.

However, one might reasonably ask whether the 'societal transformation' on offer – foreseen as both fundamental and wide-ranging but unspecific in details or implications – is something to which any society might rationally seek to commit. Besides, as Geoffrey Vickers wrote, '[T]here are limits to the possible rate at which human history can change without disintegration, since coherent change involves change in the whole set of cultural standards by which a society interprets its situation; and these standards are related to the life experience and hence the life span of individuals.'[26] The anticipated 'transformation' of US and European societies is, its advocates concede, a leap in the dark:

> It may be possible to influence the ways convergent technologies will change economics and society, on a national scale, by providing leadership and support for a nationwide, collaborative development effort. [...] This effort should have many stakeholders in education, healthcare, pharmaceuticals, social science, the military, the economy and the business sector to name a few.[27]

To recognise that a sequence of actions and defaults will place us in a position where we might be able only to *influence* forces at work on the fundamentals of our societies and yet to continue to press ahead not only circumvents our deliberative systems but is also an abrogation of the responsibilities of governance. And we can be certain that the drive to push back necessarily wide-ranging and slow-moving deliberation will not be long in delivering much-prized new products, processes and competitive advantage, but also governance issues of considerable gravity and magnitude. Mihail Rocco, the Senior Advisor for Nano-technology at the US National Science Foundation has written, 'The speed and scope of nanotechnology [research and development] already exceeds for now the capacity of researchers and regulators to fully assess human and environmental implications.'[28]

The speed and dynamism of the world – the complex interaction of human and natural systems – suggests that 'skilful incompleteness' is the most realistic governance aspiration.

Whatever might comprise the global governance of the environment cannot be confined to securing adequate political consensus and deter-mination (even if one were to regard the protracted political manoeu-vring over climate change to be an anomaly), because our physical and human systems are now so closely bound together. We must now deal not only with our capacity and propensity to wreak systemic changes on planetary ecosystems by regulating certain activities: we must also deal with a changed and changing set of circumstances. This is abun-dantly clear in the case of conservation activities.

More and more these days, conservationists are struggling like harried emergency-room doctors to protect plants and animals in the face of rapid human-induced changes. This has led some to question the very essence of what they do. Conservation is, by definition, about maintaining the status quo, yet this may no longer be possible, given that pollution, climate change, exotic species invasions, extinctions and land fragmentation are altering almost every ecosystem on the planet. [C]onservationists [are being urged] to reassess their roles. 'The point is not to think outside the box but to recognise that the box itself has moved, and in the twenty-first century will continue to move increasingly rapidly.'[29]

Our familiarity with the form of climate change negotiations (frame-work convention, subsequent protocols, national commitments) can mask not only the unprecedented scope of what will be entailed in order for them to succeed – wholesale changes in ways of life throughout the developed world – but also the extent to which atmospheric physics and chemistry will maintain the challenge, or reinforce the threat. 'Even if atmospheric composition were fixed today, global mean temperature and sea level rise would continue due to oceanic thermal inertia. Avoiding these changes requires, eventually, a reduction in emissions to substantially below present levels. For sea level rise, a substantial long-term commitment may be impossible to avoid.'[30] In this fundamental at least, global governance will remain aspirational in our lifetime.

Less dramatically but still importantly, we cannot even say if a fully globalised world is possible, and if so, what it might comprise; who might benefit – and what would be the costs – environmental, social, cultural, political; what might be the fate of the nation state – or of markets and free trade; and whether we could in some sense 'complete' globalisation, or find that one or a number of constraints limited its progress. These and related questions are all the more striking because there is no global governance of globalisation as such. Instead, we have pre-existing forms of governance that have been globalised in some ways and to certain degrees; and we have initiated forms of governance in response to certain aspects and outcomes of globalisation. We are not only generating hosts of new issues and problems: we are extending, stressing and adding complexity to the human condition. As shared aspirations, our global governance initiatives are at best likely to be 'strategies for skilful incompleteness'.[31]

10
The human rights regime as global governance

Introduction

Disputes about the concept of global governance generally take place around a shared understanding that there are two distinct but not entirely free-standing uses of the term. The first, referred to throughout this book as 'summative' global governance, depicts the overall order of the world, many important elements of which are not accounted for by the structures and dynamics of states and the international system. The second, characterised in previous chapters as 'sector specific', is not necessarily unitary or in possession of commanding political authority, but refers to order-creating and sustaining action in defined arenas of human endeavour (global finance) or consequence (health; environment). So what has come to be known as global governance can be exercised directly, or created and sustained through a combination of state/non-state and formal/informal mechanisms. Neither seems adequate on its own, either in descriptive or normative terms;[1] and a substantial portion of contestation over global governance consists of investigating highly complex and dynamic questions of political authority, practical capacity, accountability, agency and legitimacy[2] in a world in which states and the international system are necessary but not sufficient for the kinds of global order we can observe and, under the pressure of events, those we must shore up, extend or create.

Because globalisation is a condition as well as a generic term for the myriad dynamics that penetrate borders and boundaries of every kind, twenty-first century human affairs are played out in a global arena in an active, practical sense and not merely a logical one. Although governance at local, sub-national and national levels has not ceased to matter (the governance exercised by governments in particular), global order is not simply an un-deliberated aggregate of these – and considering the prospects for stable and sustainable human continuance, nor can it be. In some quarters, a degree of unease still attends the 'global governance' concept since it is not confined to any particular mode of political action, or to a defined set of political (or other) actors. But it seems likely that the profusion and dynamism of the world will continue to outpace the best efforts to deliver conceptual clarity that is at once both precise and comprehensive. The summative global governance we have created is not without the familiar and important state and international actors and hierarchies of power and every kind of political and legal mechanism, but the sources of world order run more widely and deeply:

> There is no single organizing principle on which global governance rests, no emergent order around which communities and nations are likely to converge. Global governance is the sum of myriad – literally millions of – control mechanisms driven by different histories, goals, structure, and processes [...] In terms of governance, the world is too disaggregated for grand logics that postulate a measure of global coherence.[3]

Nevertheless, the lack of a 'single organising principle' for global governance does not prevent the creation of global order (poor as this might be for some purposes and some peoples); and nor does it preclude the initiation of sector-specific forms of global governance, any more than anarchy (the absence of supranational authority in the international system) prevents states from addressing matters of shared concern.

In describing the fundamentals of global governance as an activity, the previous eight chapters have not focused on either a specific actor or set of actors – international organisation, regime, state/non-state configurations – or a single mode of action. Instead, the emphasis throughout has been on the commonalities that will be faced by the enactment of any form of global governance as understood in the definition introduced in Chapter 1: 'Efforts to bring more orderly and reliable responses to social and political issues that go beyond the capacities of states to address individually.'[4]

But what would an adequate global governance be the governance *of*? What counts as a 'social and political issue' of sufficient seriousness, extent and/or inclusiveness to warrant either summative or sector-specific global governance? Certainly the issues that generate the largest share of interest in the theoretical and practical aspects of global governance are crises, often those such as climate change and global financial turmoil in which sector-specific and summative global governances are clearly linked. However, the disjunctures between the two forms of governance are every bit as obvious, as any comprehensive set of development indicators makes plain.[5] But unlike 'international peace and security' (in which civil wars and insurgencies wreak terrible damage but without serious systemic disturbance to the international system), summative global governance that is less than global in its human inclusiveness is normatively as well as descriptively inadequate. And indeed, a good deal of political activism around the world – necessitated but also empowered by the vagaries of globalisation – centres on the injustices or inadequacies of both summative and sector-specific global governance. Although attention has focused on NGO networks and coalitions,[6] and on configurations of what has come to be known as global civil society,[7] the ideals and normative expectations that animate the oppositional currents of global politics are not the preserve of non-state and/or low-level actors – or perhaps more tellingly, 'high level' actors are not impervious to the range of uncomfortable and challenging questions that arise from 'of, by and for whom?' interrogations of global governance. The Millennium Goals can be regarded in this light – an attempt to re-prioritise if not altogether re-orient global governance; so too can the UN's Global Compact, which works to align business policies and activities with non-business principles,[8] together with the Global Governance Initiative of the World Economic Forum. Against the worldwide background of gross disparities between the well off and the impoverished, the questions and challenges are not difficult to generate; what deserves attention is what gives them their purchase – that is, what denaturalises poverty, disenfranchisement and systematic abuse and makes of them social and political issues of global import.

The facilitation and growth of global politics has generated demands that directly confront global governance arrangements and actors – some of it from the hitherto voiceless, sometimes as expressions of global solidarity. The impetus for righting or realigning global governance arises from sources that include but do not begin with the practical possibilities of exercising regulation and control on a global scale, but with something deeper: the normative expectation sustained by the institutionalisation of human rights.

In this chapter, the human rights regime will be considered as a form of global governance, and its successes and failures as an ordering, regulatory regime will be noted under each of the eight themes that have been employed to characterise more familiar forms of global governance. Compared with the global governance of the environment, or global finance, the inclusion of human rights as a form of global governance might at first appear anomalous. This is because although the panoply of human rights laws and norms certainly comprise a regime no less than the arrangements in place to reverse climate change,[9] human rights is not a realm of action but a quality of relatedness; not something over which global governance can be exercised, but criteria against which global governance ends and means can be judged. Perhaps then it is not surprising that the literature on human rights as a form of global governance is not well developed.[10] Nevertheless, human rights claims made in national and international political and legal arenas are so well established as to be routine. These claims are of kinds and on a scale that indicate the extent to which human rights already shape shared understandings and formal agreements about the acceptable ends and means of the exercise of power, including governance. And since human rights are universal, there can be little in global governance of any kind that is not informed by them, even if it is only to the extent of giving an account of its shortcomings.

The human rights regime

One need not have a Realist understanding of human nature and the human prospect to see throughout human history the persistence and prominence of violence and oppression. Yet out of the terrible destruction of World War II, human rights were articulated and subsequently codified in international law and countless national laws; and perhaps more importantly, the idea and ideal of human rights also took root as lived expectation in the hearts of probably the majority of human beings. This norm, or shared expectation, is the standard by which states no less than individuals are held to account. Leaving aside for the moment the question of how effective the enactment and enforcement of human rights laws are, it is important to acknowledge what an historic achievement it is to have the comfortable and oppressed alike believe that they are entitled to their human rights – and that any exercise of absolute power over human beings is fundamentally wrong. How this came about cannot be reduced to the virtue or brilliance of the diplomats and lawyers who drafted the Universal Declaration of Human Rights (UDHR) – which was, initially, just that: a declaration of intent.[11] Instead, the UDHR can more plausibly be seen as the culmination of centuries-long struggles to make power accountable: not only the work of philosophy and religion, but also the great political struggles of history and the fight of millions who strive for a decent life for themselves and their communities.

In the decades since 1948, human rights have been codified throughout the world to the extent that the UDHR is now generally recognised as customary international law; state adherence to human rights has become an essential element in international political exchange and contestation; and they have become a standard of legitimacy against which governance initiatives of every kind – and particularly those of non-democratic forms of governance – are challenged. Much of the power of human rights derives from the shared conviction that they are universal and inalienable, by dint of which they provide individuals and peoples everywhere with ways of interrogating politically-driven suffering; and of critiquing cultures (both from within and without). They also establish minimum standards for the proper extent and exercise of power and the basis on which we can – or should – order human relations at every level; and they provide us with ways of thinking about what it means to be a human individual and also a social being, with a view to the inviolability of human integrity.

In order for these rights to be *human* rights, they must be universal, but although this principle remains contentious, both conceptually and contextually,[12] the strength and duration of these debates is a clear indicator of the degree to which human rights have become firmly entrenched as a norm. Questions also attend the 'blind spots' of the human rights regime: 'In seeking to universalize a particular model of rights we may be promoting not only the political virtues articulated by the contract but its patterns of exclusion while promoting a tool which is not equipped to respond to many forms of systematically inflicted injury.'[13] But the most serious deficiency of the human rights regime is in the enactment of its standards, most glaringly in the privileging of negative human rights ('freedom from') over positive human rights. The latter, enshrined in The International Covenant on Economic, Social and Cultural Rights,[14] are now often referred to as 'second generation' human rights. Less euphemistically, it could fairly be said that the failure of states to honour their obligations under the Covenant is what necessitated the Millennium Development Goals. A consistent failing of such proportions reflects back on the human rights regime as a whole, which the relevant UN Committee expressed plainly at the Vienna World Conference on Human Rights in 1993:

The shocking reality...is that states and the international community as a whole continue to tolerate all too often breaches of economic, social and cultural rights which, if they occurred in relation to civil and political rights, would provoke expressions of horror and outrage and would lead to calls for immediate remedial action. In effect, despite the rhetoric, violations of civil and political rights continue to be treated as though they were far more serious, and more patently intolerable, than massive and direct denials of economic, social and cultural rights.[15]

No one familiar with the workings of the human rights regime and contemporary affairs would want to venture that human rights mark a fundamental and irreversible advance in the conduct of governance. After all, we have not managed to bring a halt to genocide, much less widespread malnutrition and its consequences. But the deficiencies of the human rights regime, rather than invalidating it as a form of global governance, places it firmly within the span of all collective efforts to secure peace, stability and sustainability. In common with other forms of governance and global governance, 'Human rights practices are not part of a progression to perfection, or its approximation, but a way of working with the systemic generation of suffering. They offer not so much an answer to the persistent problems of living together as a way of going about these problems in contemporary circumstances.'[16] What makes a compelling case for the human rights regime as a form of global governance is not their universality at a time when the defining characteristic of 'living together' is our globalised condition, but that they apply equally both to the ends and the means of any form of global governance. By the standards of human rights, human lives cannot be sacrificed to state security, to private interests or to systemic stability. We often fail in this, as we do in so much else that comprises global governance, but it matters to have a measure of success that is meaningfully and inclusively human as well as technically proficient.

The human rights regime as global governance

Global governance in most senses and in most cases will make explicit links between the local and the global; and between individuals and the national/ international realms.

The enunciation and subsequent codification of human rights was not an ending of struggles for liberty and the wider human good but their culmination, based on a principle that was to have far-reaching consequences for all forms of human relatedness: that the possession and exercise of absolute power is anathema. Because the enactment of this principle is a matter of practical politics, we can best regard human rights as having conditioned rather than transformed arenas of human interaction. The largest of these arenas with the most consistent and direct bearing on the welfare of peoples is the state; and despite the number and severity of human rights outrages still perpetrated by states and their agents, the degree to which modern statehood has been conditioned by human rights has been considerable.[17] This has taken two forms. The first is that because human rights are both inviolable and inalienable (that is, not a token of citizenship), they offer an implicit challenge to the sovereign power of states. The power that rulers and/or governments can wield over their citizens is now constrained by international law and normative expectation. Power relations between citizens and their governments can still legitimately be conditioned in numerous ways, but within boundaries set by human rights.

Altered relational parameters between citizens and states also has its counterpart at international level, most visibly and controversially in the debates about humanitarian intervention. The idea of humanitarian intervention turns on the question of whether in emergency situations states have a right to break the non-interventionist principle of international law (Article 2.4 of the UN Charter) to rescue people from life-threatening violations of their human rights – the 'right' in this case being a moral right that trumps legal prohibition, or as some would see it, honours the spirit of the law in the breach of it.[18] The political interests of states are often abstracted from these debates, and (as in so much else in human rights) these are central to whether and under what conditions states are prepared to act.[19] However, for our purposes here, what matters is the direct linkage between the national and international realms.

The second way in which human rights have conditioned modern statehood is in the expectation of democratic government – a norm that complements human rights, never more clearly than at times when people struggle against unaccountable power. After all, any drive toward democratic governance is also an effort to bring power within the orbit of law, by making governors accountable to the governed. Hence, 'Democracy should remain on the agenda of human rights proponents the world over, because without it human rights cease to be rights, they become attractive but ultimately optional norms or standards. As such they are easily put to use in a utilitarian manner by authoritarian states in pursuit of strategic interests. Without democracy, human rights are at the discretion of the sovereign, and thus not rights at all. *With* democracy, the sovereign must serve the rights of the people.'[20] The expectation of democratic governance, within the international systems as a whole as well as within sovereign boundaries, is more than a widely shared populist impulse: 'Both textually and in practice, the international system is moving toward a clearly designated democratic entitlement, with national governance validated by international standards and systematic monitoring of compliance.'[21]

We can see then that human rights as a form of global governance makes explicit links between individuals and the national/international realms, but this is not free-standing from other forms of global governance: human rights are now summoned by individuals, interest groups, peoples, and states themselves to critique and challenge many if not most sector-specific forms of global governance.[22] Human rights also crucially inform links between the local and the global levels of human interaction, the implications of which are, like many forms of global governance, difficult or contentious, or both. For example, arguments about environmental quality and integrity supported by human rights claims (and vice versa) are more often a matter of contesting powerful interests than righting unwitting harm;[23] and efforts to stop the practice of female genital mutilation align the integrity of individuals with international norms (and increasingly, national laws) but also come into conflict with embedded local beliefs and pressures.[24]

The sum of all global governances is not likely to be entirely coherent or to avoid competitive and/or antagonistic relationships.

Although summative global governance is a useful term for describing the overall order of the world, the phrase might easily suggest more consensus and coherence than is actually the case. The local, national and international provisions against organised crime can certainly be regarded as order-creating or order-sustaining, both individually and summatively. At the same time, criminal organisations and networks also create and maintain orders, sometimes on quite a considerable scale. The traffic in people and counterfeit goods, money laundering and other highly profitable activities rely on established and generally well governed, legitimate activities such as world trade and communications links. But although the order created by criminal networks is parasitic, it is order nonetheless – and governed as such, albeit by means no more legitimate than the activities themselves. Even within the span of what we can regard as legitimate forms of governance, coherence in the sense of agreed upon and coordinated governance ends and means is hardly the norm, hence clashes between the global governance of trade and international determinations to reduce global poverty;[25] and between global health and numerous forms of sectoral global governance.[26]

The worst of these clashes in recent years pitted the UN Charter remit to maintain 'international peace and security' against 'faith in fundamental human rights [and] the dignity and worth of the human person' in its Preamble. As part of the effort to secure Iraqi compliance with UN Security Council resolutions after the first Gulf War, comprehensive sanctions were imposed on the regime. Originally conceived after World War I as a way of bringing recalcitrant states to conformity with international norms without recourse to warfare, the sanctions imposed on Iraq from 1990 were the first sustained and logistically thorough exercise of what had largely remained a theory. The sanctions were to prove politically ineffective, but with disastrous human consequences, as Saddam Hussein sacrificed the human security of Iraqis for regime preservation. In fact, it was the UN's own agencies, funds and programmes that provided the most reliable and detailed account of the human costs of the sanctions.[27] By 2000, the UN Secretary General expressed matters as follows: 'I deeply regret the continuing suffering of the Iraqi people and hope that the sanctions imposed on Iraq can be lifted sooner rather than later. But this demands that we find a way, somehow, to move the Iraqi Government into compliance with the Security Council resolutions.'[28] More starkly, 'When asked on US television if she thought that the death of half a million Iraqi children was a price worth paying, [then-US Secretary of State Madeleine] Albright replied: "This is a very hard choice, but we think the price is worth it."'[29]

The dreadful, protracted human toll of sanctions against which human rights were of no avail might seem to suggest that the human rights regime is something less than a form of global governance. But what needs to be borne in mind is that the progress of human rights – and indeed, much else that comprises global governance – is played out through tensioned relationships, sometimes quite complex: between peoples and states/rulers; between states; between the global and the national/local; between power and values; between rights and responsibilities; between contested understandings of rights as opposed to entitlements; between globalisation-from-below and globalisation-from-above. Human rights, even when enshrined in international law, do not have commanding power commensurate with their moral weight, but must contend with the other actors and mechanisms of global governance – and with their purposes.[30]

Global governance needs to be relational, not merely technocratic
Human rights are not a global governance quality control check, or a *post-facto* measure of governance compatibility with, say, human security. The large, extensive network of national and international human rights laws and norms exist to exercise governance – that is, their purposes are order-creating and regulatory. What they regulate are relations of power between and over human beings; and the order that they create (or at least aspire to) is one in which there is no longer any politically-driven or systematic human deprivation. All forms of governance entail the adjustment of relations, but none deals more directly with the life chances of individuals and communities than do human rights. Unlike many other forms of global governance in which managerial oversight requires technical adjustments to quantitative indicators, human rights are starkly and immediately relational. It is for this reason that they are also intensely political.

In the case of human rights, we can substitute 'technical' for the 'technocratic' of the proposition above, which includes the various means by which human rights laws are framed, enacted, interpreted, monitored and (occasionally) enforced; and how differences between national and international human rights laws are reconciled. The importance of such mechanisms cannot be discounted on the basis of the deep and abiding normative appeal of human rights. In fact, in order for human rights to have anything more than rhetorical beauty, their relational qualities needed to begin with how they were first sited in existing social, political and legal structures:

> It is a commonplace that long lists of rights are empty words in the absence of a legal and political order in which rights can be realised. That was so well understood by the architects of the Universal Declaration of Human Rights that they endowed the 1948 document with features not usually seen in bills of rights: a right 'to take part in the government of [one's] country'; a right to 'a social and international order in which the rights and freedoms set forth in this declaration can be realized'; an acknowledgment that everyone's rights are limited by the need for 'meeting the just requirements of morality, public order and the general welfare in a democratic society'; and an express recognition of the importance of the rule of law.[31]

By having been embedded in this way, human rights not only delimit the power that individuals can wield over others but extend it to all forms of human relatedness – political, institutional, economic, cultural. In practice, human rights adherence has hardly been a triumphal progress, or even a steady one, but by dint of normative expectation and by means of appeal to national and/or international codification, they have become the measure of the legitimacy for actors as well as actions – and by that means, they frame many of the most important contestations over global governance.

The relational qualities of human rights have not remained static, not only because of the very considerable changes in the conditions of societies throughout the world since the UDHR of 1948, but also because the human rights regime itself has greatly expanded. Part of that expansion has been the growth and refinement of mechanisms to give them practical purchase, but the substance of human rights and the mechanisms developed to promote, enact, monitor and adjudicate them are highly interactive, nowhere more visibly than in the development of the European Convention on Human Rights.

The convention of today differs in various important respects from the convention negotiated back in 1949 and 1950. Some of the differences have been generated by what is called evolutionary interpretation, which treats the convention as a living document. Some have been the product of new protocols. Optional features of the convention, the right of individual petition, and the jurisdiction of the [European Court of Human Rights] have now become the rule. The institutional structure has been radically changed by Protocol 11 of 11 May 1994. More fundamentally the very function of the convention has changed. It has now become a mechanism for changing the political character of newly admitted states. Many of them lack any tradition of legal protection against abuses of state power, or of courts reviewing the legality of administrative decisions. The eastward expansion of the convention may also change the way in which states are encouraged to observe the convention. There may be greater reliance upon inspection and reporting, and less on investigating and adjudicating upon individual complaints.[32]

As a form of global governance, human rights are inescapably relational in substance, their global quality partly a given of their universality, and they have extraordinary scope since they have a bearing on most sector-specific forms of global governance. The 'technical' means for the furtherance of human rights remain important for the regime itself[33] and for the orientation and substance of global governance more broadly, but it is the fundamental relational substance of human rights which have transformed them in only 60 years from declaratory to lived expectation.

Although global governance arrangements concern state behaviours to some degree and rely on state compliance and furtherance, the regimes are not only about states.
The subject of human rights is human beings, their integrity and welfare; and human rights are inalienable, not subject to citizen entitlement that can be bestowed or revoked. This focus does not estrange individuals from citizen rights and obligations, but it does alter the basis of the relationship between citizens and their states, moving it from a blunt hierarchy of power that has persisted through most of human history to a codified recognition of inviolable human integrity. As described in a UK Foreign Office memo of 1946, 'The history of the struggles for recognition of Human Rights is as much as anything a struggle of the human being against the anonymous machinery of authority, whether of the Church or the State.'[34] It is puzzling and compelling that such a view should have emanated from a state at all (and at that time, one still intent on remaining a colonial power). What is true in the following depiction of the development of the European Convention on Human Rights applies in more general terms to states the world over acceding to and, over decades, developing the strictures of the human rights:

> [I]n general states were thought free to deal with their own people, and abuse them, as they wished; this was an aspect of the conception of state sovereignty. How did it come about that Britain, and certain other European countries, voluntarily gave up some of their autonomy? What did they think they were buying one half so precious as the goods they traded in return? For governments do not, simply out of disinterested benevolence, or through a lack of confidence in their own rectitude, voluntarily surrender power.[35]

Yet the largest part of the human rights regime is the international and national laws that place the onus of the promotion and protection of human rights on states themselves. Of course, the existence of the human rights regime does not of itself compel observance by states, as any reliable international human rights survey documents in detail;[36] indeed, states themselves are generally the most serious (systematic and egregious) abusers of human rights. But what might at first appear paradoxical – that 'Human rights are a shield against the almighty

State, but it takes a sturdy State to keep the shield in position'[37] – is considerably more complex. Historically, it is plain that the politicians and diplomats who instigated and subsequently extended the human rights regime did not fully comprehend the extent to which it would be embraced by peoples everywhere (implicitly signalling the end of colonialism), or create an entire range of difficult and often unwanted obligations. (In 1956, a UK official was to complain of the European Covenant on Human Rights '...that we have now got ourselves committed to this wretched Covenant and can't get out of it now...'[38]) At the same time, however, the recoil from the horrors of World War II was certainly a contributing factor to a more open-ended attitude toward the new international order then in the making. For instance, Article 2.7 of the UN Charter is a well crafted piece of ambiguity, stating that the UN shall not '...intervene in matters which are essentially within the domestic jurisdiction of any state' – leaving open in those years before the formalisation of human rights what might comprise 'essentially'. During the 1945 Senate hearings on the Charter, US Secretary of State John Foster Dulles argued, '[Article 2(7)] is an evolving concept. We don't know fifteen, twenty years from now what in fact is going to be within the domestic jurisdiction of nations. International law is evolving, state practice is evolving. There's no way we can definitively define in 1945 what is within domestic jurisdiction. Let's just let this thing drift a few years and see how it comes out.'[39] Where it came out was in an international ethos suffused with the expectation of human rights, the practical implications of which are still evolving, as Dulles foresaw in outline but would almost certainly never have imagined in detail. In 2001, the report of the International Commission on Intervention and State Sovereignty, 'Responsibility to Protect', set out its basic principles in terms rooted in the priorities of human rights rather than the historic prerogatives of states: 'State sovereignty implies responsibility, and the primary responsibility for the protection of its people lies with the state itself; [and] where a population is suffering serious harm, as a result of internal war, insurgency, repression or state failure, and the state in question is unwilling or unable to halt or avert it, the principle of non-intervention yields to the international responsibility to protect.'[40]

Sixty years after the signing of the UDHR, the human rights regime has grown to become a form of global governance that extends to the fundamentals of states and the international system, to the degree that a nation's human rights record is a core element in determining whether a state is 'rogue' or, through its incapacity to uphold human rights within its boundaries, 'failed'. So while it is true that human rights as global governance are, as the proposition above runs, 'not only about states', states' centrality to the success of the regime and the realisation and protection of rights has if anything grown in importance. At the same time, the human rights regime continues to shape, inform and critique national and international structures and dynamics.

Global governance will rely on normative acceptance rather than lego-political enforcement.
In common with international law generally, international human rights instruments have scant allowance for enforcement. Given the number and severity of human rights violations and still more widespread failure to enact many human rights provisions, there is reason to wonder why the human rights regime hasn't shrunk to the 'black letter' of the law – something beautiful but idle. But as reviewed in Chapter 6, laws and social norms are mutually reinforcing; and a law that needed to be enforced as a matter of routine would be so contrary to prevailing norms or countervailing circumstances as to be effectively void.

The outright failures of states to honour their human rights commitments is but one measure of the progress of human rights, much as the persistence of crime in stable societies is an important, but not necessarily predominant indicator of civic and governmental determination to secure and maintain a law-based order. From the perspective of the international system as a whole, we are confronted with a poor patchwork of progressive human rights enactment and abject failure, including flagrant violations of national and international laws. But both trends reflect the strength of normative expectation amongst peoples with respect to their own governments, between states and, in complex ways, through a dense network of UN, national and private organisations dedicated to achieving, extending, maintaining and monitoring human rights.[41] At individual and community levels, the normative expectation is now widespread and robust throughout the world; and it is at least sufficient within the international system to oblige even the most reluctant regimes to accede at least nominally to fundamental human rights obligations, with sometimes unexpected opportunities to move them beyond quick cynicism:

> Repressive governments often adapt to normative pressures for purely instrumental reasons. When the pressure decreases, they return to repression [...] Sometimes, however, they start institutionalizing

human rights norms into domestic law and change their discursive practices. This in turn opens space for the domestic opposition to catch the government in its own rhetoric. At this point, instrumental and communicative rationality intertwine. It becomes very hard for the government to deny the validity of human rights norms.[42]

However, such possibilities must be viewed against a still broad and quite hardened resistance to human rights norms that is occasionally little short of contemptuous. In an attempt to make the human rights regime a wider and more consistently honoured fixture of national and international life, the UN replaced the largely discredited UN Commission on Human Rights by a new, elected Human Rights Council.

The election requirement was an attempt to improve the membership, which previously only required nomination by a country's regional group. However, although some abuser states chose not to run and several who did run were not elected, the first Council still includes nine countries ranked Not Free by Freedom House in its most recent survey of political rights and civil liberties. Four of these nine, moreover, are among Freedom House's 'Worst of the Worst' regimes. These four – China, Cuba, Russia, and Saudi Arabia – also are among five countries that UN Watch identified, before the May 9, 2006 election, as particular threats to the Council's legitimacy. Sadly, all four received well over the 96-vote threshold that was supposed to prevent violators from winning membership.[43]

Humanitarian intervention can be counted as human rights enforcement and, as reviewed above, its legitimacy has been asserted over the non-interventionist stricture of the UN Charter. However, humanitarian intervention is still subject to the political cost/benefit calculus of capable states, and there is no evidence that any state confronts gross violations of human rights as a law/morality conundrum abstracted from political considerations. Besides, whether individual states or the international community respond to large-scale, deliberately inflicted human suffering, the cases themselves are a measure of our failures of enactment. Less dramatically, the responsibility for our grossly inequitable world and the human rights failure it represents is more evenly distributed – the international community's 'deafening silence'.

Nevertheless, even in the face of political recalcitrance and the intractable problems[44] that beset the many genuine efforts to enact human rights, the regime persists, supported and furthered by a normative commitment to an idea and ideal that is unique in global governance: linking ancient and contemporary; local and global; and creating bonds of solidarity that are the deepest source of progressive political change. *The Human Development Report* of 2007/08 draws explicitly on the strength of the human rights norm for the advancement of a sector-specific global governance initiative – halting climate change:

> The drafters of the Universal Declaration of Human Rights were looking back at a human tragedy, the second World War, that had already happened. Climate change is different. It is a human tragedy in the making. Allowing that tragedy to evolve would be a political failure that merits the description of an 'outrage to the conscience of mankind'. It would represent a systematic violation of the human rights of the world's poor and future generations and a step back from universal values. Conversely, preventing dangerous climate change would hold out the hope for the development of multilateral solutions to the wider problems facing the international community. Climate change confronts us with enormously complex questions that span science, economics and international relations. These questions have to be addressed through practical strategies. Yet it is important not to lose sight of the wider issues that are at stake. The real choice facing political leaders and people today is between universal human values, on the one side, and participating in the widespread and systematic violation of human rights on the other.[45]

Global governance systems must deal with or be able to accommodate large-scale violations/disruptions.
The human rights regime has faced large-scale violations through the continuance of genocide; and 'disruptions' in the form of numerous smaller-scale violations of human rights and the failure to enact positive human rights, in the form of the poverty and malnutrition still suffered by hundreds of millions of people. It is perhaps fitting to characterise unmet challenges as failures, but there is little in sectoral forms of global governance that is a matter of routine maintenance, or against which there are not substantial claims based on harm, incursion or exclusion. So the failures of the human rights regime do not give it unique standing as a form of global governance. But the human rights regime is more than the sum of the national and international laws that comprise it: it is also an idea and an ideal. Perhaps the only comfort that can be had from the terrible genocides that have occurred

during the existence of the regime is that the human rights ideal has remained undiminished, testament to the breadth and depth of normative expectation. And in the aftermath of violent conflict, the inauguration or re-establishment of a culture of human rights is widely regarded as the sine qua non of post-conflict reconstruction.[46]

In the face of gross violations of human rights, the regime is not wholly dependent on the resilience of the norm: as a form of global governance it must respond much as others do when confronted with violations, emergencies or unforeseen developments; and like them, it is largely dependent on the political willingness of states to do so. Although states and the international system have been most remiss in preventing and/or responding in timely fashion to large-scale repression and systematic killing, they have nevertheless taken steps to extend and tighten the legal provisions for dealing with the perpetrators of such outrages, most notably through the creation of the International Criminal Court. Whether or not this will have the desired deterrent effect,[47] the extension of prosecutions from *ad hoc* tribunals[48] to a standing fixture of the international system is a welcome one, not least in respect of shoring up the norm against human rights outrages and opening out the arena of international law.[49]

What remains uncertain and worrying is whether belated forms of 'dealing with' gross violations of human rights – and tolerating the disenfranchisement of a sizeable portion of humanity from the prospect of a decent life – is something that human rights laws and norms can accommodate while retaining their viability, or a political accommodation that might test to destruction both legal purchase and normative elasticity.

Global governance must be highly adaptive in respect of changing human circumstances.

Archaeological remains of the mass graves of violently killed people (including children) date back to neolithic times;[50] and repressive and coercive forms of rule do not require the means of high technology – nor did the genocide in Rwanda in 1994. Similarly, the fulfilment of basic human needs, now recognised as positive human rights, has not changed fundamentally over the course of recorded history. So unlike the global governance of the fast-paced world of global finance, or our rapidly changing physical environment, any requirement for the adaptability of the human rights regime might seem to be largely a matter of adjustment to the small particulars of long-familiar issues. However, relations of power are not confined to the governance exercised by tyrants; human integrity is not ensured by the provision of basic human needs; and the human rights regime is not fixed, its boundaries (both definitional[51] and jurisdictional[52]) are extendable – and a great deal of legal, political and practical consequence can hang on the determination of an issue as a matter of human rights. For that reason, within states one can witness arguments which turn on whether a claim is a human right or a discretionary, citizen right.

Globalisation is driving many of the larger changes in human circumstances, and as reviewed in earlier chapters, this has frequently resulted in individuals, communities and environments being subjected to change that is unbidden and sometimes disruptive and/or harmful. The deleterious environmental and cultural impacts of many forms of globalisation provide a particularly compelling context for the contestation of collective human rights – and by extension, for a critique of the legitimacy and conduct of a great many international enterprises, public and private.

The global effects of many of irreversible choices and defaults generate a focus on moral and political responsibility, which has begun to emerge in the development of the human rights regime and international jurisprudence. For example, international covenants dealing with the human rights of indigenous peoples[53] will in many cases need to stand as the bulwark for cultural survival: in some instances 'adaptation' to the forces pressing in on them will amount to cultural annihilation. And the drive for the (legal) right to a healthy environment[54] and what has come to be known more broadly as environmental justice also includes important jurisprudence about obligations to future generations.[55]

However, the greatest challenges to the adaptability of the human rights regime are likely to arise from rapid scientific and technological developments, principally but not solely driven by the revolution in the life sciences. The Universal Declaration on the Human Genome and Human Rights,[56] produced in 1997 signals an outline awareness of this, but subsequent advances together with the acceleration of technological convergence has already begun to pose very considerable social, ethical and human rights challenges. These include opportunities for physical and cognitive enhancement through genetic manipulation[57] that will generate a host of very difficult questions about human integrity, equity and justice. At the same time, adaptations of benign scientific and technological advances for wide-ranging repressive and coercive purposes are unlikely to remain a peripheral matter, either in considerations of national and international security,[58] or with respect to the compass of human rights.[59]

There is no doubt that the human rights regime will need to be highly adaptive in the face of rapid changes in our physical and social environments. The overarching question is whether the necessarily slow and inclusive social and political discussions will be able to keep pace with our propensity and capacity to generate change. This, too, the human rights regime shares with other forms of global governance.

However extensive the coverage, global governance arrangements will remain aspirational to some degree.

No plausible and humane human order can achieve peace, stability and sustainability in the absence of governance. Human numbers, human propensities and a global environment narrowed, shaped and made more fragile by human activity require global governance even to maintain such stability and security as we currently enjoy. The most reliable trajectories for our global orders indicate the need for more governance, coordinated effectively and enacted consistently.[60]

Currently, a great deal of attention is focused on adjusting the relationship between human activity and the dynamics of the natural world, but necessary though it is to mitigate the physical damage we have already brought about on a global scale and at least to slow the pace of debilitating change, we cannot lose sight of the impulses and interests that drive accumulations of power. Many of these are either fuelled by and/or impact directly on the natural world (illegal resource extraction, for example) and nearly all fall within the compass of the human rights regime, whether in conformity or violation. These will not disappear; nor, it seems, will the most vile abuses of power in the form of cruel and inhumane behaviours. The growth and progress of the human rights regime over 60 years has been an impressive achievement, but it is not irreversible, as the resurgence of torture confirms, including discussions even in the liberal press as to whether and under what circumstances it should be allowed.[61]

The largest part of global governance does not deal with malign intent and pathological abuses of power, but with the complexities and tensions that arise as integral to human social existence:

Human rights as a principle of popular politics express the indeterminacy and openness of society and politics. They undermine the attempt to police some social identities and sanction others and their indeterminacy means that the boundaries of society are always contested and never coincide fully with whatever crystallisations, power and legal entitlement impose. Human rights enclose both a principle of unity and homogeneity and its opposite, the former symbolised by the legal form, the latter by the struggles of people under the ill-defined banner of humanity.[62]

Human rights provides us with a means – not the only means, but a vital one – of mediating those complexities and tensions as we now so often must, on a global scale, as a form of global governance.

Conclusion: The human rights regime and the 'of, by and for whom?' of global governance

There is often a great deal of urgency connected with global governance initiatives – most recently the intense efforts of governments around the world to prevent a systemic collapse of global finance in the autumn of 2008. At other moments and in other sectors, the exercise appears more remote and technocratic, as in the once reassuring 'architecture of global finance' metaphor. Neither set of circumstances encourages the question, 'global governance of, by and for whom?' Instead, political pressures, popular expectations, scientific naivety and the abstraction of sector-specific governance from its contexts has given us a summative global governance that lacks the coherence and consistent political backing necessary to stave off catastrophes that will have cascading consequences. But against the social and political inertia of a comfortable *status quo*, there will always be those who attempt to subject our social and political arrangements to the scrutiny of values. Throughout history, the most important point about these challenges is not whether there are any universal values, but asserting the importance of the questions, 'What values?; Whose values?'; and 'On what authority?' The human rights regime makes questions of this character a permanent fixture of national and international life – questions to which the human rights regime itself is subjected in the form of the debate on Universal Human Rights.

This means that contestation over the ends and means of global governance are not left to victims (or theorists) and that a remarkably wide and detailed regime is already in place to scrutinise and if necessary legally challenge governance arrangements. As an increasing proportion of forms of human relatedness take on global connections, the absence of democratic controls at that level (and the remoteness of international organisations) makes the 'global governance of, by and for whom?' question compelling in both ethical and political terms; and the human rights regime gives it legal form and political substance.

As a form of global governance, the human rights regime is no more powerful, more coherent or less subject to the shifting tides of political interests than other forms of global governance. But it is unique in having been embraced by peoples everywhere as a normative expectation. We cannot govern global governance as though from above, but we can direct its purposes and its means. By setting limits on the legitimate exercise of power and specifying inalienable standards of human dignity, the human rights regime shapes both the limits and the responsibilities of all other forms of global governance. The human rights regime encodes the widely shared and deeply held aspiration that we shall not make an ungovernable world, but it is not a guarantee against failure.

Notes

Chapter 1

1 One expression of this was from former UK Prime Minister Tony Blair: 'If [we face] a global threat, it needs a global response, based on global rules', Tony Blair, speech given by the Prime Minister in Sedgefield, 5 March 2004. Available at: http://politics.guardian.co.uk/iraq/story/0,12956,1162991,00. html; see also Bjørn Lomborg (ed.) *Global Crises, Global Solutions* (Cambridge: Cambridge University Press, 2004).

2 Press Conference by President Bush, Prime Minister Goran Persson of Sweden, 14 June, 2001, available at: http://www.whitehouse.gov/news/releases/ 2001/06/20010614-1.html

3 Robert Jackson, *The Global Covenant: Human Conduct in a World of States* (Oxford: Oxford University Press, 2000), p.36.

4 See for example Rodney Bruce Hall and Thomas J. Biersteker (eds) *The Emergence of Private Authority in Global Governance* (Cambridge: Cambridge University Press, 2002).

5 Jim Whitman, *The Limits of Global Governance* (London: Routledge, 2005).

6 Jennifer Sterling-Folker, 'Realist global governance: Revisiting *cave! hic dragones* and beyond', in Alice D. Ba and Matthew J. Hoffmann (eds) *Contending Perspectives on Global Governance: Coherence, Contestation and World Order* (Abingdon: Routledge, 2005), pp.17–38.

7 Margaret P. Doxey, *International Sanctions in Contemporary Perspective*, 2nd edn. (London: Macmillan Press Ltd, 1996).

8 President William J. Clinton, *State of the Union Address*, 25 January 1994, available at: http://www.washingtonpost.com/wp-srv/politics/special/states/ docs/sou94.htm; White House Press Release, 'President and Prime Minister Blair Discussed Iraq, Middle East', 12 November 2004. Available at: http:// www.whitehouse.gov/news/releases/2004/11/20041112-5.html.

9 See for example Raymond Cohen, 'Pacific Unions: A Reappraisal of the Theory that "Democracies Do Not Go to War with Each Other"', *Review of International Studies*, Vol. 29, No. 3, July 1994; Christopher Layne, 'Kant or Cant: The Myth of the Democratic Peace', *International Security*, Vol. 19, No. 2, Fall 1994.

10 James Rosenau, 'Governance, Order and Change in World Politics', in James Rosenau and Ernst-Otto Czempiel (eds) *Governance Without Government: Order and Change in World Politics* (Cambridge: Cambridge University Press, 1992), pp.13–14.

11 Robert L. Ostergard, Jr. (ed.) *HIV/AIDS and the Threat to National and International Security* (Basingstoke: Palgrave, 2007).

12 Geoffrey Vickers, *Responsibility – Its Sources and Limits* (Seaside, California: Intersystems, 1980), p.71 (italics original).

13 See for example Rorden Wilkinson and Steve Hughes (eds), *Global Governance: Critical Perspectives* (London: Routledge, 2003).

14 Markus Lederer and Philipp S. Müller (eds) *Criticizing Global Governance* (Basingstoke: Palgrave, 2005).

15 Sir John Houghton, 'Global Warming, Climate Change and Sustainability: Challenge to Scientists, Policy Makers and Christians', The John Ray Initiative Connecting Environment, Science and Christianity (Briefing Paper 14, 2007), p.2. Available at: http://www.jri.org.uk/brief/Briefing14_print.pdf

16 Indicative studies include Rorden Wilkinson and Steve Hughes (eds) *op cit*; and Anthony McGrew and David Held (eds) *Governing Globalization: Power, Authority and Global Governance* (Cambridge: Polity, 2002).

17 The Commission on Global Governance, *Our Global Neighbourhood* (Oxford: Oxford University Press, 1995), p.4.

18 Leon Gordenker and Thomas Weiss, cited in Klaus Dingwerth and Philip Pattberg, 'Global Governance as a Perspective on World Politics', *Global Governance*, Vol. 12, No. 3 (July–September 2006), p.195.

19 Margaret P. Karns and Karen A. Mingst, *International Organisations: The Politics and Processes of Global Governance* (Boulder: Lynne Rienner, 2004).

20 WHO (Regional Office for the Western Pacific), *SARS: How a Global Epidemic Was Stopped* (WHO, 2006).

21 Jim Whitman, 'The Global Governance of Epidemics: Possibilities and Limitations', in Stella R. Quah (ed.) *Crisis Preparedness: Asia and the Global Governance of Epidemics* (Stanford: Walter H. Shorenstein Asia-Pacific Research Center Books/Brookings Institution, 2007), p.29.

22 W. Andy Knight, *A Changing United Nations: Multilateral Evolution and the Quest for Global Governance* (Basingstoke: Palgrave, 2000).

23 James P. Muldoon, *The Architecture of Global Governance: Introduction to the Study of International Organizations* (Boulder: Westview Press, 2003).

24 James N. Rosenau, 'Governance in the Twenty-First Century', *Global Governance* 1 (1995), p.15; James N. Rosenau and Ernst-Otto Czempiel (eds) *op cit*.

25 Ken Menkhaus, 'Governance Without Government in Somalia', *International Security*, Vol. 31, No. 3 (Winter 2006–07), pp.74–106.

26 William Korey, *NGOs and the Universal Declaration of Human Rights: A Curious Grapevine* (Basingstoke: Macmillan, 1998).

27 Susan K. Sell, 'Intellectual Property Rights', in David Held and Anthony McGrew, *op cit*, pp.179–80; see also Peter Drahos and John Braithwaite, *Information Feudalism: Who Owns the Knowledge Economy?* (New York: W.W. Norton & Co, 2003).

28 Mary Kaldor, 'The Idea of Global Civil Society', Martin Wright Memorial Lecture, 31 October, 2002. Available at: http://www.lse.ac.uk/Depts/global/Publications/PublicationsProfKaldor/TheIdeaofGlobalCivilSocietybyMaryKaldor.pdf

29 Mary Kaldor, Denisa Kostovicova and Yahia Said, 'War and Peace: The Role of Global Civil Society', in Mary Kaldor, Martin Albrow, Helmut Anheier and Marlies Glasius (eds) *Global Civil Society 2006/07* (London: Sage, 2007), p.111. See also the yearly succession of *Global Civil Society* volumes.

30 John Keane, *Global Civil Society?* (Cambridge: Cambridge University Press, 2003); Martin Shaw, *Global Civil Society and International Relations* (Cambridge: Polity Press, 1994).

31 Mary Kaldor, *Global Society: An Answer to War* (Cambridge: Polity, 2003).

32 Amory Starr, *Naming the Enemy: Anti-corporate Movements Confront Global-ization* (London: Zed Books, 2000).
33 James Rosenau, 'Change, Complexity, and Governance in Globalizing Space', in Jon Pierre (ed.) *Debating Governance* (Oxford: Oxford University Press, 2000), p.193.
34 Susan Strange, *The Retreat of the State* (Cambridge: The Diffusion of Power in the World Economy (Cambridge: Cambridge University Press, 1996).
35 Rodney Bruce Hall and Thomas J. Biersteker (eds) *op cit*, pp.7–8.
36 James Rosenau, 'Change, Complexity, and Governance in Globalizing Space', *op cit*, p.186.
37 Richard Falk, *On Humane Global Governance: Toward a New Global Politics* (Cambridge: Polity, 1995).
38 Jörg Friedrichs, 'Global Governance as the Hegemonic Project of Trans-atlantic Civil Society', in Markus Lederer and Philipp S. Müller (eds) *op cit*, pp.47, 53–4 (italics original).
39 Mark Duffield, *Global Governance and the New Wars: The Merging of Develop-ment and Security* (London: Zed Books, 2001), p.50.
40 *Ibid*, p.12.
41 Martin Wolf, *Why Globalization Works* (Yale: Yale University Press, 2005); Jagdish Bhagwati, *In Defence of Globalization* (Oxford: Oxford University Press, 2005).
42 Robert Gilpin, 'A Realist Perspective on International Governance', in Anthony McGrew and David Held (eds) *op cit*, pp.237–48.
43 Anthony McGrew and David Held (eds) *op cit*; Jan Aart Scholte, *Global-ization: A Critical Introduction* (Basingstoke: Palgrave, second edition, 2005).
44 Markus Lederer and Philipp S. Müller (eds) *op cit*.

Chapter 2

1 For this quotation and its applicability in this context, I am indebted to Ronnie D. Lipschutz (with James K. Rowe), *Globalization, Governmentality and Global Politics: Regulation for the Rest of Us?* (Abingdon: Routledge, 2005), p.4.
2 David Halloran Lumsdaine, *Moral Vision in International Politics: The Foreign Aid Regime 1949–1989* (Princeton: Princeton University Press, 1993).
3 The *Make Poverty History* campaign: http://www.makepovertyhistory.org/
4 Robert D. Loevy a.o. (eds) *The Civil Rights Act of 1964: The Passage of the Law That Ended Racial Segregation* (Albany: State University of New York Press, 1997).
5 Amy Gutmann and Dennis Thompson, *Why Deliberative Democracy?* (Prince-ton: Princeton University Press, 2004). See also deliberative-democracy.net, available at: http://www.deliberative-democracy.net/about/
6 Robert E. Paehlke, *Democracy's Dilemma: Environment, Social Equity and the Global Economy* (Boston: MIT Press, 2003), p.31.
7 E. Lauterpacht, Memorandum prepared for the UN Secretariat, UN Doc. A/CN.4/1/Rev.1, February 10, 1949, pp.19–20, reprinted in D.J. Harris (ed.) *Cases and Materials in International Law* (fifth edition) (London: Sweet & Maxwell, 1998), pp.140–2.

8 Mats R. Berdal and David M. Malone (eds), *Greed and Grievance: Economic Agendas in Civil Wars* (Boulder: Lynne Rienner Publishers, 2000).

9 Greenpeace, *Carving up the Congo* (April 2007). Available at: http://www. greenpeace.org/raw/content/international/press/reports/carving-up-the-congo-exec.pdf.

10 See for example, Jason Burke, 'Mugabe's loggers to ravage rainforest', *The Observer*, 26 August 2001; Paul Brown, 'Indonesian rainforests pulped to extinction', *The Guardian*, 11 February 2002.

11 Remarks by Chairman Alan Greenspan at the Annual Dinner and Francis Boyer Lecture of The American Enterprise Institute for Public Policy Research, Washington, D.C., December 5, 1996. ttp://www.federalreserve.gov/BOARDDOCS/SPEECHES/19961205.htm

12 Rory Carroll 'Emigrants from Latin America send home £32bn lifeline', *The Guardian*, 19 March 2007.

13 United Nations Environment Programme, Environment Alert Bulletin: 'Tourism Expansion: increasing threats or conservation opportunities?' (April 2005), available at: http://www.grid.unep.ch/product/publication/download/ew_tourism.en.pdf.

14 John Braithwaite and Peter Drahos, *Global Business Regulation* (Cambridge: Cambridge University Press, 2000).

15 David Kennedy, 'Challenging Expert Rule: The Politics of Global Governance', *Sydney Law Review*, Vol. 27, No. 5 (March 2005), p.2.

16 Ramesh Thakur and Luk Van Langerhove, 'Enhancing Global Governance Though Regional Integration', *Global Governance*, Vol. 12, No. 3 (July–September 2006), p.233.

17 Jim Whitman, *The Limits of Global Governance* (London: Routledge, 2005).

18 The Pew Research Center Survey Reports, 'Little Consensus on Global Warming: Partisanship Drives Opinion', 12 July 2006. Available at: http://people-press.org/reports/display.php3?ReportID=280

19 UK Parliament, Environmental Audit Committee, 'Reducing Carbon Emissions from Transport', 19 January 2006. Available at: http://www.parliament.uk/parliamentary_committees/environmental_audit_committee/eac_19_01_06c.cfm

20 Matthew Tempest, 'Blair Rules Out Air Fuel Tax', *The Guardian*, 8 February 2005. Available at: http://politics.guardian.co.uk/green/story/0,,1408376,00.html.

21 James Rosenau, *Along the Domestic-Foreign Frontier: Exploring Governance in a Turbulent World* (Cambridge: Cambridge University Press, 1997), p.4.

22 'Skype crash raises peer-to-peer fear', *New Scientist*, 25 August 2007, p.25.

23 Andrew Clark, 'Goldman Sachs bails out hedge fund with $3bn', *The Guardian*, 14 August 2007, p.22; Richard Wray and Ashley Seager, '£800m hedge fund bail-out adds to City's jitters over Barclay's', *The Guardian*, 1 September, 2007, p.34.

24 Nils Pratley, 'With blood in the water, look to bigger fish', *The Guardian*, 17 August 2007, p.27

25 Crispen Odey quoted in Nils Pratley, 'Odey the prophet of loss', *The Guardian*, 29 August 2007, p.24.

26 BBC News, 'SEC vows to rein in hedge funds', 26 July 2006. Available at: http://news.bbc.co.uk/1/hi/business/5216556.stm

27 BBC News Online network, 'Greenspan defends hedge fund buy-out', http://news.bbc.uk/hi/english/business/the_economy/newsid_184000/184505.stm

28 See for example the statement by UK Prime Minister Gordon Brown, 'The issue about transparency in relation to some of the financial instruments has been raised and is going to be discussed widely in the international community. We would support greater transparency.' Ashley Seager, 'Brown calls for greater clarity in financial products', *The Guardian*, 5 September 2007. Little more than a month earlier, 'Private equity firms [...] escaped the threat of tighter regulation and demands for closer scrutiny of pay and fees after a review rejected imposing public company-style rules on the industry.' Philipp Inman, 'Private equity escapes statutory scrutiny', *The Guardian*, 18 July 2007, p.21.

29 Timothy Garton Ash, 'Like it or loathe it, after 10 years Blair knows exactly what he stands for', *The Guardian*, 26 April 2007.

30 Paul Brown, 'Melting ice cap triggering earthquakes', *The Guardian*, 8 September 2007.

31 George Monbiot, 'Ministers know emissions trading is a red herring and won't work', *The Guardian*, 19 December 2006.

32 *The Economist*, 'Doffing the cap', 16 June 2007, p.90.

33 Patrick Wintour, 'Miliband plans carbon trading "credit cards" for everyone', *The Guardian*, 11 December 2006; and Patrick Wintour and Ashley Seager, 'Firms face compulsory carbon quotas', *The Guardian*, 6 December 2006.

Chapter 3

1 G8 Information Centre, St Petersburg Summit Documents, 'Fighting High-Level Corruption' (16 July 2006), available at: http://www.g7.utoronto.ca/summit/2006stpetersburg/corruption.html

2 Jan Kooiman (ed.) *Governing as Governance: New Government-Society Interactions* (London: Sage, 1993), p.2.

3 Volker Schneider and Frank M. Häge, 'Europeanization and the Retreat of the State', *Journal of European Public Policy*, Vol. 15, Issue 1 (January 2008), pp.1–19.

4 James N. Rosenau and Ernst-Otto Czempiel, *Governance Without Government: Order and Change in World Politics* (Cambridge: Cambridge University Press, 1992).

5 See successive editions of the yearly *Global Civil Society* – most recently, *Global Civil Society, 2006–07* (London: Sage).

6 Hidemi Suganami, *The Domestic Analogy and World Order Proposals* (Cambridge: Cambridge University Press, 1989), p.1.

7 Alexander King and Bertrand Schneider, *The First Global Revolution: A Report of the Council of Rome* (New York: Pantheon Books, 1991), pp.181–2.

8 The Commission on Global Governance, *Our Global Neighbourhood* (Oxford: Oxford University Press, 1995), pp.2–3.

9 David Held, Anthony McGrew, David Goldblatt and Jonathan Perraton, *Global Transformations: Politics, Economics and Culture* (Cambridge: Polity, 1999), p.85.

10 Margaret P. Karns and Karen A. Mingst, *International Organisations: The Politics and Processes of Global Governance* (Boulder: Lynne Rienner, 2004).

11 Robert O. Keohane and Joseph Nye, Jr., 'Transgovernmental Relations and International Organizations', *World Politics* (27) 1974; and more recently, Thomas Risse-Kappen, *Bringing Transnational Relations Back In: Non-state Actors, Domestic Structures and International Institutions* (Cambridge: Cambridge University Press, 1995); Kendall Stiles (ed.) *Global Institutions and Local Empowerment: Competing Theoretical Perspectives* (Basingstoke: Macmillan, 2000).

12 To capture both the integrative and fracturing capacities of these dynamics, James Rosenau coined the term, 'fragmegration'. James Rosenau, *Along the Domestic-Foreign Frontier: Exploring Governance in a Turbulent World* (Cambridge: Cambridge University Press, 1997).

13 Mary Kaldor, Denisa Kostovicova and Yahia Said, 'War, Peace and the Role of Global Civil Society', in Mary Lador, Martin Albrow, Helmut Anheier and Marlies Glasius (eds) *Global Civil Society 2006/7* (London: Sage, 2007), pp.94–109.

14 Anne Marie Clark, *Diplomacy of Conscience: Amnesty International and Human Rights Norms* (Princeton: Princeton University Press, 2001).

15 Jonathan A. Fox and L. David Brown (eds), *The Struggle for Accountability: The World Bank, NGOs and Grassroots Movements* (Cambridge: MIT Press, 1998).

16 Helen Yanacopulos, 'Patterns of Governance: The Rise of Transnational Coalitions of NGOs', *Global Society*, Vol. 19, No. 3 (2005), pp.247–66.

17 Rodney Bruce Hall and Thomas J. Biersteker (eds), *The Emergence of Private Authority in Global Governance* (Cambridge: Cambridge University Press, 1992).

18 Martin Shapiro, 'Administrative Law Unbounded: Reflections on Government and Governance', *Indiana Journal of Global Legal Studies*, 8 (2001), p.369.

19 David Kennedy, 'Challenging Expert Rule: The Politics of Global Governance', *Sydney Law Review*, Vol. 27, No. 5 (March 2005), pp.5–28; Anne-Marie Slaughter, *A New World Order* (Princeton: Princeton University Press, 2004).

20 Anne-Marie Slaughter, *ibid*, p.2.

21 *Ibid.*

22 John Braithwaite and Peter Drahos, *Global Business Regulation* (Cambridge: Cambridge University Press, 2000).

23 Kelley Lee (ed.), *Health Impacts of Globalization: Towards Global Governance* (Basingstoke: Palgrave, 2003).

24 United Nations Millennium Goals, available at: http://www.un.org/millenniumgoals/

25 Nick Paton Walsh, 'Putin throws lifeline to Kyoto as EU backs Russia joining WTO', *The Guardian*, 22 May 2004.

26 The Commission on Human Security, available at: http://www.human-security-chs.org/

27 Tom Jones, 'Policy Coherence, Global Environmental Governance and Poverty Reduction', *International Environmental Agreements: Politics, Law and Economics* (2) 2002, p.391.

28   Organisation for Economic Co-operation and Development, Special Dialogue between Members of the ECSS and Non-Members: Key Elements of OECD's Work On Governance Issues, DIAL/ECSS(2000)5, p.3. Available at: http://www.olis.oecd.org/olis/2000doc.nsf/809a2d78518a8277c125685d005300b2/c125685b0057c558c12568ec004fc5f5/$FILE/10078151.PDF
29   *Ibid.*
30   Vic George and Paul Wilding, *Globalization and Social Welfare* (Basingstoke: Palgrave, 2002), p.182.
31   John Ralston Saul, *The Collapse of Globalism* (London: Atlantic Books, 2005), p.25.
32   The Report of the World Commission on Dams, 'Dams and Development: A New Framework for Decision-Making', November 2000, available at: http://www.dams.org//docs/report/wcdreport.pdf
33   Mike Moore, *A World Without Walls: Freedom, Development, Free Trade and Global Governance* (Cambridge: Cambridge University Press, 2003); Jagdish Bhagwati, *In Defense of Globalization* (Oxford: Oxford University Press, 2007).
34   Mark Townsend and Paul Harris, 'Now the Pentagon tells Bush: climate change will destroy us', *The Observer*, 22 February 2004, available at: http://observer.guardian.co.uk/international/story/0,6903,1153513,00.html
35   Paul Rogers, *Losing Control: Global Security in the Early Twenty-first Century* (London: Pluto Books, 2002).
36   'Rudd takes Australia inside Kyoto', BBC News, 3 December 2007, available at: http://news.bbc.co.uk/1/hi/world/asia-pacific/7124236.stm; Deborah Zabarenko, 'Bali climate deal paves way for hotter U.S. debate', *Washington Post*, 16 December 2007, available at: http://www.washingtonpost.com/wp-dyn/content/article/2007/12/16/AR2007121600612.html
37   Charles E. Lindblom, 'The Science of "Muddling Through"', *Public Administration Review*, Vol. 19, No. 2 (1959), p.80.
38   C.S. Holling and Steven Sanderson, 'Dynamics of (Dis)harmony in Ecological and Social Systems', in Susan Hanna, Carl Folke and Karl-Goran Maler (eds), *Rights to Nature: Ecological, Economic, Cultural and Political Principles of Institutions for the Environment* (Washington, D.C.: Island Press, 1996), p.59.
39   Yishai Blank, 'Localism in the New Legal Order', *Harvard International Law Journal*, Vol. 47, No. 1 (Winter 2006), p.272.

Chapter 4

1   Mona Sue Weissmark, *Justice Matters: Legacies of the Holocaust and World War II* (Oxford: Oxford University Press, 2004).
2   William B. Schwartz, *Life Without Disease: The Pursuit of Medical Utopia* (Berkeley: University of California Press, 2000).
3   Richard Bookstaber, *A Demon of Our Own Design: Markets, Hedge Funds and the Perils of Financial Innovation* (Hoboken: John Wiley & Sons, 2007).
4   Cited in Laurie Garrett, *The Coming Plague: Newly Emerging Diseases in a World Out of Balance* (New York: Farrar, Straus and Giroux, 1994), p.30.
5   Geoffrey Vickers, unpublished manuscript on Western culture, 1970 (approx.), p.29.

6 R. Buckminster Fuller, *Critical Path* (London: Hutchison, 1983), p.127.

7 *Ibid*, p.217.

8 Edwin Black, *War Against the Weak*: *Eugenics and America's Plan to Create a Master Race* (New York: Thunder's Mouth Press, 2003).

9 See for example, Hugh Lacey, *Is Science Value Free?* (London: Routledge, 1999).

10 For a fascinating study on this theme, see James C. Scott, *Seeing Like a State*: *How Certain Schemes to Improve the Human Condition Have Failed* (New Haven: Yale University Press, 1999).

11 Robin McKie and Juliette Jowit, 'Can science really save the world?', *Observer*, 7 October 2007. Available at: http://observer.guardian.co.uk/focus/story/0,,2185343,00.html; see also, Oliver Morton, 'Climate change: is this what it takes to save the world?', *Nature*, 447 (10 May 2007), pp.132–6.

12 Jacques Ellul, *The Technological Society* (London: Jonathan Cape, 1965); and *The Technological Bluff* (Grand Rapids: William B. Erdmans Publishing, 1990); Lewis Mumford, *The Pentagon of Power* (New York: Harcourt Brace Jovonovich, 1970); James Brook and Iain A. Boal, *Resisting the Virtual Life*: *The Culture and Politics of Information* (San Francisco: City Lights Books, 1995).

13 Mumford, *ibid*, p.291. For the latest rendering of this kind of thinking, see Ray Kurzweil, *The Singularity is Near*: *When Humans Transcend Biology* (London: Gerald Duckworth & Co, 2005).

14 *Ibid*.

15 John Cornwell, *Hitler's Scientists: Science, War and the Devil's Pact* (London: Penguin, 2003).

16 Henri Poincaré, quoted in Lacey, *op cit*, p.1.

17 Danielle Egan, 'We're going to live forever', *New Scientist*, 13 October 2007, p.16.

18 Quoted in Mumford, *op cit*, p.271.

19 Jim Whitman, 'The Governance of Nanotechnology', *Science and Public Policy*, 34(4), June 2007, pp.273–83.

20 M.C. Roco and W.S. Bainbridge, 'Executive Summary', in NSF/DOC-sponsored report, Converging Technologies for Improving Human Performance: Nanotechnology, Biotechnology, Information Technology and Cognitive Science (Arlington, Virginia, 2002), available at http://www.wtec.org/ConvergingTechnologies/Report/NBIC_report.pdf , p.xiii.

21 *Ibid*, p.9.

22 For a further examination of the National Science Foundation/Department of Commerce report, see Jim Whitman, 'The Governance of Converging Technological Systems', *Bulletin of Science, Technology and Society*, Vol. 26, No. 5 (October 2006), pp.398–409.

23 *Ibid*, p.22.

24 Jacques Ellul, *The Technological Society*, *op cit*, p.133.

25 Alfred Nordmann (Rapporteur), *Converging Technologies – Shaping the Future of European Societies* (2004), p.3. Available at: http://www.ntnu.no/2020/pdf/final_report_en.pdf.

26 *Ibid*, p.4. Italics added.

27 Chris Mooney, 'Requiem for an Office', *Bulletin of the Atomic Scientists*, Vol. 61, No. 5 (September/October 2005), pp.40–9.

28   Chris Mooney, *The Republican War Against Science* (New York: Basic Books, 2005), p.53.
29   Jim Whitman, 'The Challenge to Deliberative Systems of Technological Systems Convergence', *Innovation: The European Journal of Social Sciences*, Vol. 20, No. 4 (December 2007), pp.329–43.
30   M. Chow and D. Fernandez, 'Intellectual Property Strategy in Bio-informatics', *Proc. Virt. Conf. Genom. And Bioinf.*, North Dakota State University, 15–16 October 2001.
31   *Ibid.*
32   Bent Flyvbjerg, *Megaprojects and Risk: An Anatomy of Ambition* (Cambridge: Cambridge University Press, 2003), pp.89–90.
33   Sheila Jasanoff, '(No?) Accounting for expertise', *Science and Public Policy*, Vol. 30, No. 3 (June 2003), p.158.
34   *Ibid.*
35   I am indebted to Catherine Rhodes of the Department of Peace Studies, Bradford University for this information.
36   Sarah Gibbon and Carlos Novas (eds), *Biosocialities, Genetics and the Social Sciences: Making Biologies and Identities* (London: Routledge, 2007).
37   Mark A. Rothstein (ed.), *Genetic Secrets: Protecting Privacy and Confidentiality in the Genetic Era* (New Haven: Yale University Press, 1998).
38   Richard Bookstaber, *op cit.*
39   John de la Mothe (ed.), *Science, Technology and Governance* (London: Continuum, 2001).
40   Richard Wray, 'China overtaking US for fast internet access as Africa gets left behind', *The Guardian*, 14 June 2007; Pippa Norris, *Digital Divide: Civic Engagement, Information Poverty and the Internet Worldwide* (Cambridge: Cambridge University Press, 2001).
41   Zygmunt Bauman, *Postmodern Ethics* (Oxford: Blackwell, 1993), pp.198–9.
41   Geoffrey Vickers, *Value Systems and Social Process* (London: Tavistock Publications, 1998), p.217.
42   *Ibid*, p.219.
43   Peter Unger, *Living High and Letting Die: Our Illusion of Innocence* (Oxford: Oxford University Press, 1996).
44   Zygmunt Bauman, *ibid*, pp.198–9.
45   Geoffrey Vickers, *Value Systems and Social Process* (London: Tavistock Publications, 1998), pp.170–1.
46   Geoffrey Vickers, *Freedom in a Rocking Boat: Changing Values in an Unstable Society* (London: Penguin Press, 1970), p.116.
47   David Kennedy, 'Challenging Expert Rule: The Politics of Global Governance', *Sydney Law Review*, Vol. 27, No. 5 (March 2005), p.15.
48   *Ibid*, p.28.
49   A.W. DePorte, *Europe Between the Superpowers: The Enduring Balance* (New Haven: Yale University Press, 1986), p.59.

Chapter 5

 1   Colin Hay, 'What Place for Ideas in the Structure-Agency Debate? Globalisation as a "Process Without a Subject"', published in *First Press*, available at: http://www.theglobalsite.ac.uk/press/109hay.htm

2 Margaret P. Karns and Karen A. Mingst, *International Organizations: The Politics and Processes of Global Governance* (Boulder: Lynne Rienner Publishers, 2004); Paul F. Diehl, *The Politics of Global Governance: International Organizations in an Interdependent World*, third edition (Boulder: Lynne Rienner Publishers, 2005); James P. Muldoon, *The Architecture of Global Governance: An Introduction to the Study of International Organizations* (Boulder: Westview Press, 2003).

3 Yozo Yokota, 'What is Global Governance?', Keynote lecture, NIRA International Forum: 'Global Governance – In Pursuit of a New International Order', July 12–13, 2004, available at: http://nira.go.jp/newse/paper/globalg/en-08.html (accessed 3 January 2006).

4 Lawrence S. Finklestein, 'What is Global Governance?', *Global Governance*, 1 (1995), p.369.

5 Ramesh Thakur and Luk Van Langerhove, 'Enhancing Global Governance Though Regional Integration', *Global Governance*, Vol. 12, No. 3 (July–September 2006), p.233.

6 David A. Westbrook, *City of Gold: An Apology for Global Capitalism in a Time of Discontent* (London: Routledge, 2004), p.5.

7 For a discussion of this, see Philippe Sands, *Lawless World: America and the Making and Breaking of Global Rules* (London: Penguin Books, 2005), Chapter 5, pp.95–116.

8 Willem Buiter, 'What did you do in the open market today, daddy?', *Financial Times*, 13 December 2007.

9 Martin Wolf, 'Why regulators should intervene in bankers' pay', *Financial Times*, 16 January 2008.

10 Richard Bookstaber, *A Demon of Our Own Design: Markets, Hedge Funds, and the Perils of Financial Innovation* (Hoboken: John Wiley & Sons, 2007), pp.259–60.

11 Kern Alexander, Rahul Dhumale and John Eatwell, *Global Governance of Financial Systems: The International Regulation of Systemic Risk* (Oxford: Oxford University Press, 2005).

12 Martin Wolf, *op cit.*

13 Steven Drobny, *Inside the House of Money: Top Hedge Fund Traders on Profiting in the Global Markets* (Hoboken: John Wiley & Sons, 2006), p.213.

14 David Kennedy, 'Challenging Expert Rule: The Politics of Global Governance', *Sydney Law Review*, Vol. 27, No. 5 (March 2005), p.7.

15 A good account of this is Naomi Klein, *The Shock Doctrine: The Rise of Disaster Capitalism* (London: Penguin, 2007).

16 Rosemary Foot, S. Neil MacFarlane and Michael Mastanduno (eds), *US Hegemony and International Organizations* (Oxford: Oxford University Press, 2003).

17 Geoffrey R.D. Underhill, 'Global Governance and Political Economy: Public, Private and Political Authority in the twenty-first century', in Hohn N. Clarke and Geoffrey R. Edwards (eds), *Global Governance in the Twenty-first Century* (Basingstoke: Palgrave, 2004), p.125.

18 Alison Brysk, *Human Rights and Private Wrongs: Constructing Global Civil Society* (Abingdon: Routledge, 2005).

19 James N. Rosenau and Ernst-Otto Czempiel (eds), *Governance Without Government: Order and Change in World Politics* (Cambridge: Cambridge University Press, 1992), p.7.

20 Paul Brown, 'US cities snub Bush and sign up to Kyoto: Dozens of mayors, representing more than 25 million Americans, pledge to cut greenhouse gases', *The Guardian*, 17 May 2005.

21 'United Kingdom and California Conclude Agreement on Global Warming', *The American Journal of International Law*, Vol. 11, No. 4 (October 2006), pp.933–4.

22 Bioworld Today, 'High Court Spurns Challenge; California Stem Cells Marching On', available at: http://www.pillsburylaw.com/bv/bvisapi.dll/portal/ep/newsReleaseDetail.do/pub/200752192723156/ruleType/PUB_FIR MNEWS_MENTIONS/channelId/-8593/9208

23 Kopin Tan, 'Stem Cells' Powerful Promise', *Barron's* (7 May 2007), p.30.

24 Citigroup Inc., (Press release), 'Leading Wall Street Banks Establish The Carbon Principles', February 04, 2008. Available at: http://www.citigroup.com/citigroup/press/2008/080204a.htm

25 Marie-Claude Smouts, 'Multilateralism from Below: A Prerequisite for Global Governance', in Michael G. Schechter (ed.), *Future Multilateralism: The Political and Social Framework* (Basingstoke: Palgrave, for the United Nations University Press, 1999), p.292.

26 *Ibid*, p.298.

27 B.S. Chimni, 'International Institutions Today: An Imperial Global State in the Making', *European Journal of International Law*, Vol. 15, No. 1 (2004), pp.1–37.

28 Jan Aart Scholte, *Globalization: A Critical Introduction* (Basingstoke: Palgrave, 2000); for 'spheres of authority', see James Rosenau, *Along the Domestic-Foreign Frontier: Exploring Governance in a Turbulent World* (Cambridge: Cambridge University Press, 1997).

29 Niels G. Noorderhaven, 'Transaction, Interaction, Institutionalisation: Toward a Dynamic Theory of Hybrid Governance', *Scandinavian Journal of Management*, Vol. 11, No. 1 (1995), pp.43–4.

30 Jon Pierre (ed.), *Debating Governance* (Oxford: Oxford University Press, 2000), p.3.

31 R.A.W. Rhodes, *Understanding Governance: Policy Networks, Governance, Reflexivity and Accountability* (Buckingham: Open University Press, 1997), p.17. See also Jan Kooiman, *Governing as Governance* (London: Sage, 2003); and R.A.W. Rhodes, 'The New Governance: Governing Without Government', *Political Studies*, Vol. 4, No. 4 (September 1996), pp.652–68.

32 Ann Marie Clark, *Diplomacy of Conscience: Amnesty International and Changing Human Rights Norms* (Princeton: Princeton University Press, 2001); Jonathan Fox and L. Dave Brown (eds), *The Struggle for Accountability: World Bank, NGOs and Grassroots Movements* (Boston: MIT Press, 1998); William E. DeMars, *NGOs and Transnational Networks: Wild Cards in World Politics* (London: Pluto Press, 2005).

33 Helen Yanacopulos, 'Patterns of Governance: The Rise of Transnational Coalitions of NGOs', *Global Society*, Vol. 19, No. 3 (2005), pp.247–66.

34 Jim Whitman, 'Global Governance as the Friendly Face of Unaccountable Power', *Security Dialogue*, Vol. 33, No. 1 (March 2002), pp.45–57.

35 Anne-Marie Slaughter, *A New World Order* (Oxford: Oxford University Press, 2004), pp.3–4.

36 *Ibid*, pp.6–7.

37 David Held and Mathias Koenig-Archibugi (eds), *Global Governance and Public Accountability* (Oxford: Blackwell, 2005).

38 Christoph Engel, 'Hybrid Governance Across National Jurisdictions as a Challenge to Constitutional Law', in Talia Einhorn (ed.), *Spontaneous Order, Organization and the Law: Roads to a European Civil Society* (Liber Amicorum Ernst-Joachim Mestmäcker) (The Hague: T.M.C. Asser Press, 2003), pp.145–6; See also: Steven Bernstein, 'Can non-state global governance be legitimate? An analytical framework', *Regulation and Governance*, Vol. 1, No. 4 (December 2007), pp.347–71.

39 Maxwell A. Cameron, Brian W. Tomlin and Robert J. Lawson (eds), *To Walk Without Fear: The Global Movement to Ban Landmines* (Ontario: Oxford University Press, 1998). See also: William Korey, *NGOs and the Universal Declaration of Human Rights: A Curious Grapevine* (Basingstoke: Palgrave, 2003); Zoe Pearson, 'Non-Governmental Organizations and the International Criminal Court: Changing Landscapes of International Law', *Cornell International Law Journal*, 39 (2006), pp.243–84.

40 Allen Buchanan and Robert O. Keohane, 'The Legitimacy of Global Governance Institutions', *Ethics and International Affairs*, Vol. 20, No. 4 (2006), pp.405–37.

41 Terry Macalister, 'Investment fund giants demand 90% reduction in carbon emissions', *The Guardian*, 15 February 2008.

Chapter 6

1 Stephan J. Gould, 'Ten Thousand Acts of Kindness', in *Eight Little Piggies* (London: Jonathan Cape, 1993), pp.275–83.

2 Cass R. Sunstein, 'Social Norms and Social Roles', *Columbia Law Review*, Vol. 96, No. 4 (1996), pp.929–30 (Italics original).

3 Peter Wilson, 'The English School and the Sociology of International Law: Strengths and Limitations', paper presented to the annual British International Studies Association conference, University of Birmingham, 15–17 December 2003.

4 Ethan A. Nadelmann, 'Global Prohibition Regimes: The Evolution of Norms in International Society', *International Organization*, Vol. 44, No. 4 (Autumn 1990), p.480.

5 *Ibid*, p.483.

6 Mervyn Frost, *Ethics in International Relations: A Constitutive Theory* (Cambridge: Cambridge University Press, 1996), p.105.

7 David J. Bederman, 'Constructivism, Positivism, and Empiricism in International Law', *Georgetown Law Journal*, Vol. 89, No. 2 (January 2001), pp.469–99.

8 Martha Finnemore and Kathryn Sikkink, 'International Norm Dynamics and Political Change', *International Organization*, Vol. 52, No. 4 (Autumn 1998), p.916.

9 Jeffrey Pfeffer and Gerald D. Salanick, *The External Control of Organizations: A Resource Dependency Perspective* (London: Longman, 1978), p.149.

10 David Black, 'The long and winding road: international norms and domestic political change in South Africa', in Thomas Risse, Stephen C. Ropp and

Kathryn Sikkink (eds), *The Power of Human Rights*: *International Norms and Domestic Change* (Cambridge: Cambridge University Press, 1999), pp.78–108.

11   Rosalyn Higgins, *The Development of International Law Through the Political Organs of the United Nations* (Oxford: Oxford University Press, 1963) p.5.

12   Margaret E. Keck and Kathryn Sikkink, *Activists Beyond Borders*: *Advocacy Networks in International Politics* (Ithaca: Cornell University Press, 1998); Ann Marie Clark, *Diplomacy of Conscience*: *Amnesty International and Changing Human Rights Norms* (Princeton: Princeton University Press, 2001).

13   Harold Hongju Koh, 'Bringing International Law back Home' (The 1998 Frankel Lecture), *Houston Law Review*, 35 (1998–99), pp.647–53.

14   Maxwell A Cameron Robert J. Lawson and Brian W. Tomlin (eds), *To Walk Without Fear: The Global Movement to Ban Landmines* (Ontario: Oxford University Press, 1998).

15   Harold Hongju Koh, *op cit*, pp.650–1.

16   Michael Barnett and Martha Finnemore, *Rules for the World*: *International Organizations in Global Politics* (Ithaca: Cornell University Press, 2004), p.7.

17   This delineation appears in Martha Finnemore and Kathryn Sikkink, *op cit*, p.891.

18   David Kennedy, 'Challenging Expert Rule: The Politics of Global Governance', *Sydney Law Review*, Vol. 27, No. 5 (March 2005), p.6. Also instructive in this regard is John Braithwaite and Peter Drahos, *Global Business Regulation* (Cambridge: Cambridge University Press, 2000); and for a case-specific study, see Steffen Bauer, 'The United Nations and the Fight against Desertification: What Role for the UNCCD Secretariat?', in Pierre Marc Johnson, Karel Mayrand and Marc Paquin (eds), *Governing Global Desertification*: *Linking Environmental Degradation, Poverty and Participation* (Aldershot: Ashgate, 2006), pp.73–87.

19   Harold Hongju Koh, *op cit*, p.654.

20   Frederic L. Kirgis, Jr., 'Technological Challenge to the Shared Environment: United States Practice', *American Journal of International Law*, Vol. 66 (1972), p.316.

21   Benjamin Schwarz, 'Managing China's Rise', *Atlantic Monthly*, 295 (2005), available at: http://www.theatlantic.com/doc/200506/schwarz

22   The Montreal Protocol on Substances that Deplete the Ozone Layer, available at: http://ozone.unep.org/pdfs/Montreal-Protocol2000.pdf

23   HSBC Climate Confidence Index 2007, available at: http://www.hsbc.com/1/PA_1_1_S5/content/assets/newsroom/hsbc_ccindex_p8.pdf

24   *Ibid*.

25   International Energy Agency (press release), 'The Next 10 Years are Critical – the World Energy Outlook Makes the Case for Stepping up Co-operation with China and India to Address Global Energy Challenges', available at: http://www.iea.org/textbase/press/pressdetail.asp?PRESS_REL_ID=239

26   Jan Kooiman, *Governing as Governance* (London: Sage, 2003), p.4.

27   Helge Jörgens, 'Governance by Diffusion – Implementing Global Norms Through Cross-National Imitation and Learning', in William M. Lafferty and Edward Elgar (eds), *Governance for Sustainable development*: *The Challenge of Adapting Form to Function* (2004). Available at: http://papers.ssrn.com/sol3/papers.cfm?abstract_id=652942

28   James N. Rosenau, *Along the Domestic-Foreign Frontier*: *Exploring Governance in a Turbulent World* (Cambridge: Cambridge University Press, 1997), p.41.

29   John Gerard Ruggie, 'Reconstituting the Global Public Domain – Issues, Actors, and Practices', *European Journal of International Relations*, Vol. 10, Issue 4 (2004), p.504.
30   Steven Bernstein and Benjamin Cashore, 'Can Non-state Global Governance Be Legitimate? An Analytical Framework', *Regulation and Governance*, Vol. 1, Issue 4 (December 2007), p.348. See also Ronnie D. Lipschutz and Cathleen Fogel, '"Regulation for the Rest of Us?" Global Civil Society and the Privatization of Transnational Regulation', in Rodney Bruce Hall and Thomas J. Biersteker (eds), *The Emergence of Private Authority in Global Governance* (Cambridge: Cambridge University Press, 2002), pp.115–40.
31   Tobias Webb, 'Does it pay to get into bed with business?', *The Guardian*, 25 February 2005, available at: http://www.guardian.co.uk/environment/2005/feb/25/activists.ethicalmoney
32   United Nations Global Compact, available at: http://www.unglobalcompact.org/
33   Virginia Haufler, *A Public Role for the Private Sector: Industry Self-regulation in a Global Economy* (Washington, D.C.: Carnegie Endowment for International Peace, 2001).
34   Michael Manson, 'Transnational Environmental Obligations: Locating New Spaces of Accountability in a Post-Westphalian Global Order', *Transactions of the Institute of British Geographers*, Nr. 26 (2001), pp.407–29.
35   James Rosenau, *op cit*, p.11.
36   Tom Jones, 'Policy Coherence, Global Environmental Governance and Poverty Reduction', *International Environmental Agreements: Law and Economics* 2 (2002), p.398.
37   Aarti Gupta, 'When Global is Local: Negotiating the Safe Use of Biotechnology', in Sheila Jasanoff and Marybeth Long Martello, *Earthly Politics: Local and Global in Environmental Governance* (Cambridge, Mass.: MIT Press, 2004), p.143.
38   Charles E. Lindblom, 'A Century of Planning', in Michael Kenny and James Meadowcroft (eds), *Planning Sustainability* (London: Routledge, 1999), p.61.

Chapter 7

1   Usman Hannan and Hany Besada, 'Dimensions of State Fragility: A Review of the Social Science Literature', The Centre for International Governance Innovation, Working Paper 33 (November 2007); Robert H. Jackson, *Quasi-States: Sovereignty, International Relations and the Third World* (Cambridge: Cambridge University Press, 1993).
2   Report of the International Commission on Intervention and State Sovereignty, 'The Responsibility to Protect', available at: http://www.iciss.ca/report-en.asp
3   See the *Financial Times'* 'Enron Homepage', available at: http://specials.ft.com/enron/FT31GI7Q80D.html
4   Andrew Clark, 'Sold for $2 a share: rescue at a 94% discount for Bear Stearns, a bank once worth $140 billion', *The Guardian*, 17 March 2008.
5   David Cho, Neil Irwin and Peter Whoniskey, 'US Forces Nine Major Banks to Accept Partial Nationalization', *Washington Post*, 14 October 2008.

6   Angus Shaw, 'Zimbabwe inflation passes 100,000%, officials say in Harare', *The Guardian*, 22 February 2008.
7   http://theclimategroup.org/our_partners/
8   See the position adopted by Swiss re, available at: http://www.swissre.com/pws/about%20us/knowledge_expertise/top%20topics/our%20position%20and%20objectives.html?contentIDR=c21767004561734fb900fb2ee2bd2155&useDefaultText=0&useDefaultDesc=0
9   Gabriel M. Leung, 'Global Public Health Research Preparedness against Emerging and Reemerging Infectious Diseases', in Stella R. Quah (ed.) *Crisis Preparedness: Asia and the Global Governance of Epidemics* (Stanford: the Brookings Institution for the Walter H. Shorenstein Asia-Pacific Research Center, 2007), p.142.
10 Nana N. Poku, Alan Whiteside and Bjorg Sandkjaer (eds), *AIDS and Governance* (Aldershot: Ashgate, 2007).
11 Jim Whitman, 'Disseminative Systems and Global Governance', *Global Governance*, Vol. 11, No. 1 (Jan–March 2005), pp.85–102.
12 Interview with Yra Harris, Chicago Mercantile Exchange, in Steven Drobny, *Inside the House of Money: Top Hedge Fund Traders on Profiting in the Global Markets* (Hoboken: John Wiley & Sons, 2006), p.203.
13 *Ibid*, p.204.
14 *Ibid*.
15 BBC News, 'Northern Rock to be Nationalised', 17 February 2000–8, available at: http://news.bbc.co.uk/1/hi/business/7249575.stm
16 BBC News, 'Central banks fight credit crisis', 11 March 2008, available at: http://news.bbc.co.uk/1/hi/business/7289815.stm
17 Kern Alexander, Rahul Dhumale and John Eatwell, *Global Governance of Financial Systems: The International Regulation of Systemic Risk* (Oxford: Oxford University Press, 2004).
18 John Braithwaite and Peter Drahos, *Global Business Regulation* (Cambridge: Cambridge University Press, 2000), pp.88–142.
19 A useful survey of the 'international discourse on adaptation to climate change' can be found in E. Lisa F. Schipper, 'Climate Change Adaptation and Development: Exploring the Linkages', Tyndall Centre for Climate Change Research, Tyndall Centre Working Paper No. 107 (July 2007), available at: http://www.tyndall.ac.uk/publications/working_papers/twp107.pdf
20 White House, *The National Security Strategy of the United States of America* (2002), p.15. Available at: http://www.whitehouse.gov/nsc/nss.html
21 *Ibid*, p.16.
22 International Institute of Finance, 'Interim Report of the IIF Committee on Market Best Practices', April 2008, p.1. Available at: http://www.iif.com
23 John Madeley, *Hungry for Trade: How the Poor pay for Free Trade* (London: Zed Books, 2000).
24 Jagdish N. Bhagwati, *Free Trade Today* (Princeton: Princeton University Press, 2003); Joseph E. Stiglitz and Andrew Charlton, *Fair Trade For All: How Trade Can Promote Development* (Oxford: Oxford University Press, 2005).
25 Peter Singer, 'Famine, Affluence and Morality', *Philosophy and Public Affairs*, Vol. 1, No. 3 (Spring 1972), pp.229–43; Peter Unger, *Living High and Letting Die: Our Illusion of Innocence* (Oxford: Oxford University Press, 1996).

26 Douglas H. Boucher, *The Paradox of Plenty: Hunger in a Bountiful World* (Oakland: Institute for Food and Development Policy/Food First Books, 1999), p.334. A halving of malnutrition by 2015 is also one of the UN's Millennium development Goals. More recently, see Declaration of the High-Level Conference on World Food Security from the June 2008 Food Summit in Rome, which contains the following: 'Members of WTO reaffirm their commitment to the rapid and successful conclusion of the WTO Doha Development Agenda and reiterate their willingness to reach comprehensive and ambitious results that would be conducive to improving food security in developing countries. Implementing an aid for trade package should be a valuable complement to the Doha Development Agenda to build and improve the trading capacity of the developing countries.' Available at: http://www.fao.org/fileadmin/user_upload/foodclimate/HLCdocs/declaration-E.pdf

27 Debora MacKenzie, 'What price more food?', *New Scientist*, 14 June 2008, p.28.

28 Chris McGreal, 'Egypt: bread shortages, hunger and unrest', *The Guardian*, 27 May 2008.

29 Aljazeera.net, 'Manila urges end to rice export ban', 29 April 2008, available at: http://english.aljazeera.net/NR/exeres/84B4ED9E-DD71-4C2D-BA12-626A80052D09.htm

30 UN Food and Agriculture Organisation, 'Soaring Food Prices: Facts, Perspectives, Impacts and Actions Required', April 2008, p.4. Available at: http://www.fao.org/fileadmin/user_upload/foodclimate/HLCdocs/HLC08-inf-1-E.pdf

31 The White House, 'Twenty In Ten: Strengthening America's Energy Security' (2007 State of the Union Policy Initiatives). Available at: http://www.whitehouse.gov/stateoftheunion/2007/initiatives/energy.html

32 EurActiv.com, 'EU cuts back on biofuel crop subsidies', 18 October 2007. Available at: http://www.euractiv.com/en/sustainability/eu-cuts-back-biofuel-crop-subsidies/article-167713

33 FAO Newsroom, 'FAO sees major shift to bioenergy: Pressure building for switch to biofuels', 25 April 2006. Available at: http://www.fao.org/newsroom/en/news/2006/1000282/index.html

34 John Vidal, 'Crop switch worsens global food price crisis', *The Guardian*, 5 April 2008.

35 Bill Van Auken, 'Amid mounting food crisis, governments fear revolution of the hungry', *World Socialist Website*, 15 April 2008, available at: http://www.wsws.org/articles/2008/apr2008/food-a15.shtml; see also Geoffrey Lean, 'Multinationals make billions in profit out of growing global food crisis', *The Independent*, 4 May 2008.

36 John Vidal, *op cit.*

37 Otto Spengler, 'Rice, death and the dollar', *Asia Times*, 22 April 2008. Available at: http://www.atimes.com/atimes/Global_Economy/JD22Dj01.html

38 John Vidal, 'Global food crisis looms as climate change and fuel shortages bite', *The Guardian*, 3 November 2007.

39 UN News Centre, 'Global food crisis could have been avoided – UN development experts', 6 May 2008. Available at: http://www.un.org/apps/news/story.asp?NewsID=26578&Cr=food&Cr1=crisis

40 Government of Australia, Rural Industries Research and Development Corporation (press release), 'Asian animal protein demand creates opportunities for Australian agriculture: Report', 4 December 2007. Available at: http://www.rirdc.gov.au/pub/media_releases/4dec07.html

41 *International Herald Tribune*, 'Climate change could lead to global food crisis, scientists warn', April 10, 2008. Available at: http://www.iht.com/articles/ap/ 2008/04/10/europe/EU-GEN-Hungary-Climate-Change.php

42 Julian Borger, 'Food summit fails to agree on biofuels', *The Guardian*, 6 June 2008.

43 Javier Blas, 'Food aid declines to near 50-year low', *Financial Times*, 9 June 2008. Available at: http://www.ft.com/cms/s/0/06e5b31a-3645-11dd-8bb8-0000779fd2ac.html

44 Peter Wilkin, 'Against Global Governance? Tracing the Lineage of the Anti-Globalisation Movement', in Feargal Cochrane, Rosaleen Duffy and Jan Selby (eds) *Global Governance, Conflict and Resistance* (Basingstoke: Palgrave, 2003), pp.78–95.

45 Jörg Friedrichs, 'Global Governance as the Hegemonic Project of Transatlantic Civil Society', in Markus Lederer and Philipp S. Müller (eds) *Criticizing Global Governance* (Basingstoke: Palgrave Macmillan, 2005), pp.45–68.

46 Mark Duffield, *Global Governance and the New Wars: The Merging of Development and Security* (London: Zed Books, 2002); Susanne Soederberg (2006) *Global Governance in Question: Empire, Class and the New Common Sense in Managing North-South Relations* (London: Pluto Press, 2006).

47 Jagdish Bhagwati, *In Defense of Globalization* (Oxford: Oxford University Press, 2005); Martin Wolf, *Why Globalization Works* (New Haven: Yale University Press, 2005).

48 Azizur Rahman Khan and Carl Riskin, *Inequality and Poverty in China in the Age of Globalization* (Oxford University Press, 2001); World Bank, *The Cost of Pollution in China: Estimates of Economic and Physical Damage* (Washington, D.C.: World Bank Publications, 2008).

Chapter 8

1 There is evidence to suggest that as long as 5,000 years ago, human activity was already having an impact on the earth's climate, and that this might even have forestalled a new ice age. Nevertheless, the period from the industrial revolution represents a dramatic shift in human circumstances – and the speed and unthinking ease with which we are able to bring them about. See William F. Ruddiman, *Plows, Plagues and Petroleum* (Princeton: Princeton University Press, 2005).

2 E. Beinhocker, *The Origin of Wealth: Evolution, Complexity and the Radical Remaking of Economics* (London: Random House, 2005), p.11.

3 United Nations Population Fund (UNFPA), *State of the World's Population 2007: Unleashing the Potential of Urban Growth*, available at: http://www.unfpa.org/ swp/2007/english/introduction.html

4 AFP, 'Hurricanes destroyed 109 oil platforms: US government', 4 October 2005; Jitendra Joshi (AFP), 'Bush calls for new refineries after hurricane havoc', 4 October 2005. Both available at: http://www.terradaily.com/news/energy-tech-05zzzzzzp.html

5　Jad Mouawad, 'Weather Risks Cloud Promise of Biofuel', *New York Times*, 1 July 2008.

6　Aditya Chakrabortty, 'Secret report: biofuel caused food crisis: internal World Bank study delivers blow to energy drive', *The Guardian*, 4 July 2008.

7　Raj Patel, *Stuffed and Starved*: *Markets, Power and the Battle for the World Food System* (London: Portobello Books, 2008).

8　Geoffrey Vickers, *Human Systems Are Different* (London: Harper & Row, 1983), p.17 (italics original).

9　R. Alan Hedley, 'Convergence in natural, social and technical systems: a critique', *Current Science*, Vol. 79, No. 5 (10 September 2000), p.592.

10　William H. McNeil, *The Human Condition*: *An Ecological and Historical View* (Princeton: Princeton University Press, 1980), p.74.

11　See Stephen Boyden, *Western Civilization in Biological Perspective* (Oxford: Oxford University Press, 1987); Alfred W. Crosby, *Ecological Imperialism and the Biological Expansion of Europe, 900–1900* (Cambridge: Cambridge University Press, 1986); William H. McNeil, *Plagues and Peoples* (Oxford: Blackwell, 1976).

12　Jim Whitman, *The Limits of Global Governance* (Abingdon: Routledge, 2005).

13　Brian Goodwin, 'All for one, one for all', *New Scientist*, 13 June 1998, p.32.

14　Richard Bookstaber, *A Demon of Our Own Design*: *Markets, Hedge Funds, and the Perils of Financial Innovation* (Hoboken: John Wiley & Sons, 2007), p.230.

15　David Byrne, *Complexity Theory and the Social Sciences*: *An Introduction* (London: Routledge, 1998).

16　Robert Jervis, *System Effects*: *Complexity in Political and Social Life* (Princeton: Princeton University Press, 1997), p.34. See also John Urry, *Global Complexity* (Cambridge: Polity Press, 2003).

17　For the temporal dimension, see Barbara Adam, *Timescapes of Modernity*: *The Environment and Invisible Hazards* (London: Routledge, 1998).

18　This is recounted in Stephen S. Hall, *Mapping the Millennium: How Computer-Driven Cartography is Revolutionizing the Face of Science* (New York: Vintage Books, 1993), pp.127–38.

19　Debora MacKenzie, 'The end of civilization', *New Scientist*, 5 April 2008, pp.30–1.

20　The University of Ottawa Object-Oriented Engineering Site, available at: http://www.site.uottawa.ca:4321/oose/index.html#tightcoupling; see also Charles Perrow, *Normal Accidents*: *Living With High Risk Technologies* (Princeton: Princeton University Press, 1999).

21　Joseph Tainter, *The Collapse of Complex Societies* (Cambridge: Cambridge University Press, 1988), p. 91.

22　Joseph A. Tainter, 'Problem Solving: Complexity, History, Sustainability', *Population and Environment*, Vol. 22, No. 1 (September 2000), p.8.

23　*Ibid*, p.9.

24　See Geoffrey Vickers, *Value Systems and Social Processes* (London: Tavistock, 1968), pp.75–6.

25　Robert J. Diaz and Rutger Rosenberg, 'Spreading Dead Zones and Consequences for Marine Ecosystems', *Science*, 321, pp.926–9.

26　James Lovelock, *Gaia*: *A New Look at Life on Earth* (Oxford: Oxford University Press, 2000).

27　Lee B. Reichman (with Janice Hopkins Tanne), *Timebomb*: *The Global Epidemic of Multi-Drug-Resistant Tuberculosis* (New York: McGraw-Hill, 2003);

Laurie Garrett, *The Coming Plague*: *Newly Emerging Diseases in a World Out of Balance* (New York: Farrar, Straus & Giroux, 1994), Chapter 13.

28   Stella R. Quah (ed.), *Crisis Preparedness: Asia and the Global Governance of Epidemics* (The Brookings Institution for the Shorenstein Asia-Pacific Research Center, Stanford University, 2007).

29   http://www.un.org/millenniumgoals/

30   John Lingard, 'Agricultural Subsidies and Environmental Change', available at: http://www.wiley.co.uk/egec/pdf/GB403-W.PDF

31   http://unfccc.int/2860.php

32   G. Prins and S. Rayner, 'Time to ditch Kyoto', *Nature* (449), 25 October 2007, pp.973–5.

33   Chris Brummitt, 'UN climate chief says US-EU deadlock over emissions cuts threatens climate summit', 13 December 2007, available at: http://climate.weather.com/articles/emissions121307.html

34   Article 7.6 of the Framework Convention on Climate Change states, 'Any body or agency, whether national or international, governmental or non-governmental, which is qualified in matters covered by the Convention, and which has informed the secretariat of its wish to be represented at a session of the Conference of the Parties as an observer, may be so admitted unless at least one third of the Parties present object'. Text available at: http://unfccc.int/not_assigned/b/items/1417.php

35   Andrew Simms, 'World hunger needs a simple solution rather than hi-tech GM food', *The Guardian*, 4 August 2003.

36   Jerry Taylor, 'Sustainable Development: A Dubious Solution in Search of a Problem', The Cato Institute, *Policy Analysis*, No. 449 (26 August 2002).

37   Helen Yanacopulos, 'Patterns of Governance: the Rise of Transnational Coalitions of NGOs', *Global Society*, Vol. 19, No. 3 (2005), pp.247–66; Ann Marie Clark, *Diplomacy of Conscience: Amnesty International and Changing Human Rights Norms* (Princeton: Princeton University Press, 2001).

38   James N. Rosenau and Ernst-Otto Czempiel (eds), *Governance Without Government: Order and Change in World Politics* (Cambridge: Cambridge University Press, 1992); James N. Rosenau, *Along the Domestic-Foreign Frontier: Exploring Governance in a Turbulent World* (Cambridge: Cambridge University Press, 1997).

39   James N. Rosenau, 'Governance in the Twenty-first Century', *Global Governance*, Vol. 1, No. 1 (Winter 1995), p.14.

40   For a fascinating study of the practical politics of improving standards of regulation in global business, see John Braithwaite and Peter Drahos, *Global Business Regulation* (Cambridge: Cambridge University Press, 2000), especially chapter 26, in which they discuss 'Five strategies for intervening in global webs of regulation to ratchet-up standards in the world system', from p.612.

Chapter 9

1   Mark Rupert, *Ideologies of Globalization*: *Contending Visions of a New World Order* (London: Routledge, 2000).

2   Krishna Guha, Daniel Dombey and James Politi and Michael MacKenzie, 'Bail-out faces flak from wary Congress', *Financial Times,* 24 September 2008.

3 Ron Suskind, 'The Crisis Last Time', *New York Times*, 24 September 2008.

4 *Ibid.*

5 Nils Pratley, 'The day the ticking time bombs went off', *The Guardian*, 16 September 2008.

6 Nassim Nicholas Taleb, 'The Fourth Quadrant: A Map of the Limits of Statistics', *Edge*, 15 September 2008. Available at: http://www.edge.org/3rd_culture/ taleb08/taleb08_index.html

7 Louis W. Pauly, 'Global finance, political authority, and the problem of legitimation', in Rodney Bruce Hall and Thomas J. Biersteker (eds) *The Emergence of Private Authority in Global Governance* (Cambridge: Cambridge University Press, 2002), pp.76–90.

8 James Grant, 'The Buck Stopped Then', *New York Times*, 23 September 2008.

9 Andrew Clark, 'Confidence nosedives after latest collapse', *The Guardian*, 27 September 2008.

10 Louis W. Pauly, *op cit*, p.88.

11 Deutsche Welle, 'German environment minister warns against exploiting Arctic', 29 August 2007. Available at: http://www.dw-world.de/dw/article/0,2144,2756813,00.html; Cleo Paskal, 'How climate change is pushing the boundaries of security and foreign policy', Chatham House Briefing Paper, June 2007. Available at: http://www.chathamhouse.org.uk/publications/papers/view/-/id/499/

12 The Commission on Global Governance, *Our Global Neighbourhood* (Oxford: Oxford University Press, 1995), pp.2 and 4.

13 James N. Rosenau, *Distant Proximities*: *Dynamics Beyond Globalization* (Princeton: Princeton University Press, 2003).

14 Alice D. Ba and Matthew J. Hoffmann (eds), *Contending Perspectives on Global Governance* (Abingdon: Routledge, 2005).

15 Rodney Bruce Hall and Thomas J. Biersteker (eds), *op cit*.

16 Geoffrey Vickers, *Value Systems and Social Processes* (London: Tavistock Publications, 1968), p.116. Italics original.

17 For an examination of the conceptual history of the term, see Michael Redclift, 'Sustainable development (1987–2005): An Oxymoron Comes of Age', *Sustainable Development*, 13 (2005), pp.212–27.

18 Charles E. Lindblom, 'A century of planning', in Michael Kenny and James Meadowcroft (eds) *Planning Sustainability* (London: Routledge, 1999), p.59.

19 Max Singer and Aaron Wildavsky, *The Real World Order: Zones of Peace, Zones of Turmoil* (New York: Chatham House Publishers, 1993), p.1.

20 Robert Cooper, 'The new liberal imperialism', *The Observer*, 7 April 2002.

21 Jörg Friedrichs, 'Global Governance as the Hegemonic Project of Trans-atlantic Civil Society', in Markus Lederer and Philipp S. Müller (eds), *Criticizing Global Governance* (Basingstoke: Palgrave, 2005), pp.45–68; Mark Duffield, *Global Governance and the New Wars*: *The Merging of Development and Security* (London: Zed Books, 2001).

22 Jim Whitman, 'The Challenge to Deliberative Systems of Technological Systems Convergence', *Innovation*: *The European Journal of Social Sciences*, Vol. 20, No. 4 (December 2007), pp.329–42.

23 Report of a NEST High-Level Expert Group, *Synthetic Biology*: *Applying Engineering to Biology* (Brussels: European Commission, 2005), p.5.

24 Sylvia Pagán, 'Virus synthesised in a fortnight', *New Scientist*, 14 November 2003.
25 The principal US document on technological convergence is M.C. Roco and W.S. Bainbridge, 'Executive Summary', in NSF/DOC-sponsored report, *Converging Technologies for Improving Human Performance: Nanotechnology, Biotechnology, Information Technology and Cognitive Science* (Arlington, Virginia, 2002). Available at: http://www.wtec.org/ConvergingTechnologies/Report/NBIC_report.pdf. The primary EU report is Alfred Nordmann (Rapporteur), *Converging Technologies – Shaping the Future of European Societies* (2004). Available at: http://www.ntnu.no/2020/pdf/final_report_en.pdf.
26 Geoffrey Vickers, *Human Systems Are Different* (London: Harper & Row, 1983), p.xv.
27 M.C. Roco and W.S. Bainbridge, *op cit*, p.72.
28 M.C. Roco, 'National Nanotechnology Initiative – Past, Present and Future', 20 February 2006. Available at: http://www.nano.gov/NNI_Past_Present_Future.pdf, p.31.
29 Sharon Oosthoek, 'Nature 2.0', *New Scientist*, 5 July 2008, p.33.
30 T.M. Wigley, 'The Climate Change Commitment', *Science*, Vol. 307, No. 5716 (March 2005), pp.1766–9.
31 Charles E. Lindblom, 'Still Muddling, Not Yet Through', *Public Administration Review*, November/December 1979, p.524.

Chapter 10

1 James N. Rosenau, 'Governance, Order, and Change in World Politics', in James N. Rosenau and Ernst-Otto Czempiel (eds) *Governance Without Government: Order and Change in World Politics* (Cambridge: Cambridge University Press, 1992).
2 Indicative studies include Martin Hewson and Timothy J. Sinclair (eds), *Approaches to Global Governance Theory* (Albany: State University of New York Press, 1999); Jon Pierre (ed.), *Debating Governance* (Oxford: Oxford University Press, 2000); and Alice D. Ba and Matthew J. Hoffmann (eds), *Contending Perspectives on Global Governance* (Abingdon: Routledge, 2005).
3 James N. Rosenau, 'Global Governance in the Twenty-first Century', *Global Governance*, Vol. 1, No. 1 (1995), p.13.
4 Leon Gordenker and Thomas Weiss, cited in Klaus Dingwerth and Philip Pattberg, 'Global Governance as a Perspective on World Politics', *Global Governance*, Vol. 12, No. 3 (July–September 2006), p.195.
5 See any of the yearly editions of the UN Human Development Report. The 2007/2008 report is available at: http://hdr.undp.org/en/reports/global/hdr2007-2008/; see also Caroline Thomas, *Global Governance, Development and Human Security: The Challenge of Poverty and Inequality* (London: Pluto Press, 2000).
6 Helen Yanacopulos, 'Patterns of governance: the rise of transnational coalitions of NGOs', *Global Society*, Vol. 19, No. 3 (2005), pp.247–66.
7 Randall D. Germain, *The Idea of Global Civil Society: Ethics and Politics in a Globalizing Era* (Abingdon: Routledge, 2006); Mary Kaldor and others (eds), *Global Civil Society 2006/07* (London: Sage, 2007).

8 The UN Global Compact, available at: http://www.unglobalcompact.org/ AbouttheGC/TheTENPrinciples/index.html

9 Manfred Nowak, *Introduction to the International Human Rights Regime* (Boston: Martinus Nijhoff Publishers, 2003).

10 Significant studies include: Leslie Friedman Goldstein and Cornel Ban, 'The European human-rights regimes as a case study in the emergence of global governance', in Alice D. Ba and Matthew J. Hoffmann (eds) *Contending Perspectives on Global Governance*: *Coherence, Contestation and World Order* (Abingdon: Routledge, 2005), pp.154–75; Julie Owen, 'Human Rights as Civil Religion: The Glue for Global Governance?', in Markus Lederer and Philipp S. Müller (eds), *Criticizing Global Governance* (Basingstoke: Palgave, 2005), pp.221–42; James W. Nickel, 'Is Today's International Human Rights System a Global Governance Regime?', *The Journal of Ethics*, Vol. 6, No. 4 (2002), pp.353–71; William H. Meyer and Boyka Stefanova, 'Human Rights, the UN Global Compact, and Global Governance', *Cornell International Law Journal*, 34 (2001), pp.501–21; and Stephanie Lawrence, 'Global governance, human rights and the "problem" of culture', in Rorden Wilkinson and Steve Hughes, *Global Governance*: *Critical Perspectives* (London: Routledge, 2002), pp.75–91.

11 Johannes Morsink, *The Universal Declaration of Human Rights: Origins, Drafting, and Intent* (Philadelphia: University of Pennsylvania Press, 2000).

12 Jack Donnelly, *Universal Human Rights in Theory and Practice* (Ithaca: Cornell University Press, 1989); Joanne R. Bauer and Daniel A. Bell (eds), *The East Asian Challenge to Human Rights* (Cambridge: Cambridge University Press, 1999); C. Cerna, 'Universality of Human Rights and Cultural Diversity: Implementation of Human Rights in Different Socio-Cultural Contexts', *Human Rights Quarterly*, Vol. 16, No. 4 (November 1994), pp.740–52.

13 M. Anne Brown, *Human Rights and the Borders of Suffering*: *The Promotion of Human Rights in International Politics* (Manchester: Manchester University Press, 2002), p.35.

14 Available at: http://www.unhchr.ch/html/menu3/b/a_cescr.htm

15 UN doc. E/C.12/1992/2, p.83, cited in David Beetham, 'What Future for Economic and Social Rights?', *Political Studies*, XLIII (1995), p.40.

16 M. Anne Brown, *op cit*, p.205.

17 Christian Davenport (ed.), *Paths to State Repression*: Human Rights Violations and Contentious Politics (London: Rowman & Littlefield Publishers, 2000).

18 Nicholas J. Wheeler, *Saving Strangers*: *Humanitarian Intervention in International Society* (Oxford: Oxford University Press, 2002).

19 Jim Whitman, 'After Kosovo: The Risks and Deficiencies of Unsanctioned Humanitarian Intervention', *Journal of Humanitarian Assistance*, http://www.jha.ac/articles/a062.htm (September, 2000).

20 Anthony J. Langlois, 'Human Rights Without Democracy? A Critique of the Separationist Thesis', *Human Rights Quarterly*, Vol. 25, No. 4 (November 2003), p.1019.

21 Thomas M. Franck, 'The Emerging Right to Democratic Governance', *American Journal of International Law*, Vol. 86 (1992), p.91. See also Gregory H. Fox and Brad R. Roth (eds), *Democratic Governance and International Law* (Cambridge: Cambridge University Press, 2000).

22   See for example Lance Gable, 'The Proliferation of Human Rights in Global Health Governance', *Journal of Law, Medicine and Ethics*, Vol. 35 (Winter, 2007), pp.534–44; Rodolfo Stavenhagen, 'The Rights of Indigenous Peoples: Closing a Gap in Global Governance', *Global Governance*, Vol. 11 (2005), pp.17–23; Jean Grugel and Enrique Peruzzotti, 'Claiming Rights Under Global Governance: Children's Rights in Argentina', *Global Governance*, Vol. 13 (2007), pp.199–216.

23   Dinah Shelton, 'Human Rights and the Environment: Jurisprudence of Human Rights Bodies', Background paper No. 2, Joint UNEP-OHCHR Expert Seminar on Human Rights and the Environment, 14–16 January 2002. This and the other five background papers are available at: http://www.unhchr.ch/environment/index.html

24   Center for Reproductive Rights, 'Female Genital Mutilation (FGM): Legal Prohibitions Worldwide' (January 2008), available at: http://www.reproductiverights.org/pub_fac_fgmicpd.html

25   Oxfam, *Rigged Rules and Double Standards*: *Trade, Globalization and the Fight Against Poverty* (2002), available at: http://www.oxfam.org.uk/what_we_do/issues/trade/downloads/trade_report.pdf.

26   Kelly Lee (ed.), *Health Impacts of Globalization*: *Towards Global Governance* (Basingstoke: Palgrave, 2003).

27   World Health Organisation, *The Health Conditions of the Population in Iraq since the Gulf Crisis* (March 1996), available at: http://www.who.int/disasters/repo/5249.html; see also Geoff Simons, *The Scourging of Iraq*: *Sanctions, Law and Natural Justice* (Basingstoke: Palgrave, 2002).

28   UN Secretary-General, in Address to International Rescue Committee, Reflects on Humanitarian Impact of Economic Sanctions, UNIS/SG/2719 (16 November 2000). Available at: http://www.unis.unvienna.org/unis/pressrels/2000/sg2719.html

29   Jonathan Pilger, 'Squeezed to Death', *The Guardian*, 4 March 2000. Available from: http://www.guardian.co.uk/theguardian/2000/mar/04/weekend7.weekend9

30   One small and belated consequence of the experience of the Iraq sanctions regime is a developing interest in 'smart' sanctions. See for example David Cortright and George A. Lopez (eds), *Smart Sanctions: Targeting Economic Statecraft* (London: Rowman & Littlefield Publishers, 2002).

31   Mary Ann Glendon, 'The Rule of Law in the Universal Declaration of Human Rights', *Northwestern Journal of International Human Rights*, Vol. 2 (Spring 2004), p.2.

32   A.W. Brian Sampson, *Human Rights and the End of Empire*: *Britain and the Genesis of the European Convention* (Oxford: Oxford University Press, 2001), pp.2–3.

33   Anne Gallagher, 'Making Human Rights Treaty Obligations A Reality: Working With New Actors and Partners', in Philip Alston and James Crawford (eds) *The Future of Human Rights Monitoring* (Cambridge: Cambridge University Press, 2000), pp.201–8.

34   A.W. Brian Sampson, *op cit*, p.12.

35   *Ibid.*

36   Human Rights Watch, *World Report 2008* (New York: Seven Stories Press, 2008).

37 Rick Lawson 'Out of Control: State Responsibility and Human Rights: Will the ILC's definition of "Acts of State" Meet the Challenges of the Twenty-first Century?', in Monique Castermans-Holleman, Jacqueline Smith and Freid van Hoof (eds) *The Role of the Nation-state in the 21st Century: Essays in Honour of Peter Baehr* (Leiden: Martinus Nijhoff Publishers, 1999), p.91.

38 Quoted in A.W. Brian Sampson, *op cit*, p.11.

39 Cited in David Scheffer, 'Humanitarian Intervention versus State Sovereignty', in United States Institute of Peace, Peacemaking and Peacekeeping: Implications for the United States Military – Special Middle East Program in Peacemaking and Conflict Resolution, Washington D.C., 1993, p.12.

40 http://www.iciss.ca/pdf/Commission-Report.pdf

41 Andrew Clapham, 'UN Human Rights Reporting procedures: An NGO Perspective', in Philip Alston and James Crawford (eds) *op cit*, pp.175–200; see also Jack Donnelly, *Universal Human Rights in Theory and Practice* (Ithaca: Cornell University Press, 2002), p.127.

42 Thomas Risse and Kathryn Sikkink, 'The socialization of international human rights norms into domestic practices: introduction', in Thomas Risse, Stephen C. Ropp and Kathryn Sikkink (eds) *The Power of Human Rights: Institutional Norms and Domestic Change* (Cambridge: Cambridge University Press, 1999), p.15.

43 UN Watch, 'Human Rights Council', available at: http://www.unwatch.org/site/c.bdKKISNqEmG/b.1518297/k.7483/Human_Rights_Council.htm. See also Philip Alston, 'Reconceiving the UN Human Rights regime: Challenges Confronting the New UN Human Rights Council', Center for Human Rights and Global Justice Working Paper (New York University School of Law), 4 November 2006.

44 Brett J. Miller, 'Living Outside the Law: How Informal Economy Frustrates Enforcement of the Human Rights Regime for Billions of the World's Most Marginalized Citizens', *Northwestern Journal of International Human Rights*, Vol. 5, Issue 1 (Fall 2006), pp.127–52.

45 Human Development Report 2007/08: *Fighting Climate Change: Human Solidarity in a Divided World*, available at: http://www.tz.undp.org/docs/hdr_20072008_summary_english.pdf

46 NEPAD Secretariat (Governance, Peace and Security Programme), 'African Post-Conflict Reconstruction Policy Framework' (June 2005), available at: http://www.nepad.org/2005/aprmforum/PCRPolicyFramework_en.pdf; N.D. White and Dirk Klaasen (eds), *The UN, Human Rights and Post-conflict Situations* (Manchester: Manchester University Press, 2005).

47 Julian Ku and Jide Nzelibe, 'Do International Criminal Tribunals Deter or Exacerbate Humanitarian Atrocities?', Hofstra University Legal Studies Research Paper No. 06-27, available at SSRN: http://ssrn.com/abstract=931567.

48 Theodor Meron, 'Reflections on the Prosecution of War Crimes by International Tribunals', *American Journal of International Law*, Vol. 100 (2006), pp.551–79.

49 Zoe Pearson, 'Non-Governmental Organizations and the International Criminal Court: Changing Landscapes of International Law', *Cornell International Law Journal*, Vol. 39 (2006), pp. 243–84.

50 Christopher Scarre, *The Human Past: World Prehistory and the Development of Human Societies* (London: Thames & Hudson, 2005), p.411.

51 M. Anne Brown, *Human Rights and the Borders of Suffering*: *The Promotion of Human Rights in International Politics*, *op cit*.

52 Dinah Shelton, 'The Boundaries of Human Rights Jurisdiction in Europe', *Duke Journal of Comparative and International Law*, Vol. 13 (2003), pp.95–153.

53 Patrick Thornberry, *Indigenous Peoples and Human Rights* (Manchester: Manchester University Press, 2002).

54 Adriana Fabra and Eva Arnal, 'Review of jurisprudence on human rights and the environment in Latin America', Joint UNEP-OHCHR Expert Seminar on Human Rights and the Environment, 14–16 January 2002, available at: http://www.unhchr.ch/environment/bp6.pdf

55 'Agora: What Responsibility Does Our Generation Owe to the Next? An Approach to Global Environmental Responsibility', *American Journal of International Law*, Vol. 84, No. 1 (January 1990), pp.190–212; Laura Westra, *Environmental Justice and the Rights of Unborn and Future Generations*: *Law, Environmental Harm and the Right to Health* (London: Earthscan, 2008).

56 Universal Declaration on the Human Genome and Human Rights, 11 November 1997, available at: http://portal.unesco.org/en/ev.php-URL_ID= 13177&URL_DO=DO_TOPIC&URL_SECTION=201.html

57 Gregory Stock, *Redesigning Humans*: *Choosing Our Genes, Changing Our Future* (New York: Houghton Mifflin, 2003); John Harris, *Enhancing Evolution*: *The Case for Making Better People* (Princeton: Princeton University Press, 2007).

58 Jürgen Altmann, *Military Nanotechnology* (Abingdon: Routledge, 2005).

59 Sean Kevin Thompson, 'The Legality of the Use of Psychiatric Neuroimaging in Intelligence Interrogation', *Cornell Law Review*, Vol. 90 (2005), pp.1601–37; Mark Wheelis and Malcolm Dando, 'Neurobiology: A case study of the imminent militarization of biology', *International Review of the Red Cross*, Vol. 87, No. 859 (September 2005), pp.553–71.

60 Lester Brown, *Plan B 3.0*: *Mobilizing to Save Civilization* (New York: W.W. Norton & Company, 2008).

61 David Walsh, 'US liberal pundits debate the value of torture', *World Socialist Web Site* (10 November 2001), http://www.wsws.org/articles/2001/nov2001/ tort-n10_prn.shtml; Andrew C. McCarthy, 'Torture: Thinking the Unthinkable', *Commentary*, July–August 2004, pp.17–24.

62 Costas Douzinas, *The End of Human Rights* (Oxford: Hart Publishing, 2000), p.375.

Index